A QUESTION
OF SEDITION

A QUESTION OF SEDITION

The Federal Government's
Investigation of the Black Press
During World War II

Patrick S. Washburn

New York Oxford
OXFORD UNIVERSITY PRESS
1986

Oxford University Press

Oxford   New York   Toronto
Delhi   Bombay   Calcutta   Madras   Karachi
Petaling Jaya   Singapore   Hong Kong   Tokyo
Nairobi   Dar es Salaam   Cape Town
Melbourne   Auckland

and associated companies in
Beirut   Berlin   Ibadan   Nicosia

Published by Oxford University Press, Inc.,
200 Madison Avenue, New York, New York 10016

Library of Congress Cataloging-in-Publication Data

Washburn, Patrick Scott.
  A question of sedition.

  Bibliography: p.
  Includes index.
  1. World War, 1939–1945—Censorship—United States.
2. Afro-American press. 3. United States. Federal
Bureau of Investigation. I. Title.
D799.U6W37 1986   071'.3   85-21683
ISBN 0-19-503984-X

Printing (last digit): 9 8 7 6 5 4 3 2 1

Printed in the United States of America
on acid-free paper

For Glenda,
Chris, and Julie

Preface

History is replete with examples of the right person being at the right place at the right time. As trite as that may sound, such fortuitous events also affect historical research. Without Donald B. Schewe's helpful response to a 1980 letter, this book probably would never have been written.

While working that summer toward a doctorate at Indiana University, I came across Walter White's autobiography, *A Man Called White*, in which he recalled a December 1942 meeting with Franklin Roosevelt. The president revealed that pressure was being applied on both the Justice Department and the White House to indict some black publishers for sedition, and White claimed that Roosevelt apparently put an end to it. Intrigued by White's story, I asked history professor George I. Juergens, an authority on the presidents and the press, where I could find more about the meeting. He explained that nothing had been written about it because historians probably had been unable to find any material other than White's account.

Having been a newspaper reporter ten and a half years, I took that as a challenge. I was going to prove to Juergens that more information could be located. And so I wrote to the Roosevelt Library in Hyde Park, New York, asking if any documents existed on White's conversation with Roosevelt. Schewe, the library's assistant director, was not encouraging in his reply on October 10, 1980. Not only could he find no notes on the meeting, but according to a check of the White House usher's diary there was no evidence that White had even seen the president at the White House in December 1942. That almost surely would have been the end of my research if Schewe had not gone further. He suggested that I might be interested in a "secret" 1943 FBI survey on blacks of 714 pages, including 30 pages specifically on the black press. After receiving the section about black publications, which came from a report that had been ignored by historians using the Roosevelt Library for over seven years, I suddenly was on my way to a dissertation and now this book. As an ironic postscript, I was frustrated time after time over the next four years in trying to document White's story about Roosevelt. Whether White's version of what took place was correct, or if the meeting even occurred, may never be known.

And so a white Southerner, who virtually had never been around blacks until he was in graduate school, was launched on what many considered an unlikely research topic. My mother, my relatives, and my friends kept asking the same questions: Why are you writing about the black press? Isn't there something else more important? And I usually would reply with a cryptic question: Why do men climb mountains? I would explain that historians, like mountain climbers, look for personal challenges that interest them. Thus, it is the search for knowledge and the belief that their findings will be important that drive historians, not the fact that they are researching a subject the public finds socially acceptable. And I would point out that the black press was extremely important in World War II because it was on the cutting edge of determining how the government would deal with sedition. The result was a milestone in American libertarian history. But such explanations usually were ineffectual, and I frequently came away feeling that I had convinced no one because their biases were permanent.

Fortunately, there were no such doubts on the part of the two historians who closely oversaw my dissertation research, Juergens and David P. Nord of Indiana's journalism school.

Functioning virtually as cochairmen, they read each chapter carefully and suggested changes that strengthened the final product, improved my writing, and taught me the ways of a historian. It was a valuable learning experience that I always will treasure. but perhaps more important was the confidence they displayed in my work. Early on, they encouraged me to look beyond merely a dissertation and go for a book. That caused me to strive for the best manuscript I could produce, rather than one that was merely passable. Richard G. Gray and Ralph L. Holsinger also must be thanked. Both served on my dissertation committee and offered insightful comments into the events discussed in this book. Every doctoral student should be as fortunate to have such support.

Debts also are owed to the numerous librarians and archivists besides Schewe who were consulted for this book. They frequently guided me through a bewildering maze of documents and secondary sources, helping me to find what I needed quickly with a minimum of searching. The libraries and archival collections included the Indiana University Library in Bloomington; the National Archives in Washington and Suitland, Maryland; the Library of Congress in Washington; the Roosevelt Library; the University of Virginia Library in Charlottesville; the Schomburg Center for Research in Black Culture in New York; the University of Notre Dame Archives in South Bend, Indiana; the Moorland–Spingarn Research Center at Howard University in Washington; and the Beinecke Rare Book and Manuscript Library at Yale University in New Haven, Connecticut.

Other debts are owed to those I interviewed, particularly publisher John H. Sengstacke of the *Chicago Defender*. Their insights and recollections of the World War II period provided valuable background material, helped me to fill in gaps, and kept me from making inaccurate historical assumptions in several important parts of this study. Others deserving of thanks are *Reader's Digest*, which helped fund my research, and the faculty and graduate students at Indiana University, who continually encouraged me and provided an excellent atmosphere in which to work. Gordon Jackson and Mary Alice Sentman were particularly supportive. The faculty at Ohio University was equally understanding as I made the final changes in the manuscript and did all the other little things that go into publishing a book. Also important were Nancy Kreisler of New York, Mr. and Mrs. John Herbert of Washington, and Mr. and Mrs. Larry Saunders of Arrington, Virginia. By generously allowing me to stay in their homes, they significantly cut the cost of my research.

The three persons with whom I have worked closely at Oxford University Press deserve special thanks. Associate Editor Wendy Warren Keebler, Editor Susan Rabiner, and Editorial Assistant Rachel Toor patiently endured my many questions and turned what could have been drudgery into a pleasurable undertaking. The fact that I already am planning my second historical book says a lot about my working relationship with them.

Finally, but certainly not least, there is my wife, Glenda, and my children, Chris and Julie. Because I wanted my dissertation to be published, I spent an extra year at Indiana University rather than trying to write under the pressure of a first-year faculty position. That turned out to be an excellent decision, but it was not made easily because of the financial implications. I was working at two part-time jobs in Bloomington while Glenda was working full-time, and our combined salaries were only slightly more than I would earn as a full-time associate professor. Nevertheless, there were few complaints, and the year turned out to be one of the most productive of my life because of the support and love I received at home. Therefore, this book is dedicated to them.

Athens, Ohio   P.S.W.
August 1985

Contents

A QUESTION
OF SEDITION

1

"Civil Liberties Are the Essence of the Democracy We Are Pledged to Protect"

Francis Biddle was not in the best of spirits in June 1945. On May 23, President Harry S Truman had asked abruptly for his resignation as attorney general, a position he had held since 1941, and had followed that up by ignoring Biddle's advice about a successor. None of that was surprising since Biddle had opposed Truman's nomination for the vice-presidency in 1944, but it was saddening nevertheless. There had been speculation that Biddle might cap an exemplary legal career by being named to the U.S. Supreme Court, and now that obviously was not to be. In an attempt to cheer him, Assistant Attorney General Herbert Wechsler sent Biddle a memorandum on June 16, only two weeks before his resignation became effective, complimenting him on his accomplishments in the Justice Department. "As a matter of historical record, it will be said of this war that with seditious prosecutions reduced by the Attorney General to an incredible minimum in contrast to the last war, an Army of 12,000,000 men was raised by the Government with no significant difficulty and turned in a performance of unprecedented perfection in the entire history of war."[1]

Those words undoubtedly pleased Biddle. A resolute defender of First Amendment rights, he had let it be known shortly after taking over at the Justice Department in 1941 that he was not going to make the same mistake as Attorney General A. Mitchell Palmer, who had instigated a controversial witch hunt for radicals and government critics, some of whom were journalists, from 1919 to 1921. "The most important job an Attorney General can do in a time of emergency is to protect civil liberties," Biddle told *New York Times Magazine* in September 1941. ". . . Civil liberties are the essence of the democracy we are pledged to protect."[2]

Most segments of the press in World War II did not provide a serious challenge to Biddle's libertarian philosophy. German, Japanese, and Italian publications in the United States were understandably shunned by much of the public, and many suffered severe and in some cases fatal circulation and advertising losses. The Justice Department, as well as numerous other government agencies, investigated them continuously but judiciously, which was a normal wartime safeguard. This caused little criticism. The government, along with the public, also had little sympathy for ultraradicals, such as fascists, some of whom published pamphlets or magazines. After an initial period of hesitancy, the Justice Department indicted and tried some of them, but even journalists, while recognizing this as a slight chipping away at freedom of the press, were not alarmed. Then, there was the mainline white press. The government generally ignored it, which was not surprising considering the publishers' overall conservatism and outspoken war support, and the rare investigations usually were conducted quietly. The Justice Department only moved publicly against one of these publications, the *Chicago Tribune*, for printing war secrets in 1942, and the case ended quickly when a grand jury refused to indict the publisher.

The black press, however, presented a dilemma. During World War I, it was relatively small and easily cowed by government pressure, and only a few publications refused to tone down to help the war effort in 1918 following a meeting with government officials. But by 1919, some black publications again became critical and cynical when they realized that fighting overseas and stressing patriotism did not guarantee equality after the war. At the same time, and of even more importance, a New York

City Post Office examiner noted "the undue feeling of triumph the negro is experiencing over the fact that he is fighting back" in black publications.[3] That turned out to be a permanent attitude, and by 1926, with the black press growing rapidly, it was called the "greatest single force in the Negro race."[4]

Nothing occurred to change that assessment by the time the United States entered World War II. If anything, the black press enjoyed unprecedented power because of an amazing rise in circulation. It thundered into 1942, almost daring the government to try to shut it down and adamantly refusing to back off as it had during World War I. As the *Pittsburgh Courier's* George Schuyler boasted in June 1942, "The old days of scared, timid, ignorant Negroes are gone forever."[5]

The black press's belligerency was a problem because many government officials considered such outspokenness only marginally legal under the existing wartime sedition statutes. Overall, the black press was more critical of the government than most of the white press, but few of the publications approached the strident views expressed by ultraradicals. Thus, no one knew how the courts would react to a sedition indictment. And furthermore, even if the black press could be suppressed, this course worried government officials because it might alienate the country's 13 million blacks, who made up 10 percent of the population. Everyone agreed that black support was necessary to win the war.

When no sedition indictments occurred, blacks were ecstatic. In December 1945, Florence Murray, editor of *The Negro Handbook*, wrote that the black press was "surprisingly free from censorship restraints" during World War II. "Editors and reporters spoke their minds in no uncertain terms on the conduct of the war as it affected the darker races, not only in this country, but all over the world," she said. She noted that a few army and navy installations had banned black papers temporarily, but the Post Office Department had not suppressed any black publications.[6]

While Murray's statements were accurate, they were misleading because they oversimplified the situation. For example, she ignored numerous complaints by black newspapers in 1942 that they were being investigated by the federal government; they warned that this was an unofficial form of censorship because of the mere threat of suppression. She also failed to mention an intriguing revelation in July 1945 by Harry S. McAlpin, the first black White House correspondent. "Plans were on foot [during World War II] . . . to completely demoralize the press by accusing it of sedition," he wrote in his weekly column in the *Atlanta Daily World*. "These plans fell through when the Department of Justice refused to cooperate with the interested military authorities and the 'keep-the-Negro-in-his-place' planners."[7] Unfortunately, McAlpin did not indicate the source of his information, and he could not recall it in a 1983 interview.[8]

After the war, occasional information kept appearing about the government's wartime investigation of the black press. One such occasion was when Walter White, executive secretary of the National Association for the Advancement of Colored People, published his autobiography, *A Man Called White*, in 1948. He, like McAlpin, revealed that the black press had faced far more of a threat of censorship during the war than Murray indicated. White said that President Franklin D. Roosevelt had told him in December 1942 "that pressure was being brought to bear on him and the Department of Justice to indict the editors of some of the more flamboyant Negro newspapers for 'sedition' and 'interference with the war effort.' " Roosevelt added that several "of the men high in government" believed that some black editors could be convicted because of their papers' "clearly biased and inaccurate" stories. White concluded that "apparently the President called in his advisers and ordered them to abandon the absurd and dangerous proposal to charge Negro editors with disloyalty." White added that the government limited or cut off newsprint supplies shortly afterward to some black newspapers, but Roosevelt ended the cutbacks in early 1943 when White told him about them.[9]

More fragmented information surfaced in 1950 in Schuyler's

Fifty Years of Progress in Negro Journalism, which briefly discussed the conflict between the government and the black press in World War II. He claimed that "the Department of Justice maintined a file on the Negro newspapers, editors and columnists," and FBI agents sometimes visited editors. He also reported that War Department officials were provided with weekly "Reports of Trends in the Colored Press."[10] Far more information about the black press investigation conducted by the War Department and the army appeared in 1966. Ulysses Lee, in a government-published book, *United States Army in World War II: Special Studies: The Employment of Negro Troops,* used extensive documentary evidence to show that the investigation began in World War I and became more intense in World War II. While the army suppressed black papers at some posts up until the end of 1943, which angered the black press, he noted that the army improved press relations in the latter half of the war by working more closely with black war correspondents and giving them more information.[11]

Although Lee's book is the most complete treatment of the government's investigation of the black press in World War II, it presents an incomplete picture by concentrating on only one agency. In addition, the lone book devoted solely to the black press during the war, Lee Finkle's *Forum for Protest* in 1975, is only of marginal help in examining the investigation because of the book's overall direction. It authoritatively discusses what the various black publications wrote during the war and what caused them to react editorially as they did, but the government's investigation is rarely mentioned. It is unclear whether Finkle was basically unaware of it or whether he discounted its extent and importance, but his book provides virtually no new information about the investigation.[12]

Government documents now available reveal that the investigation of the black press during World War II was far more massive than previously indicated by historians. In fact, an official in the Office of Facts and Figures complained in June 1942 that the investigation of blacks, which included the black press, involved so many agencies that it was a "muddle."[13] Seven agencies investigated the black press—the Justice Department, the FBI, the Post Office Department, the Office of Facts and Figures, the Office of War Information, the Office of Censorship, and the army—and an eighth agency, the War Production Board, may have attempted illegally to tone down the black press by cutting newsprint supplies to some papers. High government officials involved in the various investigations included Biddle, Roosevelt, FBI Director J. Edgar Hoover, and Postmaster General Frank Walker.

Biddle was the key individual. This book's main theme is that the black press was in extreme danger of being suppressed until June 1942, when Biddle decided quietly that no black publishers would be indicted for sedition during the war. Thus, McAlpin was correct in stating that the Justice Department saved the black press. Since there were no indictments, it is tempting to assume that Biddle merely felt the black press had not violated the sedition laws. But historical explanations are seldom that simple, and, as this book will show, the decision was more complicated than that. It involved such seemingly unrelated events as the internment of West Coast Japanese, clashes of wills and egos in the president's cabinet meetings, and a tough confrontation between Biddle and John H. Sengstacke, publisher of the *Chicago Defender* and founder of the Negro Newspaper Publishers Association. After June 1942, the FBI and the Post Office continued to investigate the black press regularly and wanted to take action against a number of the papers, but the Justice Department's steadfast refusal to act, while offering virtually no explanations, halted both threats.

Meanwhile, the other government agencies continued their investigations, and a knowledge of these agencies' actions is crucial to an understanding of the government's reaction to the black press in World War II. But these investigations were less important. While officials in these agencies revealed the general mood of wartime Washington, which *The Nation* noted was a "southern town" with southern attitudes toward blacks,[14] they simply had less power with which to harm the black press. Furthermore, they were not on center stage when it came to deciding the fate of the black press, as were the officials at the Justice Department. Biddle and his top advisers stemmed a strong, determined antiblack press threat, which came principally from the FBI, the Post Office, and the White House.

Thus, in many ways, this book necessarily focuses on Biddle, who virtually has been ignored by historians. A slender, freckle-faced, balding man who enjoyed wearing bright bow ties and wine-colored smoking jackets, he did not appear overly strong at first glance. "He looks more like a poet than like the nation's chief law officer," an *American Magazine* writer observed in April 1942.[15] But looks can be deceiving. In Biddle's case, his appearance masked a mental toughness and a stubborn determination to defend civil liberties and freedom of the press. If these traits led to unpopular actions, so be it. "He is not bothered by adverse criticism when he believes himself to be in the right," *Survey Graphic* noted in 1942. ". . . He apparently saw in his present job a chance to perform permanent service to the administration of the law at a time when the law must be protectively strong."[16] One of the main beneficiaries was the black press.

In addition, this is a study of libertarianism, which in the context of this book is defined as the freedom to criticize the government. In previous wars, such as the Revolution, the Civil War, and World War I, the government—and at times angry private citizens—openly challenged America's libertarian foundation, and press freedom sometimes suffered. But in writing about World War II, historians have implied that few libertarian problems existed. For example, Edwin Emery and Michael Emery, in *The Press and America*, concentrate on how the press cooperated with the government during the war, resulting in mainly "pro-Fascist and subversive propaganda sheets" being suppressed.[17] That is true but misleading. Government documents—many of which became available only in the 1970s, as well as some that were obtained through the Freedom of Information Act or were declassified for the first time for this study—demonstrate a strong undercurrent of antilibertarianism in the United States during World War II, particularly among many government officials who felt it was anti-American to be critical during wartime. And yet the government, with a few minor exceptions, did not move against the black press. This book explains why.

2

"The Negro Is Seeing Red"
(1917–1941)

The government's widespread investigation of the black press during World War II was not brought about solely because of a sudden, strong surge of antilibertarian feeling. Instead, the investigation's roots stretched back to the period from 1917 to 1921. During those years, wartime sedition laws were passed and applied vigorously on a large scale, and the principal law, the Espionage Act, was still in force during World War II. Another important parallel also existed between the two eras: the black press's critical attitude toward the government during both wars. Thus, although the turnover of high government officials was almost complete between the two time periods, with the important exception of J. Edgar Hoover, and the cast of black publications was somewhat altered, with some of the most strident in World War I dying and others not attaining prominence until World War II, the investigation from 1941 to 1945 was predictable. Adding to the predictability was a quiet government investigation of the black press before the Japanese bombing of Pearl Harbor. The prewar investigation was yet another sign that the government and the black press were on an unavoidable collision course. The only thing that was not predictable was the outcome.

When the United States entered World War I on April 6, 1917, an immediate clamor arose for sedition legislation. Many regarded the existing statutes as inadequate for punishing those who encouraged draft evasion. Such concerns were heightened by recollections of Civil War opposition being handled entirely, but not very well, by martial law, and by a pervasive fear of German propaganda, which already had caused Great Britain and Canada to guard against it legislatively and administratively.[1] Among those pushing for legislation was President Woodrow Wilson. He favored a mild measure that would restrict merely those persons "who cannot be relied upon and whose interests or desires will lead to actions on their part highly dangerous to the nation in the midst of a war."[2]

The result was the Espionage Act, which became law on June 15, 1917. Title I, section 3, limited freedom of expression during wartime by declaring it unlawful to make false statements that interfered with the military; to attempt to cause "insubordination, disloyalty, mutiny, or refusal of duty" in the military; or to obstruct the military recruiting or enlistment services. Anyone found guilty could be fined up to $10,000 and/or jailed for up to twenty years.[3] Of at least equal if not more importance to the press was Title XII, which allowed the postmaster general to declare any material unmailable if he felt it violated the law. Under the Classification Act of 1879, newspapers and periodicals had to appear at regularly stated intervals to qualify for a second-class mailing permit allowing them reduced postal rates. If the postmaster general withheld just one issue from the mail, however, he could revoke a second-class permit indefinitely because the publication no longer appeared regularly. Publishers, as well as government officials, knew that such a revocation probably would prove economically fatal to a publication.[4]

The Espionage Act did not stem the nation's hysteria, however. Numerous states quickly became dissatisfied with its terms and its enforcement and enacted even stricter measures. Faced with such public disenchantment, Attorney General Thomas W. Gregory pushed for an even stricter federal law, and the result was the most severe limitation in U.S. history on freedom of expression and the press. The Sedition Act of May 16, 1918, amended the Espionage Act by adding nine new offenses. They included speaking, writing, or publishing any "disloyal, profane, scurrilous, or abusive language" about topics ranging from the government to the flag to the armed forces. Also prohibited were writings or statements intended to result in "contempt, scorn, contumely, or disrepute" of the government, the Constitution, the flag, and even the armed forces' uniforms. Penalties for those convicted were identical to those under the Espionage Act.[5]

The Justice Department applied its new legal weapons vigorously. Between 1917 and 1921, it launched 2168 prosecutions under the Espionage and Sedition acts and secured 1055 convictions.[6] At least eleven persons received ten-year prison terms, six were sentenced to fifteen years, and twenty-four were given twenty years.[7]

No one was more zealous in applying the laws than Postmaster General Albert S. Burleson, a longtime Texas congressman. On June 16, 1917, only one day after the Espionage Act took effect, he secretly ordered local postmasters to forward immediately to him "unsealed matter, newspapers, etc., containing matter which is calculated to interfere with the success of any Federal loan . . . or to cause insubordination, disloyalty, mutiny, or refusal of duty in the military or naval service, or to obstruct the recruiting, draft or enlistment services . . . or otherwise to embarrass or hamper the Government in conducting the war."[8] Burleson was inundated with material from postmasters as well as concerned citizens, and he moved quickly. In a wartime scenario that would be repeated more than two decades later, little attention was focused during World War I on mainline newspapers, which were generally conservative and strongly nationalistic.[9] German-language and socialist publications faced the brunt of the attack.

By mid-July 1917, Burleson and the Post Office solicitor, William H. Lamar, had declared unmailable at least one issue each of about fifteen publications, most of which were socialist, including the *Masses*, the *International Socialist Review*, the *Appeal to Reason*, the *American Socialist*, and the *Milwaukee Leader*.[10] The government was quickly criticized for suppressing unpopular views, but Wilson denied the charge in a letter to Oswald Garrison Villard, editor of *The Nation*. "Certain copies of certain newspapers were excluded from the mails because they contained matter explicitly forbidden by law," he wrote.[11]

Burleson accomplished the greater part of his suppressions within a few months of receiving legislative authorization. By November 1917, he had either declared unmailable or revoked the second-class permits of about seventy-five publications, of which about forty-five were socialist, and the U.S. Court of Appeals upheld him in a case brought by the *Masses*.[12] Lamar justified the suppressions in *Forum* magazine in February 1918. "For us to permit an exaggerated sentimentalism [or] a misapplied reverence for legal axioms . . . ," he argued, "would be criminal not only to our soldiers, sailors, and ourselves, but to posterity."[13] By the time the war ended, the Post Office had taken action against about 100 newspapers and periodicals, about 60 percent of which were socialist.[14]

The black press, which had been in existence for ninety years when the United States entered World War I, was virtually untouched by the government, but it was far from unnoticed. This was not surprising considering the black press's new sensationalistic and critical tone.

Before the mid-1910s, the black press was small and relatively uninfluential because it lacked a large urban audience, forcing it to focus on an elite readership of literate blacks. Then, publisher Robert S. Abbott of the *Chicago Defender* began a highly successful campaign to attract Southern blacks to the North, where better job opportunities existed. The growing number of new urban subscribers resulted in a striking change in the editorial content of the Northern black press. Instead of publishing further ideological debates between black leaders about the best way to achieve equality, the *Defender* became a mass appeal publication, turning to front-page news of crime and discrimination played up under banner headlines. The black masses streaming north into city ghettos (as well as those remaining in the South) liked the new tone, which was modeled after William Randolph Hearst's and Joseph Pulitzer's newspapers, and other black papers quickly followed Abbott's lead.[15] Mainly as a result of its outspokenness, the black press became an object of intense pride and interest among blacks. "Every Negro who can read does read a race paper," Frederick G. Detweiler noted in 1922.[16]

By the time the United States entered World War I, black editors were adamant in demanding an end to discrimination. Reader approval, signaled by growing circulation figures, was only one reason. In addition, Booker T. Washington had died in 1915, ending his controversial conciliatory approach to race relations. Moreover, the black press believed the "Wilsonian rhetoric about world democracy" and saw nothing incongruous in criticizing injustices toward blacks while overwhelmingly supporting the war effort and emphasizing that blacks would gain equality more rapidly by fighting Germans.[17]

The combined criticism-and-support approach of the black press angered many government officials. Although no one denied the reality of racial injustices, such as a rise in the number of black lynchings from thirty-five in 1917 to sixty in 1918, it was considered unpatriotic to make an issue of them in wartime.

Among the critics of the black press was George Creel, chairman of the government's influential Committee on Public Information (CPI). One of the circulars distributed by Creel's agency claimed that German agents had "thousands of propagandists among the Negroes, exciting them with stories of impossible atrocities committed against the colored people."[18] Realizing that such sentiments placed the black press in danger, two blacks with high government positions, Emmett J. Scott, special assistant to the secretary of war, and Maj. J. E. Spingarn of military intelligence, suggested to Creel that he should have a Washington conference of prominent blacks, most of them journalists. The purpose, according to Scott, would be to recognize "the fact that we are at war and that Negro public opinion should be led along helpful lines rather than along lines that make for discontentment and unrest."[19] Creel liked the suggestion, and Scott sent out invitations to the conference, which was hosted jointly by the War Department and CPI.[20]

The Washington conference, from June 19 to 21, 1918, was attended by forty-one black leaders, including thirty-one black editors. In a statement at the conference's conclusion, the editors blamed black "unrest and bitterness" on the government's "apparent indifference" to black problems, not on German propaganda. However, they agreed that the defeat of Germany was of "paramount importance" and promised to try to keep black public opinion "at the highest pitch, not simply of passive loyalty but of active, enthusiastic and self-sacrificing participation in the war."[21] On the day after the conference ended, Spingarn wrote to the head of military intelligence that he believed the meeting would have "an excellent effect on the colored press, and on the other leaders of the negro race. All were pleased at having been taken into the confidence of the Government and asked for advice and co-operation."[22]

The Washington conference, which received considerable public attention, was not the government's only attempt to tone down the black press during World War I. Working behind the scenes, the government conducted a massive investigation of black papers throughout the war and applied pressure on those it considered most objectionable. The crackdown involved little subtlety.

One of the first and most heavily investigated publications was the *Chicago Defender*. Part of the reason for this was a large number of complaints about the paper from Southerners, who were angered by the *Defender*'s campaign to lure blacks, a cheap source of labor, to the North. A typical letter to the Bureau of Investigation (it was renamed the FBI in 1935) came in July 1917 from a Little Rock man who claimed that the *Defender* was causing blacks to behave "badly" and should be barred from the mail. He suggested that the paper was a German propaganda tool and concluded that "no more insidious and ingenious plan could be adopted for crippling the South and its resources."[23]

Such complaints, coupled with what the government believed to be the paper's inaccurate and inflammatory reporting of racial events, caused the Bureau of Investigation on April 9, 1917 (only three days after the United States entered the war), to order its Chicago office to conduct an investigation.[24] After talking to Abbott on April 13 about his editorial practices, an agent reported back to Washington that "Abbott in his zeal for the betterment of his people may have overstepped the bounds of propriety."[25] That was clearly the government's view when cartoonist Leslie Rogers drew black soldiers fighting Germans while white American troops shot the blacks in the back. Abbott avoided going to jail on that occasion only by buying liberty bonds and encouraging their purchase in the *Defender*.[26]

In May 1918, the army's Military Intelligence branch, which was one of the most active investigatory agencies, applied pressure to the *Defender*.[27] Maj. W. H. Loving, a black, visited Abbott in Chicago and told him "he would be held strictly responsible and accountable for any article appearing in his paper in the future that would give rise to any apprehension on the part of the government."[28] This worried Abbott, and he wrote Loving several days later to assure him of the *Defender*'s patriotism:

> You know through your reading of the *Defender* the attitude of this paper towards the government. I say with absolute certainty, that without a doubt, it has never at anytime spoken disloyal, and is entirely guiltless of the attack centered on it. . . . I have more than once advised my staff writers to refrain from expressing their views on problems that would precipitate national strife, or inculcate in the heart of any member of my race the spirit of revolt against the laws of the national or state governments.[29]

Upon receipt of Abbott's letter, Loving wrote his superiors that "the tone of this reply is all that we can expect, if the writer lives up to it, and I shall endeavor and try to see that he does."[30]

However, both historian Lee Finkle and Roi Ottley, Abbott's biographer, note that the *Defender* remained militant throughout the war.[31]

At least two other black newspapers, the *Baltimore Afro-American* and the *St. Louis Argus*, were also warned in 1918 that they might be suppressed if their editorial tones did not change.[32] The U.S. attorney in Baltimore assured the U.S. attorney general that the editor of the *Afro-American* in an interview "expressed great contrition and most elaborate promises to eliminate such stuff hereafter from his paper."[33]

The government's most notable success in toning down the black press during the war was with the NAACP's *The Crisis*, edited by the militant W. E. B. Du Bois. After the United States entered the war, Du Bois was highly critical of President Wilson, the U.S. Civil Service Commission, the adjutant general, and the War Department.[34] A typical editorial appeared in the January 1918 issue:

> We raise our clenched hands against the hundreds of thousands of white murderers, rapists, and scoundrels who have oppressed, killed, ruined, robbed, and debased their black fellow men and fellow women, and yet, today, walk scot-free, unwhipped of justice, uncondemned by millions of their white fellow citizens, and unrebuked by the President of the United States.[35]

In May 1918, the army's Military Intelligence division placed *The Crisis* on a secret list of publications to be excluded from soldiers' reading rooms.[36] Then, in early June, the division informed the NAACP's Charles H. Studin, who was in charge of eliminating objectionable material in *The Crisis* before it went to press, that the magazine was in danger of being suppressed because a large number of complaints had been received about it. "[The government] can not tolerate carping and bitter utterances likely to foment disaffection and destroy the morale of our people for the winning of the war," the letter concluded.[37] Studin, obviously alarmed, replied that "no pains will be spared to make all future issues of this magazine comply with the wishes of the Government both in letter and spirit." He also assured military intelligence that those working at the magazine were "loyal to the last degree."[38] As a final means of control, an agent for the American Protective League, a group of amateur sleuths who voluntarily helped the Justice Department, visited *The Crisis* in June and talked with the publication's business manager about patriotism.[39]

The NAACP board immediately ordered Du Bois to confine *The Crisis* to only "facts and constructive criticism" and insisted that he must present all editorial material to a legal consultant before publication.[40] Du Bois quickly changed his tone, writing the famous "Close Ranks" editorial in July in which he exhorted blacks, for the remainder of the war, to "forget our special grievances and close our ranks shoulder to shoulder with our own white fellow citizens and the allied nations that are fighting for democracy."[41] The major black newspapers immediately attacked him. They not only felt he was abandoning the traditional NAACP position of fighting discrimination, but they insisted that such articles were necessary because they were the only outlet for black frustration and were a major reason for the recent circulation increases of the black press.[42] But Du Bois refused to retreat for the remainder of the war, and in September he elaborated on his new position:

This Association and this magazine stand today exactly where they have stood during the eight years of their work; viz., for the full manhood rights of the American Negro. . . .

The [July] editorial seeks to say that the first duty of an American is to win the war and that to this all else is subsidiary. It declares that whatever personal and group grievances interfere with this mighty duty must wait.

It does not say that these grievances are not grievances, or that the temporary setting aside of wrongs makes them right. . . .

The Crisis says, first your Country, then your Rights! . . .

God knows we have enough left to fight for, but any people who by loyalty and patriotism have gained what we have in four wars ought surely to have sense enough to give that same loyalty and patriotism a chance to win in the fifth.[43]

Du Bois's concession to the government would not be forgotten. It would again become an issue with the black press when the United States entered World War II.

No government documents indicate whether the threats to suppress the black press during World War I were merely bluffs. However, the black press could not have taken the threats lightly, since the government moved against two black publications.

The first occasion was in late 1917. After black soldiers participated in a Houston riot in which fifteen persons were killed, the army hanged thirteen of those involved and sentenced forty-one others to life imprisonment. When the *San Antonio Inquirer* criticized the hangings, the Justice Department charged the editor, G. W. Bouldin, with violating the Espionage Act because the article attempted "to cause insubordination, disloyalty, mutiny, and refusal of duty." Although Bouldin had not written the article and had not been in San Antonio when it appeared, he was found guilty and sentenced to two years at Leavenworth.[44] In 1919, a federal appeals court refused to overturn the decision.[45]

The second publication was *The Messenger*, a socialist monthly magazine in New York. Two young blacks, A. Philip Randolph and Chandler Owen, had launched the publication in November 1917 as a "magazine of scientific radicalism." Their goal was

to appeal to reason, to lift our pens above the cringing democracy of the times, and above the cheap peanut politics of the old reactionary Negro leaders. . . . Patriotism has no appeal for us; justice has. Party has no weight with us; principle has. Loyalty is meaningless; it depends on what one is loyal to. Prayer is not one of our remedies; it depends on what one is praying for.[46]

The magazine, which at first carried the subtitle "The Only Radical Negro Magazine in America," was against the war and opposed both major political parties. Besides socialism, it applauded Russia's bolshevik revolution and hinted that "such an upheaval might be good for America," it praised radical trade unionism, and it demanded government action "to ensure civil liberties and protections, guarantee absolute social equality including intermarriage, and protect the rights of blacks to arm themselves in their own defense."[47]

Randolph and Owen had problems with the government during a coast-to-coast antiwar speaking tour in the summer of 1918. On August 4 in Cleveland, while one was speaking to an audience and the other was selling *The Messenger*, they were arrested by federal agents and charged with treason. In addition, 100 copies of the magazine were confiscated. The two men spent two and a half days in jail until a leading Socialist Party lawyer arrived to get them out on bail and handle their defense. The court proceeding was brief.

> The judge before whom they were brought refused to believe that the two young-looking "boys" could possess the knowledge and intelligence to write the inflammatory editorials in the magazine presented as evidence by the prosecutor, and preferred to think that unscrupulous persons had used the names of the two to cover their real identity. Showing the best of judicial (and racial) paternalism, the judge dismissed the charges and, so he thought, sent the two home to their parents. Safely out of the courtroom, they proceeded instead to their next speaking engagement, by then minor martyrs in the anti-war movement.[48]

They were more fortunate than their magazine. The July issue carried an unsigned editorial, "Pro-Germanism Among Negroes," which noted that the government suspected a link between black discontent and German propaganda. The editorial claimed, however, that the real reason for discontent was that blacks faced "peonage, disfranchisement, Jim-Crowism, segregation, rank civil discrimination, injustice of legislatures, courts and administrators." "We should like to assist the government investigate this pro-Germanism among Negroes," it concluded. "It might bring to light the fact that they [blacks] are still so absorbed in suppressing American injustices that their minds have not yet been focused upon Germany."[49] Randolph felt the editorial was merely "satirical and sarcastic," which made it harmless, but the postmaster general did not agree.[50] *The Messenger* had its second-class mailing permit revoked, and it was not restored until mid-1921.[51] Nevertheless, the magazine continued to publish for three years despite higher mailing costs.

When the armistice was signed on November 11, 1918, ending World War I, it appeared that the government's investigation of the press—and the threat of suppression—was over. After all, the Espionage and Sedition acts apparently had lapsed with the end of hostilities, as Wilson was quick to point out. On November 27, he instructed Burleson to end all censorship, which the postmaster general promised to do, and on February 28, 1919, Wilson reiterated his order. "I cannot believe that it would be wise to do any more suppressing," the president declared. "We must meet these poisons in some other way."[52] But Burleson was not about to stop, and his mood was reflected at other agencies. The government's investigation of the press, particularly black publications, escalated.

Part of the reason was that the United States technically remained at war with Germany until Congress passed a joint resolution terminating hostilities in 1921.[53] Thus, it could be argued that the wartime statutes were still in effect. An even more important reason for the continued investigation of the black press, however, was the "Red Scare" that followed the armistice. Intolerance of dissent spread rapidly, particularly against those who sympathized with the Russian Revolution, and blacks inevitably were drawn into the conflict. When a series of race riots electrified the country in 1919, bolshevism was included among the many factors responsible for the outbreaks. The charge was not surprising. A small but vocal number of black publications, including the now-famous *The Mes-*

senger, favored any solution that would end discrimination, including bolshevism if necessary. For example, *The Negro World* of New York City told its readers in July 1919 that oppressed peoples must "avail themselves of every weapon [bolshevism] that may be effective in defeating the fell motives of their oppressors."[54]

Such statements, which heightened the belief that racial unrest was caused by bolshevist agitation, were not ignored by the government. Between 1919 and 1921, the government's investigation of the black press continued unabated, spurred on by numerous complaints from Southern congressmen as well as private citizens. The army's Military Intelligence, the Post Office, and the Bureau of Investigation all took active roles. During this period, black editors were interviewed by government agents,[55] secret surveillances of black journalists took place,[56] several black publications were held up by the Post Office pending rulings on their mailability,[57] lists of subscribers of at least two black publications were secretly checked,[58] and both Military Intelligence and the Bureau of Investigation compiled regular reports on radical activities, including what the black press was writing.[59] The government supplemented its investigation with public attacks on the black press. For example, the *New York Times* noted in July 1919 that a federal official had shown it an unnamed black magazine that he claimed was seeking to cause discontent. He told the *Times* that such black publications appealed to "the ignorant" and sought "openly" to cause problems "that may lead to results that all good citizens will deplore."[60]

While the government's investigation of the black press from 1919 to 1921 was merely a continuation of what had occurred in the two previous years, it was not without significance. The reason was the presence of J. Edgar Hoover. The government's close monitoring of the black press in World War II almost surely would have been less extensive if he had not been involved intimately in the "Red Scare" investigations.

Hoover had a meteoric rise at the Department of Justice. An

honor student whom his classmates called "Speed" because he was always in a hurry, he got his Bachelor of Law degree from George Washington University in 1916 and his Master's in 1917, when he was admitted to the bar. On July 26, 1917, he became a clerk at the Department of Justice, but he was in that position less than six months.[61] With the nationwide "Hun scare" resulting in a work overload at the department, the attorney general named John Lord O'Brien, a Republican from Buffalo, as a special assistant for war work. Hoover, who was an aide to O'Brien, was placed in charge of an enemy alien registration section, despite having had no experience in that type of work.[62] Jay Robert Nash has noted:

> Hoover worked tirelessly at his job. His chance to prove his integrity and ingenuity had arrived. With him it was not a case of "rounding up the usual suspects." He worked day and night rooting out would-be spies, saboteurs, and slackers who had not responded to the draft. . . . By 1919, Hoover had . . . acquired a reputation for dedication to duty.[63]

Hoover's life took a dramatic turn on the night of June 2, 1919, when two unidentified anarchists were blown up in Washington while placing a bomb on the doorstep of the new U.S. attorney general, A. Mitchell Palmer. Eight other explosions occurred on the same night at government buildings and at the homes of political and business leaders in New York; Cleveland; Newtonville, Massachusetts; Paterson, New Jersey; Boston; Pittsburgh; and Philadelphia. At each bombing site, police found the same printed message:

> The powers that be make no secret of their will to stop here in America the worldwide spread of revolution. The powers that be must reckon that they will have to accept the fight they have provoked. A time has come when the social question's solution can be delayed no longer; class war is on, and cannot cease but with a complete victory for the international proletariat. . . . There will have to be bloodshed; we will not dodge; there will have to be murder; we will kill; . . . there will have to be destruction; we

will destroy. . . . We are ready to do anything and everything to suppress the capitalist class—THE ANARCHIST FIGHTERS.[64]

Palmer, who was not injured in the blast at his home, reacted quickly. Within forty-eight hours, he named the former head of the Secret Service, William J. Flynn, as the new director of the Bureau of Investigation, "with carte blanche to deal with the situation throughout the country in his own way."[65] To help Flynn, Palmer appointed Francis P. Garvan of New York as assistant attorney general in charge of investigations and prosecutions, and Hoover as head of the newly created General Intelligence Division (GID). Operating under Garvan, the GID was ordered to "concentrate on a study of subversive activities—to determine their scope and decide what prosecutorial actions should be taken. . . . All information gathered by Flynn's agents bearing on radicalism would be funneled to it."[66] These duties led to the GID often being called the antiradical division of the Justice Department.[67]

Hoover approached his new job with such tireless enthusiasm that one reporter described him as a "slender bundle of high-charged electric wire."[68] He immediately immersed himself in the works of Karl Marx, Friedrich Engels, Leon Trotsky, and V. I. Lenin, and these readings led to his lifelong belief that communism posed a serious threat to the United States.[69] At the same time, he moved at a rapid pace in collecting information on radical persons, publications, and organizations. In Hoover's first hundred days, the GID prepared biographies on 60,000 radicals, and in less than a year and half it had a card catalogue listing more than 450,000 radicals.[70] Palmer boasted that the file represented "a greater mass of data upon this subject than is anywhere else available."[71] Who appeared in the GID's file and whether the information was accurate was unknown by those not close to the operation because the cards and biographies were classified and unavailable for public scrutiny. All Hoover would tell the Senate was that the biographies included persons "showing any connection with an ultraradical body or movement," especially "authors, publishers, editors, etc."[72] The mention of journalists was not surprising. The GID regularly checked on 625 newspapers that it considered radical, including 251 that it labeled ultraradical.[73]

The GID unquestionably read black publications closely. In September 1919, for example, Hoover noted in a letter that both *The Crisis* and *The Messenger* "are well known to me." He added that "if possible something should be done to the editors of these publications as they are beyond doubt exciting the negro elements in this country to riot and to the committing of outrages of all sorts."[74] Such prosecutions, however, posed a problem. Assistant Attorney General R. P. Stewart explained to a South Carolina congressman in September 1919 that the government only prosecuted publications "when it is reasonably satisfied that a conviction can be secured, as it is believed that the loss of such cases does more harm than good."[75]

Throughout the fall of 1919, the Justice Department pondered whether it had the grounds to move legally against the most objectionable black publications, particularly *The Messenger* and *The Crisis*. Using *The Messenger* as an example, the Justice Department viewed prosecution under Title I, section 3, of the Espionage Act as almost certain to fail because the government had no evidence that the magazine was published "to weaken the war making power of the Government."[76] That left one option: prosecution under section 6 of the Criminal Code, which made it illegal to conspire to forcefully overthrow the U.S. government. But a successful prosecution using the Criminal Code also was unlikely, as the U.S. attorney for New York explained in December 1919:

> The purpose and object of the publication [*The Messenger*] is to prevent the lynching of negroes and their oppression and discrimination against them. . . . If the purpose stated be the true and be the sole purpose for which the magazine is published, there is nothing unlawful in its publication. This is the only purpose that can be established if the only evidence relied upon be the magazine itself. It is not unlawful to arm, to train, nor to

strike for a lawful purpose. Armed resistance to mobs bent on lynching and committing other acts of violence upon negroes is of course lawful.[77]

Since existing statutes provided doubtful prospects for a successful case against the black press, Palmer and Hoover took a different tack. Some sentiment already had been expressed in Congress for a peacetime sedition act, which the United States had not had since the Alien and Sedition acts lapsed in 1801. Feeling strongly that such an act was necessary, Hoover put together two lengthy reports on blacks and communism, which Palmer submitted to the Senate in November 1919 and to the House in June 1920.[78] The 1919 report, titled "Radicalism and Sedition Among Negroes As Reflected in Their Publications," contained the following analysis:

> Among the most salient points to be noted in the present attitude of the Negro leaders are . . . the identification of the Negro with such radical organizations as the I.W.W. and an outspoken advocacy of the Bolsheviki or Soviet doctrine. . . . The Negro is "seeing red," and it is the prime objective of the leading publications to induce a like quality of vision upon the part of their readers.[79]

The report also claimed that "the number of restrained and conservative [black] publications is relatively negligible." To substantiate that statement, the GID gave Congress large amounts of what it considered objectionable material from black newspapers and magazines, particularly *The Messenger*, which it called "the most able and the most dangerous of all the Negro publications."[80]

The black press was appalled and angered at the GID's onslaught. A typical comment came fom publisher Robert L. Vann of the *Pittsburgh Courier*. "The only conclusion therefore is: As long as the Negro submits to lynchings, burnings and oppressions, and says nothing, he is a loyal American citizen," wrote Vann. "But when he decides that lynchings and burnings shall cease even at the cost of some human bloodshed in America, then he is a Bolshevist."[81]

Hoover's report to the Senate, along with the highly publicized New York Legislature's Lusk Committee hearings on "subversives" (including the black press), helped generate extensive congressional activity. Between late 1919 and early 1920, seventy peacetime sedition bills were introduced.[82] In the House, all of the proposals were combined into the Graham Bill, which called for a $10,000 fine and/or twenty years in prison for "any person who sought to overthrow or destroy the government or prevent or delay the United States government." The Senate version, known as the Sterling Bill, was passed quickly and sent to the House, which combined the two pieces of legislation into the Graham–Sterling Bill and began committee hearings.[83]

Public opinion crystallized quickly against the bill. The press overwhelmingly attacked it as a danger to free speech and free press and pointed out that the country would be limiting democracy severely in its haste to control bolshevism. Justice Oliver Wendell Holmes also condemned the bill, stating that "with effervescing opinions, as with the not yet forgotten champagne, the quickest way to let them get flat is to let them get exposed to the air." In addition, Samuel Gompers and Zechariah Chafee, Jr., added their influential voices to the groundswell of criticism. The opposition was so devastating that Palmer admitted that the bill was too strict and should be modified, but the House Rules Committee went even further. It reported unfavorably on the bill, and no action was ever taken.[84]

Thus, the threat of suppression, which had hung over the black press since 1917, was lifted and would not descend again until World War II. Furthermore, the Sedition Act was repealed in 1921, leaving only the milder but still dangerous Espionage Act. There were indications, however, that the government was unlikely to tolerate unpopular beliefs during future wars any more than it had during World War I. As the U.S. Supreme Court said in 1919 in the famous *Schenck* decision:

The question in every case is whether the words used are used in such circumstances and are of such a nature as to create a clear and present danger that they wll bring about the substantive evils that Congress has a right to prevent. It is a question of proximity and degree. When a nation is at war many things that might be said in time of peace are such a hindrance to its effort that their utterance will not be endured as long as men fight and that no Court could regard them as protected by any constitutional right.[85]

In still another important ruling two years later the Supreme Court upheld the right of the postmaster general to revoke a publication's second-class mailing permit if there was a violation of the law.[86] This confirmed that the Post Office's power during the next war would again be substantial.

The significance of the period from 1917 to 1921 as a fore-runner of what would occur during World War II was substantial. The black press came out of the four-year period with a radical reputation. That reputation was not warranted by many black magazines and newspapers, but the government, and particularly Hoover, was in the grip of national hysteria over communism and not in a mood to make fine distinctions among publications. Thus, the GID's push for a peacetime sedition act left the impression that the entire black press was troublesome, even un-American. But a radical reputation based on a con-nection with communism was not the only legacy that followed the black press into World War II. There was also the govern-ment investigation. Once begun on a large scale, it did not end simply because there was no war or no perceived threat to democracy from a different ideology. Documentary evidence strongly suggests—and in some cases confirms—that both the Bureau of Investigation and the army investigated black pub-lications vigorously throughout the entire period between the wars. In the case of the former, the investigation was not un-expected in light of Hoover's belief in the dangerous nature of black publications.

At the outset, Attorney General Harlan Fiske Stone attempted to control the young zealot. When he appointed Hoover as the agency's acting director in 1924, he pointed out that the Bureau was merely to be "a fact-gathering organization" with investigatory decisions to be made solely by the U.S. attorney general.[87] "The Bureau of Investigation is not concerned with political or other opinions of individuals," said Stone. "It is concerned only with their conduct and then only with such conduct as is forbidden by the laws of the United States."[88]

Coinciding with this statement, Stone abolished the Department of Justice's GID.[89] Whether the Bureau took over the GID's files and continued collecting information on radicals and subversives (including the black press) is unknown. Some historians have concluded that "Stone's resolute actions curtailed bureau intelligence activity" until the mid-1930s,[90] but in the late 1920s a small group of congressmen already was accusing Hoover of eavesdropping on them because they were critical of the Bureau.[91]

What has been established is that by 1933 Hoover once more was collecting information quietly on suspect groups and persons. In that year, Secretary of State Cordell Hull requested an investigation of pro-Nazi organizations in the United States, and in 1934 President Roosevelt widened the investigation to include fascist organizations.[92] Then, in late summer of 1936, the president requested information on all subversive groups, particularly Communists.[93] In a memo to his staff, Hoover cautioned that "this investigation . . . should, of course, be handled in a most discreet and confidential manner."[94] Thus, the FBI, as had been the case with the GID from 1919 to 1921, could legally investigate anyone without outside interference.

The New Yorker in 1937 noted the rumors circulating about Hoover:

> One hears in Washington that Hoover has secret dossiers on all left-wingers and is just awaiting a chance to clap them in concentration camps. Hoover pooh-poohs such stories. In discussing them, he points out that the Sedition Act has long since been

repealed and that it is now anyone's privilege to advocate overthrow of the government, so long as no overt act is committed.
He doesn't believe that the law should be so broad-minded, but
says that as long as it is, he considers it no business of his to
gather evidence on agitators, and insists that he has not done so.
The supposed secret dossiers, he says, do not exist. . . . Yet there
remains an undercurrent of feeling that somehow he is doing
something to undermine the citadel of liberty.[95]

As rumors continued to increase, Hoover acquired still more
power. In 1939, the president announced that the FBI had taken
charge of all investigations relating to espionage, sabotage, and
neutrality violations.[96] In the following year, Roosevelt authorized the FBI to use "warrantless wiretaps and bugs against
persons suspected of subversive activities against the government of the United States, including suspected spies."[97] At the
same time, on its own, the FBI began opening mail.[98]

By then the GID was back in the news. On January 5, 1940,
Hoover told the House Appropriations Subcommittee that he
had reactivated the GID in 1939 when Roosevelt increased the
FBI's investigatory authority. He continued:

We have also initiated special investigations of persons reported
upon as being active in any subversive activity or in movements
detrimental to the internal security. In that connection, we have
a general index, arranged alphabetically and geographically, available at the Bureau, so that in the event of any greater emergency
coming to our country we will be able to locate immediately these
various persons who may need to be the subject of further investigation.[99]

Hoover's statement caused a national uproar, particularly in
Congress, where New York Republican Representative Vito
Marcantonio criticized the FBI for putting together "a system
of terror by index cards."[100] Hoover survived with his power
intact, however, when Roosevelt indicated publicly that Hoover
had his support.[101]

Hoover's enormous investigatory power, coupled with his

1919 to 1921 experiences and the president's concern with investigating subversive groups, leaves little doubt that the black press was watched closely by the FBI throughout the entire period between the wars. Other reasons were the massive but largely ineffective efforts of the Communists and the Japanese in the interwar years to enlist black support. The government investigated these attempts secretly and continuously for two decades before the United States entered World War II and noted on several occasions that the black press published highly subversive articles.

In 1939, for example, the FBI obtained a confidential report, "Japanese Propaganda Among the Negro People," which had been prepared for the Chinese government. The report pointed out that the *Baltimore Afro-American* (mistakenly called the *Boston Afro-American*) had written that "it is plain now that the objective of the Japanese Government is to boot the white races out of China, and set up an Asiatic Monroe Doctrine through which Japan can control the destinies of the Far East. The *Afro-American* fully believes Japan is justified in the foregoing objectives." The *Amsterdam News* of New York was also quoted: "If Japan goes down, every black man's right will go down with her."[102]

The report failed to mention whether such pro-Japanese comments were common in the late 1930s in black publications. But Lee Finkle, who has made the most thorough study of the black press in World War II, has noted that black newspapers "openly praised the Japanese" for several years before the bombing of Pearl Harbor. While some papers enjoyed seeing the Dutch pushed out of Asia and others viewed this as merely one exploiter taking over from another, virtually all of the black press agreed that Japan was the dominant eastern nation just as the United States was the dominant western power. Furthermore, many in the black press considered Asia as Japan's natural sphere of influence and urged the United States not to become involved.[103] It is unlikely that the FBI ignored such attitudes.

Nor were they ignored by the army. In July 1941, Military Intelligence forwarded to Hoover a black special agent's report claiming that "Japanese and Communist press agents are releasing news in all available negro publications and in some cases, Communists or Communist sympathizers are employed on the editorial staffs of these papers." The agent, who said that he had been asked by a Japanese newspaper editor to write news releases for the black press, labeled five black journalists (including three on the influential *Pittsburgh Courier*) as either Communists, communist sympathizers, or radicals. He concluded that "the source of this subversive activity [should] be investigated at the earliest possible moment."[104]

Although the FBI probably heeded the special agent's advice, documentary evidence on this point is lacking. It is known that FBI agents already had visited the *Courier* in 1940 and had lunched with the publisher and executive editor. The visit was precipitated by articles dealing with the attempts of blacks to vote in the South, and the agents complained to several of the paper's writers that the articles were "holding America up to ridicule."[105] In the same year, a citizen in Savannah complained to an FBI agent about two September issues of the *Chicago Defender*. He claimed that the paper's articles contained "propaganda" which "might possibly hinder the Government in securing registrations from negroes who come within the draft age." The papers were forwarded to Hoover, who sent them to the Justice Department in October, asking if they violated any federal statute. A month later he was informed that the *Defender* was operating within the law.[106]

While little is known about the FBI's prewar investigations of the black press, numerous documents indicate that the army investigated the black press extensively throughout 1941, seeking ways to control it as officers complained about articles hurting black troop morale. The army's concern began in 1938 and was brought on primarily by a new force in black journalism, the *Pittsburgh Courier*. The paper had not been investigated by the government during 1917 through 1921 because it had been small, with limited influence, and highly patriotic. Publisher Robert Vann was not only an ardent anti-Communist who favored deporting "anarchists," but he continually stressed the loyalty of blacks to America despite all injustices.[107] Following the war, however, the *Courier* increased rapidly in national influence among blacks. One of the major reasons was that Vann looked for issues with circulation appeal, even if it meant changing the paper's previous editorial policy, and then devoted considerable editorial space to those issues.[108] In 1938, the *Courier* discovered such an issue: the virtual exclusion of blacks from the army. The paper began campaigning vigorously to have blacks represented in the army in numbers proportionate to their 10 percent share of the population. The campaign made little headway, however. At the end of 1939, the paper noted that only 4451 black enlisted men and five black officers were in uniform, compared to 229,636 white enlisted men and 1359 white officers.[109]

In April 1940, the *Courier* began to devote even more space to the campaign, using front-page articles in every edition and often adding further comments on the editorial page. Readers also were urged to send letters and telegrams to congressmen demanding the end of "military taxation without representation" in all branches of the armed services. In addition, the *Courier* organized a committee, which appeared before the Senate Subcommittee on Military Appropriations to request that the 1941 Military Establishment Bill include "a general 10-percent strength for Negro enlisted men and officers in the Regular Army." Rayford W. Logan, a Howard University professor who headed the committee, told the senators that blacks wanted to "be given the opportunity to exercise their rights."[110]

Although the Senate refused to act on the request, Roosevelt signed a Conscription Bill in September 1940 that contained a nondiscrimination clause. The *Courier* was pleased and boasted about its part in the bill's passage, but the pleasure was brief. On October 9, the White House released a policy statement about black troops which granted what the *Courier* sought: proportional representation in the army and more black commissioned officers. But the statement also declared that "the policy of the War Department is not to intermingle colored and white enlisted personnel in the same regimental organizations." As Finkle has noted, this "became a national insult to black citizens, and black papers reflected their indignation on every front page."[111]

The black press's criticism broadened to include numerous types of discrimination in the army, and complaints from army officers increased. In January 1941, the head of the Philadelphia quartermaster depot noted an "unjustified editorial" in the *Philadelphia Tribune* which said that his department discriminated in hiring black workers. He pointed out, however, that the editorial's damage was offset when Military Intelligence (known internally as G-2) persuaded the *Pittsburgh Courier* to run a two-page feature on black workers in its Philadephia edition.[112] In the same month, Military Intelligence in Chicago reported that John Sengstacke, publisher of the *Chicago Defender*, was encouraging blacks to become conscientious objectors as a protest against the armed forces' racial segregation policy.[113] Still another G-2 report from Rhode Island in February complained that articles in the *Courier* and the *Providence Chronicle* were stressing discrimination.[114]

Then, on April 26, the Richmond and Baltimore editions of the *Afro-American* published the army's "General Classification Test 1 A," which was a series of questions and problems used to classify enlisted men. The army was understandably alarmed and sent an officer to interview publisher Carl Murphy on May 16. Murphy pointed out that the test, which he had received from an unidentified reader, was not marked "restricted" or "confidential," and he thought it was "obsolete" because it was dated 1940. Therefore, the interviewer concluded that the paper had not intended to harm the army. However, the discussion ranged much broader than that. The Military Intelligence agent also questioned Murphy extensively about his feelings toward "certain political factions and alleged subversive organizations, which were reputed to have communistic leanings."[115]

During the same period, Percival Prattis, the executive editor of the *Courier*, was visiting thirteen army camps and writing a lengthy series of "exposes" about black soldiers. His articles noted that often brutal white military policemen were stationed with black troops and that blacks frequently would be assigned to clean up one part of a camp and then be transferred to some other area.[116] The post intelligence officer at Camp Claiborne in Louisiana complained in June that the articles were "radical" and inaccurate and would cause problems among black troops, and he recommended that the FBI should investigate Prattis. Acknowledging that Prattis could not be controlled totally by the army because of freedom of the press, the officer also suggested that "in no instances should this man and his photographer be permitted to wander around any military reservation without an officer in control of the situation."[117]

While evidence is lacking to show if the officer's latter recommmendation was followed, it is known that the War Department immediately asked the FBI to investigate the *Pittsburgh Courier*. The Bureau finally responded on November 29, 1941, that its investigation had failed to show that the *Courier* was "engaged in questionable activities with reference to the national defense program." In its report, the FBI noted a "confidential" letter (supplied by an informant) that *Courier* President Ira F. Lewis had written to one of the paper's columnists on June 3:

> The *PITTSBURGH COURIER* has . . . tried to be decent and reasonably conservative. In short, we have never believed in red, scare-head headlines; we have never believed that the Negro could be helped a whole lot by appealing directly to the prejudice within a Negro. We subscribe to the theory that to appeal to the prejudice in the Negro is but to heighten the prejudice in a white man.
>
> With the foregoing in mind, we are writing to advise that we think this is a very nice country in which to live. We know that all is not right here for any group; at the same time we believe that we can do better here than we can anywhere else. . . . We are going to continue to intelligently protest, but our basic policy

in this emergency will be the policy that will be characteristic of all good Americans—the support of the President and the country's foreign policy.[118]

While the FBI's investigation was continuing, the army received still further complaints about articles exposing discrimination in not only the *Courier* but also the *Richmond Afro-American* and the *Amsterdam News*.[119] The articles caused Under-Secretary of War Robert P. Patterson to protest bitterly in September to the director of civilian defense that some black papers were promoting

> social gains which have not been attained in the country as a whole and using the Army as a means of promoting such gains among the civilian population. I believe you will agree with the War Department that such activities are most unfortunate, because they materially impede the War Department in its present desire to build promptly and efficiently an Army capable of defending the nation in the existing crisis and organized so that it will fit into the accepted social order of this country.[120]

While black problems in the military were a major issue in the black press before the war, papers also focused on discrimination in civilian life as well as the continued violence against blacks, particularly lynchings.[121] Some isolationist publications quickly supported this push for black equality, tying it in with their campaigns to keep the United States out of the war. For example, the *New York Daily News* ran full-page photographs of the Ku Klux Klan and Southern black sharecroppers with captions that included, "Should We Fight to Save the World . . . While These Things Continue at Home?" "Tell your president, senators, and congressmen," the paper declared, "that you want democracy to work properly at home before you fight for it abroad." *Scribner's Commentator* carried similar articles with headlines such as, "Should Negroes Save Democracy?" These articles worried government officials, who feared that "subversive influences would find a fertile field for fifth column activities among a disaffected Negro population."[122]

By late 1940, black editors shared the government's concern that black morale could become a problem. A special committee studying black newspapers stressed that the press must "do everything possible" to become "a powerful and effective force in maintaining the traditional loyalty of the Negro to his country."[123] Thus, in the summer of 1941, with the U.S. involvement in the war appearing increasingly likely, most of the black press began telling readers that they must fight in any future war, although that did not mean they had to give up the battle against discrimination at home. The *Chicago Defender* praised a speech by Dr. Harold M. Kingsley of Chicago's Church of the Good Shepherd, in which he said, "It is sound wisdom that we fight both of these battles at the same time." The paper went on to urge blacks to defend "the system that hoisted us out of slavery." In the same vein, the *Philadelphia Tribune* said that a struggle against discrimination in the United States should be the "second thing" that blacks should consider important if war occurred. "The second element . . . is not inconsistent with the fight for the security of America, it supplements the first," the *Tribune* explained.[124]

The black press never advised, however, giving up the fight against discrimination. Quite simply, good reasons existed for continuing. For example, the *Pittsburgh Courier*'s Prattis noted in 1946 that readers had always demanded a crusading medium:

The Negro reporter is a fighting partisan. He has an enemy. That enemy is the enemy of his people. The people who read his newspaper . . . expect him to put up a good fight for them. They don't like him tame. They want him to have an arsenal well-stocked with atomic adjectives and nouns. They expect him to invent similes and metaphors that lay open the foe's weaknesses and to employ cutting irony, sarcasm and ridicule to confound and embarrass our opponents. The Negro reader is often a spectator at a fight. The reporter is attacking the reader's enemy and the reader has a vicarious relish for a fight well fought.[125]

Such expectations by readers posed a monetary dilemma for black publishers and editors. Unlike their white counterparts, black newspapers had virtually no lucrative advertising accounts because white advertisers generally ignored them. As a result, they were forced to depend on circulation for economic survival. Thus, while black publishers did not want to be viewed as unpatriotic by the government, they risked a "fatal loss of prestige, confidence and circulation" if they toned down their publications. "It [the black press] is and must be responsive to the wishes of its readers because it is more dependent upon them than other newspapers," one of the country's leading black columnists, the *Courier*'s George Schuyler, noted after the war.[126] Still another reason existed for the black press's outspoken attitude. Prattis and others have claimed that its crusading articles resulted in fewer racial problems—not more, as the government felt—because this approach provided "a release for pent-up bitterness and aggression felt by Negroes."[127]

Thus, the stage was set for a collision that had its genesis more than twenty years before. Black publications, charging hard at discriminatory evils, were growing in circulation and influence. When Roosevelt entered office in 1933, they had an average circulation of 600,000. That more than doubled to 1,276,600 by 1940 and would reach 1,808,060 by the end of World War II. But circulation figures alone understate the papers' influence. Even before the war, more than a third of the black families subscribed to a black paper. Even more revealing is research that has estimated that between 3½ and 6 million of the nation's 13 millon blacks read the newspapers each week during the war, with large Northern black papers, such as the *Courier* and the *Defender*, being read the most frequently.[128] Why they were read so avidly was no secret. The black press was the only place where blacks could get news about themselves because the white press virtually ignored blacks, other than in terms of crimes. This, in turn, played into the hands of the black publishers seeking to build ever-escalating circulations.

Then there was the government, a powerful giant held largely in check by the absence of a war. It was locked on the eve of World War II into an investigatory pattern that had been established more than twenty years earlier. Quite simply, the government felt the black press was uncomfortably friendly to the Japanese as well as to Communists and other radicals, and to ignore such signs could be dangerous if a war occurred. This made extensive investigations mandatory. But there was an even more fundamental reason for the collision. The black press's critical nature irritated government officials, who had long ago formed beliefs about what constituted appropriate press comment. To some officials in Washington, the black press had gone too far, even for peacetime.

So a collision was inevitable. The bombing of Pearl Harbor was all that would be needed to set the drama into motion.

3

"A Good Chance to Clean Up . . . Vile Publications"

(December 1941–February 1942)

Although the collision between the government and the black press was unavoidable, the drama unfolded slowly, almost leisurely, in the first three months of the war. That was understandable. With the United States rocked back on the defensive on December 7, 1941, by the surprise attack on Pearl Harbor, much needed to be done immediately. The first priority was to move against the principal internal threats, such as suspected enemy agents.[1] While this did not involve the press, subtle, ominous signs warned that the government would not tolerate criticism any more in the present war than it had in the previous one.

Nowhere was this mood more evident than at the White House. On December 8, President Roosevelt ordered FBI Director J. Edgar Hoover to take over "censorship matters" temporarily until a director of censorship could be named. Hoover promptly recommended that only "voluntary" newspaper and radio censorship be imposed.[2] A week later, when Byron Price, executive news editor of the Associated Press, was appointed to the position, Roosevelt issued the following statement:

All Americans abhor censorship, just as they abhor war. But the experience of this and of all other nations has demonstrated that some degree of censorship is essential in war time, and we are at war. . . .

It is necessary that prohibitions against the domestic publication
of some types of information, contained in long-existing statutes,
be enforced.[3]

On January 15, 1942, Hoover's recommendation of voluntary
press censorship was put into practice when Price announced
a wartime code of practices for newspapers, magazines, and
periodicals. Its crux was contained in one sentence: "A maxi-
mum of accomplishment will be attained if editors will ask
themselves with respect to any given detail, 'Is this information
I would like to have if I were the enemy?' and then act ac-
cordingly."[4] The press was not alarmed. Not only did it view
censorship as a normal wartime practice, but most publishers
wanted to help the war effort. Even before Price announced his
wartime code, Stephen T. Early, the president's press secretary,
wrote the Associated Press's Kent Cooper that it was "amazing
. . . to see the press and radio asking for rather than standing
solidly against such a thing as censorship."[5]

Behind the scenes, however, there was concern that Roosevelt might use the war as an excuse to stamp out anything he
did not like in the press. U.S. Attorney General Francis Biddle
cautioned the president on December 9 that it would be unwise
to establish domestic censorship,[6] but he quickly became worried that Roosevelt was not going to heed his advice. "I don't
think the President has any clear idea of censorship," he noted
privately after a December 19 cabinet meeting, "and still believes that Price is going to censor newspapers—which, of course,
is not the fact, the President not even having that power."[7]
Biddle's notes do not indicate whether he attempted to explain
to the president the government's limits in applying the Espionage Act to the wartime press.

Given the pressing concerns of the war's early months, Roosevelt's antipress reaction was understandable. And yet it surely
must have shocked Biddle because of the president's well-known
love of the press, which has been noted by numerous historians.
Graham J. White has written, for example, that Roosevelt's

affection for reporters was "deep and unfeigned."[8] Strikingly informal, he continually joked with them, he occasionally played cards with them, and he called them by their first names, frequently engaging in small talk. But, perhaps most telling, he was available to them as no president before or since. In his twelve years in office, he met with the press 998 times, an average of 83 times a year. He looked forward to the questioning and the verbal jousting, and he knew what made good copy. Many reporters realized that he was subtly manipulating them, not only to get what he wanted in the press, but to get it there when he wanted it. Nonetheless, they liked him because he made their jobs easier.[9]

Yet Roosevelt's antipress reaction was more than understandable. It was predictable. The president was a complex man who not only loved the press but also had a history of hostility to it that stretched back to the 1920s. There were numerous reasons. As with all presidents, some of his favorite schemes had been attacked unmercifully by the press, even thwarted, which clearly did not endear journalists to him. Furthermore, by the time the United States entered World War II, he had endured bitter press criticism year after year about his New Deal programs as well as countless accusations that he was deliberately attempting to bring the country into the war on the side of England and France. Leading the way in the rough treatment, sometimes with inaccurate and unfair articles, were such antiadministration organs as the *Chicago Tribune*, the *New York Daily News*, and the *Washington Times–Herald*. He felt that the publishers of those three newspapers deserved "neither hate nor praise—only pity for their unbalanced mentalities."[10] White argues that such attacks by Roosevelt, while conceived in anger, also may have been calculated carefully to put the press on the defensive, thus encouraging "introspection or timidity."[11]

Still other reasons for his anger were more fundamental to his political beliefs. Although Roosevelt had no press training other than in college on the *Harvard Crimson*, he considered himself an expert on journalism—and reporters tended to agree.

As columnist Heywood Broun once said, Roosevelt was "the best newspaperman who has ever been President of the United States."[12] It was not surprising, therefore, that he frequently lectured newsmen on how to do their jobs, particularly focusing on ethics. He believed unequivocally that it was unethical to include interpretation in news articles because it distorted the truth. In his view, a writer's opinions should be confined to editorial columns. This was crucial, claimed Roosevelt, in applying Jeffersonian logic, because the press's primary role in a democracy should be to act as a pipeline, carrying the best available government information to the people, who were capable of understanding complex government issues and making intelligent decisions if they were provided with the facts. But if the information was embellished with interpretation, Roosevelt continued, the press threatened to break a vital informational circuit which was important to the functioning of a democracy.[13]

With those views, it was not surprising that Roosevelt was ready to silence his, and what he considered the country's, journalistic enemies when war broke out. As Biddle noted two decades later, Roosevelt was "a great man," but he had faults, including a "streak of vindictiveness."[14] His intimate knowledge of the press made him all the more formidable as an adversary. While much of that knowledge had been gathered by his continual association with journalists over almost twenty years, he also had access to the reports of the Division of Press Intelligence. Established in July 1933 at the insistence of Presidential Secretary Louis Howe, it read and clipped articles from approximately 400 of the country's largest daily newspapers and issued daily mimeographed bulletins in which news and editorial comment about the government were described and indexed.[15]

Nor were those his only sources of prewar press information. Since the mid-1930s, Roosevelt had occasionally used the FBI to investigate publications and journalists, as well as broadcast stations, that he felt might be "subversive." The first known occasion was in 1934, when Roosevelt asked the FBI to investigate William Dudley Pelley, who had created an anti-Semitic, anti-Communist, and anti-Roosevelt organization, the "Silver Shirts of America," whose aim was to make Pelley dictator of the United States. As part of his activities, Pelley edited numerous publications throughout the 1930s, including *Liberation*, the *Silver Legion Ranger*, and *Pelley's Weekly*.[16]

Then, in May 1940, Roosevelt learned that KGEI, a San Francisco radio station, had broadcast an untrue story about native unrest in the Dutch East Indies. The broadcast, which was heard in the East Indies, had resulted in strong complaints from Dutch officials, who pointed out that the natives were anti-German and anti-Japanese. "Please have a careful check made on the ownership and management of this station," Roosevelt wrote Hoover. The latter responded two days later that the unrest was in the West Indies, not the East Indies, and the error had been made by the International News Service, whose bulletins were read over KGEI.[17] Still another investigation was launched at Roosevelt's suggestion in November 1940, when the FBI looked at left-wing journalist George Seldes and his semimonthly newspaper, *In Fact*. Hoover's report said that Seldes, "although not a Communist of his own admission, is regarded as a close follower of the Communist doctrines."[18]

Such journalistic reports, of course, were only a minuscule part of the massive prewar information-gathering effort by Hoover, whose investigations ranged widely to include congressmen, former President Herbert Hoover, British Prime Minister Winston Churchill, and businessmen who promoted nationalism over internationalism. Kenneth O'Reilly has noted that, while Roosevelt was not "insensitive" to civil liberties, he sometimes understandably blurred "the distinction between national security and his own political prospects as the United States sped toward World War II."[19] Equally important, as Wayne S. Cole has pointed out in his study of Roosevelt and the isolationists, was the president's view of power. "He accepted constitutional constraints on presidential powers, but his was a decidedly loose constructionist view of the Constitution," Cole has written. "He believed the president of the United States had the responsibility and authority to lead." Cole also has noted that Roosevelt's patriotism and "conceptions of national interest" were important in determining his actions.[20] Therefore, feeling that the country was threatened, it was not unusual for him to encourage Hoover's investigations. In mid-1940, for example, the president asked his secretary, Edwin M. Watson, to write Hoover, "thanking him for all the reports on investigations he has made, and tell him I appreciate the fine work he is doing."[21]

With the onset of the war, Roosevelt was quick to take advantage of the situation and attack the press. He angrily went after publishers and journalists who had opposed him in the past or who had dared to write stories that he felt were detrimental to the country's war effort. As Biddle quickly discovered, the president believed all rights, including freedom of the press, "should yield to the necessities of war. Rights came after victory, not before."[22] Historian Richard W. Steele has criticized Roosevelt because his press actions from 1940 to 1945 were "needlessly restrictive and stemmed as much from personal preference and political expedience as from a realistic appraisal of national interests."[23] Arthur Schlesinger, Jr., has cautioned, however, against taking too harsh a view of Roosevelt's willingness to intrude on constitutional rights immediately before and during World War II:

> These were desperate times. Desperate times rarely produce rational behavior. . . . One wishes, as one does with Lincoln [during the Civil War], that he had acted at the time with the wisdom and restraint available to historians after the peril has passed. But Lincoln and Roosevelt had to reckon with the gravest threats to the life of the republic, and they could not foretell the outcome. . . . Whatever Lincoln and Roosevelt felt compelled to do under the pressure of crisis did not . . . corrupt their essential commitment to constitutional ways and democratic values.[24]

The president's views on the role of the wartime press quickly became apparent on December 10, 1941, when Joseph Patterson, the publisher of the *New York Daily News*, came to Washington hoping to see Roosevelt. He told Early that "he had been wrong in his isolationist policy—that he wanted to confess his error to the President."[25] Patterson must have realized that he would receive a chilly reception. On December 4, he had run a *Chicago Tribune* story that had caused a national uproar and infuriated government leaders by reporting the contents of a "Top Secret" document outlining the country's plans to enter the European war. When Patterson was ushered into Roosevelt's office, the president quickly brought tears to his eyes by angrily reading a series of 1941 *Daily News* editorials which were critical of the administration. Patterson, who remained standing throughout Roosevelt's fifteen-minute tirade, later called his comments "pretty severe criticism."[26]

That episode was followed two days later by a Roosevelt-orchestrated attack on Drew Pearson and Robert S. Allen, whose "Washington Merry-Go-Round" column was nationally syndicated. In a column sent to subscribers for use several days later, they named the specific U.S. losses at Pearl Harbor and called it the "largest naval defeat in this nation's history." When several newspapers wired the White House asking if they should use the column, Roosevelt instructed Early to have Hoover inform the columnists that "if they continue to print such inaccurate and unpatriotic statements that the Government will be compelled to appeal directly to their subscribers and to bar them from all privileges that go with the relationships between the Press and the Government." After a meeting with Hoover, Pearson and Allen killed the column.[27]

The next to feel Roosevelt's ire was magazine magnate Henry Luce, who owned *Time*, *Life*, and *Fortune*. The two men had never been close, and sometimes their relationship even approached hostility. Only a month before Pearl Harbor, for example, *Time* had published an article critical of the Chilean government, which the U.S. ambassador in Chile felt was a significant help to the Nazis in their anti-American propaganda. Roosevelt had publicly criticized *Time*, which caused Luce to write the president in December that "the drubbing you handed out to *Time* before December 7 was as tough a wallop as I ever had to take. If it will help you win the war I can take worse ones. Go to it! and God bless you." Roosevelt replied in a letter that he appreciated Luce's patriotism and sportsmanship.[28]

Almost immediately, however, another problem arose. A December 15 article in *Life* erroneously labeled a Brazilian air base as a U.S. field, angering Brazilian officials who felt that their country's sovereignty had been violated. Under-Secretary of State Sumner Welles complained to Roosevelt, who instructed Early to speak to Luce about the article. After a January 10 meeting in Washington, Early told Roosevelt that Luce was "truly distressed" at causing the government problems. "Time after time during our discussions, Mr. Luce expressed an eagerness to cooperate—to serve his Country 'on all fronts,' " wrote Early. But an issue of *Time* on January 12 resulted in still another complaint from Chilean officials, who resented the statement that the United States was starting a "round-up" to "corral" the American republics into a homogeneous "herd." Roosevelt, in a January 17 memorandum to Early, agreed that Chile had a right to be upset and labeled such articles "unpatriotic." "Honestly, I think that something has got to be done about Luce and his papers," he continued angrily.[29] No government action was ever taken during the war, however.

In the war's first three months, Roosevelt's most notable comment about the press, the significance of which would not become apparent for several months, was in a memorandum to Hoover on January 21. Noting that Pelley had started a new publication, *The Galilean*, and that some of the material appeared "pretty close to being seditious," Roosevelt made an ominous suggestion. "Now that we are in the war," he wrote, "it looks like a good chance to clean up a number of these vile publications."[30] Just which publications he was referring to, other than Pelley's, he did not say.

Roosevelt's comment to Hoover is particularly revealing because the FBI director had no power to "clean up" anything. Just as when he had taken over the Bureau in 1924, his activites were limited to investigations and arrests. Only the attorney general could prosecute cases. Yet documents show that in the war's first three months Roosevelt continually sought out Hoover, not Biddle, when he was angered at the press overstepping what he felt were its wartime boundaries.

Roosevelt avoided Biddle for several reasons. For one, the president had worked closely with Hoover since the mid-1930s on investigations, and the two liked and understood each other. It was natural for the president to encourage such a relationship, which was to his political advantage because of the type and amount of otherwise unobtainable information that Hoover provided. Then, too, Roosevelt had long since realized that the way to get action from an attorney general, particularly on something that he might otherwise hesitate to do, was to present him with a fait accompli. Biddle recalled two decades later:

> Not infrequently he [Roosevelt] would call Edgar Hoover about something that he wanted done quickly, usually in a hurry; and Hoover would promptly report it to me, knowing the President's habit of sometimes saying afterward, 'By the way, Francis, not wishing to disturb you, I called Edgar Hoover the other day about . . .'[31]

An even more compelling reason for Roosevelt's avoidance of Biddle in the war's first three months must have been his uncertainty about the attorney general's wartime attitude on freedom of speech and the press. Thus, while applying pressure subtly through Hoover, he adopted a wait-and-see attitude toward Biddle, who had been attorney general only since

September 1941. Roosevelt surely suspected the outcome. To virtually no one's surprise, Biddle turned out to be far more of a libertarian than the president.

A wealthy Philadelphian who had graduated cum laude from Harvard Law School in 1911, Biddle began shaping his libertarian philosophy in the following year when he served as secretary for Supreme Court Justice Oliver Wendell Holmes. As the *New York Times* noted thirty years later, "that experience was the dominant one in Francis Biddle's life. It gave point and direction to all his subsequent mental growth."[32] He came away with a profound commitment to the protection of civil liberites, and over the next two decades in private practice established himself as a defender of underdogs, whom he often represented without a fee.[33]

After several years in various federal positions, Biddle became the Justice Department's solicitor general in January 1940, the acting attorney general in June 1941 after Robert H. Jackson moved up to the Supreme Court, and then the attorney general three months later. Although Biddle had an excellent legal reputation, there were reservations about his appointment. New Dealers were concerned that he was "too scrupulous to be Attorney General in a crisis"; Roosevelt asked Jackson if Biddle would be "tough enough" or "too liberal"; and Hoover was worried that Biddle's liberal background would make him "soft" on Communists.[34] In addition, some suspected that Biddle might even fire Hoover.[35] Nevertheless, his appointment went through smoothly to no one's surprise, as the *New York Times* explained:

> The newest Cabinet officer comes as near fulfilling President Roosevelt's prescription for highly placed public servants as any man in the New Deal. He is first of all a stanch liberal, intellectually as well as practically. He is well grounded and respected in his profession, the law, and he has a high ideal of public service. Moreover, the circumstance of his patrician lineage and Groton–Harvard upbringing endow him with a peculiar kinship to the President's own pattern of life.[36]

Biddle, who resolved on the day he was sworn in to "guard against the desire for popularity, for public approval,"[37] quickly established himself as a defender of civil liberties, including freedom of speech. Only twelve days after becoming attorney general, he spoke to the California State Bar Association and reminded the group of what Holmes had written in a case shortly after World War I: "We do not lose our right to condemn either measures or men because the country is at war."[38] That sentiment was followed three days later by a *New York Times Magazine* portrait of Biddle. "In so far as I can, by the use of the authority and the influence of my office, I intend to see that civil liberties in this country are protected; that we do not again fall into the disgraceful hysteria of witch hunts, strike breakings and minority persecutions which were such a dark chapter in our record of the last World War," Biddle told the *Times*.[39]

If Roosevelt still thought that Biddle's attitude toward civil liberties might change when he was faced with the reality of a war, he was mistaken. On December 20, 1941, the Justice Department dismissed Espionage Act complaints against three men for "alleged seditious utterances." One of them had said that Roosevelt should be impeached for asking Congress to declare war, and another had claimed that the president supported Hitler. In announcing the dismissals, Biddle noted that "free speech as such ought not to be restricted." The majority of the press applauded his statement enthusiastically. At the same time, Biddle instructed all U.S. attorneys that there would be no further prosecutions for seditious utterances during the war without prior approval of the Department of Justice.[40]

Any final doubts about the department's wartime course must have been dispelled in a Washington radio address by Assistant Attorney General Wendell Berge on January 11, 1942. While noting that the government planned to prosecute speech violations when they were illegal or interfered with the war effort, Berge added:

I submit that the safest and most effective way to counteract the misguided mutterings of the relatively few people who have not joined with us heart and soul in our mighty effort to win this war is by intelligent and vigorous reply to such people's talk, that is, when what they say is important enough to warrant reply. . . .

We have set ourselves against those pressures and influences which cry for the prosecution of those people who are merely exercising their right of free speech guaranteed by the First Amendment of the Constitution, and whose utterances are not in themselves seditious and cannot be shown to constitute any direct interference with the conduct of the war. I believe that the people of this country are overwhelmingly behind us in this policy, and I believe that it will further be vindicated when later it can be considered in historical perspective. . . .

The Department of Justice expects . . . that freedom of speech and other constitutionally guaranteed freedoms shall emerge from this war more deeply ingrained in our way of life than ever before.[41]

Thus, two camps existed with opposing views on the value of libertarianism in wartime. In one was Roosevelt, who did not want to hear about legal technicalities when the United States was engaged in a war for survival. He wanted immediate action against all sedition, oral as well as written, and in Hoover he had just the man to pursue a vigorous course. Standing in the president's way was Biddle, who, as some critics had feared, took constitutional guarantees seriously. He was not about to be pushed onto shaky legal ground by anyone, not even Roosevelt. Like wary fighters circling and assessing their opponent, they viewed each other at long range in the war's opening months. Roosevelt continuously hinted through Hoover for action against seditionists; Biddle continuously held back. The issue would be joined in March 1942.

Into this tense scenario came the black press. It quickly became apparent that the black press's critical tone since 1938 toward the government, and particularly the military, was not about to lessen. The NAACP's *The Crisis* noted in January 1942, in an editorial widely quoted and praised by the black press, that it would not return to the "Close Ranks" position it had been pressured into by the government in World War I:

> *The Crisis* would emphasize with all its strength that now is the time not to be silent about the breaches of democracy here in our own land. Now is the time to speak out, not in disloyalty, but in the truest patriotism, the patriotism with an eye—now that the die is cast—single to the peace which must be won.
>
> Of course, between the declaration of war and the making of a just peace there lies the grim necessity of winning the conflict. To this task the Negro American quickly pledged his fullest support. Be it said once more that black Americans are loyal Americans; but let there be no mistake about the loyalty. It is loyalty to the democratic ideal as enunciated by America and by our British ally; it is not loyalty to many of the practices which have been—and are still—in vogue here and in the British empire. . . .
>
> If all the people are called to gird and sacrifice for freedom, and the armies to march for freedom, then it must be for freedom for everyone, everywhere, not merely for those under the Hitler heel.[42]

Shortly afterward, a black journalist predicted in *Common Ground* that any editor who dared to print a "Close Ranks" editorial would lose influence with black readers.[43]

At the same time, the black press attacked the navy with renewed vigor for continuing to accept blacks only as messboys. The *Pittsburgh Courier*, the country's largest and most influential black paper, turned this policy into a cause célèbre on January 3. It revealed that during the Japanese attack on Pearl Harbor a black messboy, Dorie Miller, had carried his wounded captain to safety and then had fired a machine gun at enemy airplanes until he had run out of ammunition. "Is it fair, honest or sensible that this country, with its fate in the balance, should continue to bar Negroes from service except in the mess department of the Navy, when at the first sign of danger they so dramatically show their willingness to face death in defense of the Stars and Stripes?" the *Courier* asked.[44]

Throughout the remainder of the winter and the spring, the *Courier* campaigned for Miller to receive the Congressional Medal of Honor. That was denied, but in May he was presented with the Navy Cross, his service's highest award.[45] The *Courier* was not placated. One week after Miller received the decoration, George Schuyler questioned in a front-page column why it took five months for him to be honored and why he was not brought back to the United States, like some of the white heroes at Pearl Harbor, to boost morale and help War Bond sales. "But no, the spirit of jim crow still rules in high places," said Schuyler. "It must be comforting to Hitler, Mussolini and the Japanese."[46] In late July, the *Courier* still demanded the return of Miller with antagonistic words: "The Navy finds Dorie Miller too important waiting table in the Pacific to return him so that his people might see him."[47] The paper finally got its wish in December 1942, when Miller returned home on leave.[48]

Of far more importance than the articles about Miller, however, was the *Courier's* Double V campaign, which began in February 1942. While the criticism in the Miller incident focused only on the Navy, the Double V was directed at all discrimination against blacks. This infuriated government leaders, who feared that the campaign might result in blacks, who made up 10 percent of the country's population, refusing to support the war effort at the very moment when they were most needed.

The campaign was sparked by James G. Thompson, a twenty-six-year-old cafeteria worker at the Cessna Aircraft Corporation in Wichita. In January, he wrote to the editor of the *Courier* to express his views on patriotism:

Like all true Americans, my greatest desire at this time . . . is for a complete victory over the forces of evil which threaten our existence today. Behind that desire is also a desire to serve this, my country, in the most advantageous way.

Most of our leaders are suggesting that we sacrifice every other ambition to the paramount one, victory. With this I agree; but I also wonder if another victory could not be achieved at the same time. . . .

Being an American of dark complexion . . . these questions flash through my mind: "Should I sacrifice my life to live half American?" "Will things be better for the next generation in the peace to follow?" "Would it be demanding too much to demand full citizenship rights in exchange for the sacrificing of my life?" "Is the kind of America I know worth defending?" "Will America be a true and pure democracy after this war?" "Will colored Americans suffer still the indignities that have been heaped upon them in the past?" . . .

I suggest that while we keep defense and victory in the forefront that we don't lose sight of our fight for true democracy at home.

The V for victory sign is being displayed prominently in all so-called democratic countries which are fighting for victory over aggression, slavery and tyranny. If this V sign means that to those now engaged in this great conflict, then let we colored Americans adopt the double VV for a double victory. The first V for victory over our enemies from without, the second V for victory over our enemies from within. For surely those who perpetuate these ugly prejudices here are seeking to destroy our democratic form of government just as surely as the Axis forces.[49]

Thompson's words had an immediate impact. In the next weekly issue of the *Courier* on February 7, four Double V drawings appeared, a Double V campaign was announced a week later on the front page, and within a month the newspaper was running more than 340 column inches per issue of Double V stories, photographs, and drawings.[50] The campaign's rapid acceleration and its appeal, which was demonstrated by the telegrams and letters that inundated the *Courier*, were not surprising. Thompson's letter suggested nothing radically new, but its "double VV" expression captured the imagination of blacks by vividly stating their anger at being treated like second-class citizens. Almost immediately, a national cohesiveness developed as numerous black newspapers began pushing the Double V campaign. But no one pushed it harder than the *Courier*, which became increasingly bold and even more critical of the government with the campaign's success. "WE HAVE A STAKE IN THIS FIGHT. . . . WE ARE AMERICANS, TOO!" trumpeted the *Courier* on its front page on February 14.[51]

It is doubtful that Roosevelt and Biddle were unaware of the burgeoning discontent in the black press and the intensified drive for equal rights. After all, Hoover was diligently pursuing his investigations and reporting on them in a monthly "General Intelligence Survey," which looked at activities in the United States by Germans, Japanese, Italians, French, Slavs, Poles, Spaniards, Portuguese, Puerto Ricans, Filipinos, Koreans, and Communists. Early wartime issues of the survey did not mention the black press (although it would show up prominently as the war progressed), but blacks appeared from the first, always in the Communist section. In the February 1942 survey, for example, the FBI noted that "it has been ascertained that the Party is definitely intensifying its original drive to recruit new members from among the negro race."[52]

The fact that the black press virtually did not appear in White House or Justice Department documents during the first three months of the war may have been because it seemed a minor problem compared to others confronting the administration. Or it is possible that the black press was not even considered a problem because government officials were so used to ignoring blacks.[53] But the more likely explanation is that the black press was too hot an issue to discuss on the record, even in a confidential memorandum. If such discussions had leaked out, the country's black population could have been alienated. Thus, any comments about the black press, particularly by Roosevelt, probably were deliberately not written down. The president frequently had meetings or conversations of which no written transcripts were made because of the delicate or controversial subjects discussed.[54]

The army, however, was apparently less concerned about information leaks regarding the black press. It frequently expressed its displeasure, both publicly and behind the scenes.

On December 8, in a conference that had been scheduled before the bombing at Pearl Harbor, army officials met in Washington with twenty black columnists, editors, and publishers from eleven black publications and the Associated Negro Press. The meeting's purpose was to attempt to improve relations between the black press and the army. Gen. George C. Marshall could only spend several minutes with the group because of the sudden demands thrust upon him by the war, but he impressed the visitors when he praised black men already in the army and announced that a black division might be formed. He added that he was "not personally satisfied" with the progress made toward ending discrimination in the army.[55]

The black journalists' optimism turned to anger an hour later, however, when Col. Eugene R. Householder, of the adjutant general's department, read from a prepared statement:

> The Army is not a sociological laboratory; to be effective it must be organized and trained according to principles which will insure success. Experiments to meet the wishes and demands of the champions of every race and creed for the solution of their problems are a danger to efficiency, discipline and morale and would result in ultimate defeat.[56]

Householder went on to criticize the black press for "frequently" writing about alleged mistreatment of blacks in the service, only to have the allegations disproved by subsequent army investigations. He noted that such inaccuracies hurt morale and placed the army in an untenable position, since an official refutation "proves unavailing in erasing such feeling" and "would only engender more and more controversy." He recommended that before publishing any future stories about service inequities toward blacks, journalists should query the army, which would expedite an investigation into the facts and then report back to the press, thus eliminating factual errors. Householder continued:

If this procedure is generally adopted by all of the Negro press, it will make for better morale, both among the Negro troops and their people at home. Moreover, it will serve to strengthen the credibility in the War Department of the Negro press which has suffered because of the publication of unfounded reports.[57]

That was not the only attack. To compound their annoyance, the journalists also had to sit through a tirade by Brig. Gen. Benjamin O. Davis, who was the first black to achieve his rank largely because of the backing of the black press. He accused them of "sowing discontent in the minds of the soldiers" through the use of "propaganda."[58]

The conference received mixed reviews in the black press. Although Householder's comments about a "sociological laboratory" were understood to mean that the army was not going to change its racial policy, most of the editors played up the announcement of a new black division and suggested that there would be "steady but slow progress" in ending discrimination in the army. The *Newark (N.J.) Herald–News*, however, said the conference should "properly be placed in a compartment and marked 'File and Forget.' . . . It convinced no one, not already convinced, that racial segregation or color proscriptions have any place in the official policy of a nation dedicated to the defense of democracy and democratic institutions."[59]

The fact that the black press continued to complain about the military, particularly after the origination of the Double V campaign in early February, was not surprising. As historian John Morton Blum has noted, the military's "unchanging policies" resulted in most of the black criticism:

Angry about military segregation, blacks detested the harassment they suffered from Military Police, the abuses they suffered from civilians in towns near cantonments, especially in the South, and the Army's endorsement of Jim Crow regulations in cities frequented by troops on liberty. Segregation on Southern trains and buses especially irritated northern blacks in training camps in Dixie.[60]

These were not the only complaints. In January 1942, for example, the War Department, under pressure from the NAACP, was forced to withdraw an order at a Pennsylvania camp which said that "any association between the colored soldiers and white women, whether voluntary or not, would be considered rape." Causing an even bigger uproar two weeks later was an army appeal for 3000 more nurses, of which only 56 could be black. Furthermore, it was announced that black nurses would be restricted to caring for black soldiers.[61]

Such complaints, which were played up on the front pages of black newspapers, did not go unnoticed by the army. From December 1941 through February 1942, military intelligence collected what it considered "inflammatory" articles from numerous black publications. These included the *Oklahoma City Black Dispatch* (which ran a headline, "War Department Aids Hitler by Letting South Wreck [sic] Prejudice on Negro Soldiers"), the *Pittsburgh Courier*, the *Chicago Defender*, the *Cleveland Call and Post*, the *Denver Star*, the *Colorado Statesman* (also published in Denver), and the *Baltimore Afro-American*, which had editions in Philadelphia, Washington, Richmond, and Newark.[62] At Camp Livingston in Louisiana, unnamed black papers were blamed in late February for lowering the morale of black soldiers by "exaggerating troop conditions and actually making false statements." In addition, "the agitation of northern Negro newspapers on race issues" was listed as one of the causes for recent riots at the camp.[63] In another serious charge, seventeen black publications were listed by Military Intelligence on February 21 as "carrying abnormally inflammatory articles, sponsored by Communists."[64] Such comments were only a prelude to what would happen soon to black publications at army posts: blacklistings of those newspapers and magazines considered subversive.

Unlike the army, two other agencies that would be deeply involved with the black press, the Post Office and the Office of Facts and Figures, had more pressing problems in the war's early months. However, the groundwork was established that would lead them shortly to black publications.

At the Post Office, Solicitor Vincent M. Miles reminded postmasters in *The Postal Bulletin* of January 15, 1942, that the Espionage Act made "seditious and disloyal matter" unmailable in wartime. He advised them to send him any publication that might violate the law, for an opinion on whether it was mailable,[65] and an avalanche of material poured into Washington. According to the postmaster's annual reports during the war, more than 17,000 publications were examined for their mailability between December 7, 1941, and June 30, 1945, and "detailed legal opinions" were prepared for each.[66]

Early wartime Post Office investigations included a wide variety of publications. For example, a reader complained in January 1942 that *The Kiplinger Washington Letter* was a "rotten piece of treasonable advertising" that "creates hysteria." A cursory examination by the Post Office, however, resulted in the ruling that it was unobjectionable. "Its purpose appears to be primarily constructive rather than destructive," concluded the examiner.[67] Not surprisingly, a majority of the early work focused on foreign-language publications and publications printed in English by various nationalities, particularly the Germans and the Japanese. Under the pressure of wartime, the Post Office proved to be exceptionally tough. In a typical incident in February 1942, the postmaster in Fresno wrote that he had been requiring the publisher of a local Japanese weekly newspaper, the *Japanese Times of Central California*, to provide him with a translation of each issue along with a signed affidavit stating that the translation was "true, correct and complete." Miles approved heartily, ignoring the fact that the Post Office probably was on questionable legal ground, and told the postmaster that his actions were "worthy of commendation."[68]

The office of Facts and Figures (OFF), meanwhile, had even

less to do with the press in the war's opening months, mainly because it was not an enforcement agency. OFF was created in July 1941 by Roosevelt as part of the Office of Civilian Defense, which was headed by Fiorello La Guardia. One of its chief duties involved sustaining morale by "collecting and analyzing information and opinion from the news media and, when appropriate, producing corrective material for distribution to the press."[69] When La Guardia's leadership proved ineffective, Roosevelt in October made OFF an independent agency, responsible to the White House, and named Archibald MacLeish, the librarian of Congress, as director.[70]

From the beginning, the government attempted to hide the fact that OFF essentially was involved in propaganda. That is apparently why Roosevelt gave it such an innocuous title.[71] La Guardia once noted, seemingly in a joking manner, that "the Office of Facts and Figures is not a propaganda agency. There are three reasons why it is not. The first is that we don't believe in this country in artificially stimulated, high-pressure, doctored nonsense, and since we don't, the other two reasons are unimportant."[72] In a more serious vein, MacLeish agreed, claiming both publicly and privately that he was against "bally-hoo methods" and would confine the agency to disseminating facts and figures that were neither "perverted nor colored." This information was to be passed on to the public by other governmental departments and agencies.[73]

When the war began, OFF immediately began conducting surveys, and "Negro Attitudes Toward the War" in January 1942 represented the first of a series of reports that year on blacks. In addition, OFF started assembling weekly media reports in February.[74] Thus, it was only natural that black newspapers quickly became a subject of government interest.

Meanwhile, as the first three months of the war drew to a close, the black press was becoming more powerful, with circulations on the rise and the Double V campaign gaining in strength and popularity each week. But black publishers had reason to be concerned. For all of the bravado in their papers, they could not ignore the pressure to conform and help the war effort while putting aside until peacetime all efforts to end discrimination. "Even the boldest Negro writers cannot say all that's in their hearts at a time like this," wrote the *Pittsburgh Courier's* J. A. Rogers in early February. "There are always underhand, Gestapo methods of cracking down on Negro publications. . . . Don't think that the Nazis have a monopoly on high-handed tactics."[75]

Rogers had no way of knowing that a black chain of five newspapers already was in danger of being suppressed. At the FBI, Hoover sought his first Espionage Act indictment of the black press before the United States had been the war two months. It stemmed from a December 20, 1941, article in the *Afro-American* newspapers in which five blacks in Richmond commented on what Japan's attitude would be toward blacks if it won the war. "The colored races as a whole would benefit," a printer said. " . . . This would be the first step in the darker races coming back into their own." Two of the other blacks agreed, which caused Hoover to ask Berge on January 30 if the *Afro-American* chain had violated any federal sedition statutes. Berge replied less than a week later that the papers were operating within the law because the answers of the three blacks were "mere expressions of individual opinion as to the possible course of future events." They were not "false statements," which would have been covered by federal statutes. "Clear" evidence also was lacking, he continued, that the statements were designed to harm the armed forces or affect recruiting or enlistment. Nevertheless, Berge encouraged an immediate investigation of the *Afro-American's* ownership as well as the "character and pertinent activities" of its editors to determine if there was a tie-in with "hostile or subversive sources." This set in motion an extensive FBI investigation of the chain which lasted almost throughout the war.[76]

Although the black press did not know of Hoover's actions, it found unsettling the continuous rumors that blacks were easy dupes for enemy propaganda. The *Pittsburgh Courier* moved as early as January 17, 1942, to counter any charges of possible disloyalty. "The Japanese, Germans, Italians and their Axis stooges know that it is futile to seek spies, saboteurs or Fifth Columnists among American Negroes," the paper declared. "Every attempt in that direction has been a miserable failure."[77] But any good to come out of that editorial probably was undone a week later when the paper ran a critical letter from a black soldier. "I doubt if the Japs are as bad as we are made to believe," he wrote. "I doubt if they would treat loyal, patriotic citizens as badly as the Negro is treated in America."[78] Why the *Courier* ran such a letter is unknown.

Despite its criticisms of the government, the black press moved quickly in a variety of ways in late 1941 and early 1942 to demonstrate its loyalty. In late February, for example, *Pittsburgh Courier* columnist Edgar T. Rouzeau became the first of many black journalists to write Roosevelt during the war to assure him of black loyalty. In his letter, Rouzeau criticized blacks "who falsely preach to the masses that this is a white man's war" with nothing to be gained by blacks. He noted that he had written a column in early February refuting that contention and claimed that "scores" of blacks wrote to the paper saying that they realized that "the salvation of the Negro race was to be found in an all-out Negro effort for the salvation of America."[79] There is no record of Roosevelt's reaction to the letter, if indeed he ever saw it.

That was not the only attempt in the war's first three months to convince the government of the black press's loyalty. On December 20, 1941, the *Chicago Defender* carried an editorial setting forth its view on the wartime role of the press:

> The Negro press will not blemish its magnificent record of sound patriotism by indulging in subversive advocacy to the impairment of the national will. However, unless and until constitutional guarantees are suspended, the Negro press will continue to use its moral force against the mob in its criminal orgy, against such ultra violences as lynching, burning at [the] stake and judicial murder. It will continue to fight for those legitimate democratic

rights that have been denied the Negro. It will insist on the thesis
that the best way to save democracy is to extend it to all the
citizens without regard to color or race. Such an attitude
can hardly be construed as smacking of disloyalty and disaffection. . . .

We are for national unity. We are for victory. We are for a working
democracy. But, no one must conclude that in opposing clear cut
discriminations in civilian life or in the army and navy, that the
Negro press is disloyal. In this opposition is the essence of loyalty
and devotion to democracy—and a free press.[80]

A *Defender* official sent a copy of the editorial to Hoover, stressing that the paper wanted "to give a full pledge of allegiance
to the cause of war of the republic of the United States." Admitting that the paper was worried that its numerous articles
on discrimination might result in it being censored, the official
therefore invited the FBI to contact the paper if there was a
question about anything that was published. "We will withhold
nothing that may give you a full understanding of the facts and
motives which provoked the printing of the article," the official
promised. Hoover replied on January 3 that he appreciated the
"spirit" of the paper's letter, but he recommended that the
Defender should contact Byron Price, director of the Office of
Censorship.[81]

Whether the *Defender* followed Hoover's advice is unclear.
But Moss Hyles Kendrix, director of the National Negro Newspaper Week, wrote Price in February to inform him about the
annual observance from March 1 to March 7 and noted that it
was "especially designed to assure America of the full support
of its race papers in the war effort." John H. Sorrells, the assistant censorship director, encouraged Price to write back,
because "it seems to me that this might be a chance to say
something [about the black press] which ought to be said, at
this time." Price agreed, and after lauding the newspaper week
in a letter of February 26, he tactfully suggested what the government felt the black press's role should be in the war:

The Negro press has an opportunity in this crisis to render possibly its greatest service both to its own race and to the country. It already is evident that the propaganda bureaus of Germany and Japan will do their utmost by their customary lies and false promises to incite hatreds throughout the world. Here the Negro press is in a position to counsel sanely and wisely and to expose the progaganda for what it is.[82]

Thus, there were small but visible ripples of concern from the black press as the war's first three months concluded. Such concern was well founded. Over the next five months, Biddle and Roosevelt would clash head-on over seditionists, and the black press's future would hang in the balance.

4

"If You Want to Close Us, Go Ahead and Attempt It"

(March–August 1942)

The two men facing each other at the Justice Department in mid-June 1942 were an interesting contrast. Francis Biddle was a wealthy Philadelphian, who had attended Harvard and then established himself as a highly respected lawyer. Now, as attorney general, he held one of the country's most powerful wartime positions. John Sengstacke also had gone to college, but to the less prestigious Hampton Institute, and he was a veteran of the rough-and-tumble world of black journalism, where profit margins were small and press failures were common. As publisher of the *Chicago Defender* as well as founder of the Negro Newspaper Publishers Association in 1940, he too had power.

Against this diversity of background, the two men shared a striking similarity. Both were libertarians. *Newsweek* had noted several weeks before their meeting that Biddle was "an almost fanatical believer" in civil liberties,[1] which he had demonstrated in early 1942 by his reluctance to evacuate the West Coast Japanese to internment camps. Such stubbornness should have surprised no one. After all, Biddle was well known for being a "strict constructionist" in his constitutional views.[2] "The most important job an Attorney General can do in a time of emergency is to protect civil liberties," Biddle told the *New York Times Magazine* in September 1941 shortly after taking over at the Justice Department.[3] And yet people were surprised. Surely, his liberal friends had reasoned, his views on civil liberties would change under the exigencies of wartime, but they quickly realized, as did Roosevelt, that "to him the word 'tolerance' is more than a word."[4] That view carried over to his belief that it was permissible to criticize the government during wartime. In fact, he questioned whether there should be any sedition statutes because he felt they were "harmful."[5]

Sengstacke was equally fanatical about libertarianism. He liked to point out proudly that black newspapers had been engaged for more than 100 years in what he called a "mission"—fighting race prejudice by "calling the shots as we see them." The mere presence of a war was not about to cause his paper to abrogate its duty to blacks. There would be no backing down this time as the black press had done in World War I. To those who criticized his absolute form of libertarianism, claiming it was helping the enemy in the midst of a savage war for survival, he had a blunt answer: "We've always been Americans!" To him, that said it all, and it justified whatever his paper wrote to further the black cause.[6]

With such strong beliefs, it was inevitable that Biddle and Sengstacke would discuss libertarianism as it related to the press at their June meeting. Specifically, Biddle had been under constant pressure from Roosevelt for several months to control seditionists and had altered somewhat his position on libertarianism. He was now insistent that the black press must immediately become less critical because it was hurting the war effort. Sengstacke was equally insistent that the black press would not tone down unless the government worked more closely with it. They were two tough men in a no-nonsense confrontation, and both knew that the future of the black press was at stake.

Their meeting had its genesis in late March, when Roosevelt became irritated at the Justice Department for tolerating what he considered sedition. The president had waited with mounting impatience for Biddle to crack down ever since the bombing of Pearl Harbor but to no avail. He had tried dropping hints;

he had even tried humor. On January 5, for example, Biddle had arrived at the White House to make a report just as Roosevelt was finishing lunch with five aides and friends. Before having Biddle ushered in, the president told his guests, "You know, Francis is terribly worried about civil liberties—especially now. He has been on my neck asking me to say that the war will not curtail them too much. Now don't laugh and give me away, but I'm going to hand him a little line." Then he told Biddle with a stern face that he wanted him to draft a proclamation "abrogating so far as possible all freedom of discussion and information during the war" because "it's absolutely necessary." The attorney general, who appeared "thunderstruck," argued vigorously and eloquently against such a proclamation for five minutes, all the time pacing nervously, before the president broke into laughter and admitted it was only a joke.[7]

But two months later Roosevelt had ceased to be amused. The president had tired of Biddle's explanations of why there had been no sedition indictments; he had tired of receiving numerous letters complaining about the attorney general's "softness"; and he must have been stung by congressional criticism, which was growing.[8] For example, on March 17, Democratic Representative Hale Boggs of Louisiana blasted Biddle's "benign policy . . . toward treasonable publications" from the floor of Congress and said that such "filth" should be suppressed.[9] Thus, in early March, it was not surprising that the attorney general realized that the president considered him "out of step." But he still refused to move against the seditionists, although he knew he was incurring presidential displeasure by his inaction. "He [Roosevelt] was not much interested in the theory of sedition, or in the constitutional right to criticize the government in wartime," Biddle recalled. "He wanted this antiwar talk stopped."[10] Biddle held firm, however, not only because he believed that his interpretation of the Constitution's First Amendment was correct, but also because, as one journalist noted, his position made him "a sort of 'keeper of the President's conscience.' " Someone had to act as a check on the president's war powers or a permanent dictatorship might result, and Biddle felt obligated to provide that check, even though it placed him in an unenviable position. It was no exaggeration when a journalist described the attorney general in 1942 as occupying "the hottest spot in the government."[11]

That became apparent on March 20. Roosevelt received a confidential memorandum which noted that J. Edgar Hoover wanted to move against seditionists, but he and his agents had been "blocked by the attorney general time and time again in case after case." Therefore, he suggested that it would be "necessary" for the president to talk to Biddle before the FBI "would be permitted to act in these cases."[12] For Roosevelt, that apparently was the proverbial final straw. At a Cabinet meeting on the same day, the president promptly brought up "subversive sheets" and said something had to be done about them. Probably anticipating such a request, Biddle mentioned the possibility of withdrawing some second-class mailing permits, going to court against "the one or two possible violations" of the Espionage Act, and getting Congress to enact new legislation, enlarging the discretion of the attorney general to move against seditious propaganda. While Biddle must have cringed inwardly at merely suggesting such antilibertarian measures, he probably felt his response would dissipate the pressure. But he was wrong. In an ensuing discussion, the entire Cabinet backed Roosevelt in demanding that Biddle take "vigorous action" against seditionists.[13] It is unknown whether any particular journalists were mentioned at the meeting, or whether those who were considered seditionists included nonjournalists. However, Roosevelt's definition of seditionists undoubtedly was far broader than Biddle's.

As it turned out, the president's new hard-line approach on seditionists could hardly have come at a more inopportune time for Biddle. On the following day, *Collier's* ran an article by the attorney general, "Taking No Chances," which was an ironic title because it more aptly described Roosevelt's view toward seditionists. The attorney general once again advocated taking a soft line and not moving against those who criticized the government. After noting the government's elaborate precautions with aliens immediately after Pearl Harbor, Biddle wrote:

> I have been heartened . . . by universal encouragement from the press in our policy not to suppress expressions of opinion, however critical of the government. . . . Subversive doctrines cannot flourish on free speech. . . . Men should never, under our law, be prosecuted for their opinions, however they may disturb the beliefs we cherish or oppose the moral assumptions that most of us share. . . .
>
> That, at any rate, as Justice Holmes said over twenty years ago in a case rising out of the last war, is the theory of our Constitution. "It is an experiment," he added, "as all life is an experiment. While that experiment is part of our system I think we should be eternally vigilant against attempts to check the expression of opinions that we loathe and believe to be fraught with death unless they so imminently threaten immediate interference with the lawful and pressing purposes of the law that an immediate check is required to save the country."[14]

Such sentiments, criticized the day before by no less than the president, must have caused Biddle problems. However, documents do not show whether the attorney general ever discussed the article with Roosevelt.

After the president finally began pressing on March 20 for an end to seditious utterances and publications, he did not let up. At a March 24 press conference, he criticized some of the newspapermen and broadcasters present, whom he refused to name, as "unwittingly or wittingly" being dupes of fifth columnists by using material injurious to the war effort.[15] On the same day, he sent Biddle memoranda from Secretary of the Navy Frank Knox, who was the publisher of the *Chicago Daily News* from 1931 to 1940, and Judge Advocate General of the Navy W. B. Woodson. Both recommended that the *Chicago Tribune*, the *Washington Times–Herald*, and the *New York Daily News* be charged under the Smith Act, which was passed in 1940 to deal with peacetime sedition, for articles that appeared on December 4, 1941. The stories reported the contents of a "Top Secret" document that outlined U.S. plans to enter the European war. "A few examples made of this sort of reckless disregard of national security would do a lot, I am convinced, to improve the situation so far as newspapers are concerned," wrote Knox. Roosevelt agreed and instructed Biddle to prepare a "reply with the thought that an offensive is always better than a defensive."[16] An assistant attorney general recalled that Biddle also believed that the three papers had gone too far and wanted to go to court. However, the Justice Department staff was so busy with more important wartime matters that the papers were never charged.[17]

Roosevelt's sudden demand for action turned out to be the only time the president directly pressured Biddle in the almost four years during which he was attorney general. He recalled twenty years later that the president would frequently procrastinate when faced with decisions. "Yet when he wanted to act," continued Biddle, "particularly where the war called for speed—and war decisions almost invariably did—he would hound the responsible official, often calling him more than once personally."[18]

While such pressure was a new experience for Biddle, he had seen it applied by Roosevelt once before in the Justice Department under similar circumstances. In early 1940, shortly after Biddle became solicitor general, Roosevelt began suggesting strongly that Attorney General Robert H. Jackson should move against the country's aliens. As the German blitzkrieg had swept through Europe, Americans had become increasingly concerned that aliens were possible fifth columnists, and this led to both Congress and the states considering repressive measures against them. Jackson, who was a liberal like Biddle, quickly became concerned because he recalled uneasily the "Red Scare" days of the World War I era. He was determined to have no repetition of that period, but that presented the dilemma of how to satisfy Roosevelt. Biddle recalled that the president felt "the American people had to be reassured. The appearance was as important as the reality. . . . His Attorney General must appear to be tough, even though he was not temperamentally inclined to such a role. He must make the people feel secure against these new totalitarian threats."[19] Jackson resolved the problem by asking citizens to report sabotage and espionage, as well as other disloyal activities, to the FBI, demonstrating toughness, while at the same time cautioning everyone to remain calm. Later in the year, when Biddle headed a program that registered and fingerprinted almost 5 million aliens, he continually followed the Jackson line, stressing not only what foreigners had done for the United States but that loyal "noncitizens" must be treated the same as citizens.[20]

Therefore, Roosevelt's pressure on Biddle in 1942 was not without precedent. Biddle faced an even tougher dilemma than Jackson, however. The latter merely had had to maintain an already established semblance of toughness at the Justice Department in 1940. But by March 1942, with Biddle's outspoken advocacy of civil liberties and his refusal to move against seditionists, the semblance of toughness had deteriorated badly, and the attorney general faced the much tougher task of reestablishing it in the face of public doubt.

Contributing importantly to the public's soft image was the reluctance of Biddle and the Justice Department to evacuate 125,000 Japanese from the West Coast. By mid-January 1942, pressure was building for an evacuation of all Japanese, including not only aliens but those born in the United States as well. Californians were in the forefront of the removal campaign because they disliked business competition from the Japanese and also feared an enemy-inspired uprising. Biddle immediately resisted any evacuation, feeling that "the program was ill-advised, unnecessary, and unnecessarily cruel."[21] He also felt that a mass evacuation was illegal. "The Bill of Rights protects not only American citizens, but all human beings who live on American soil," Biddle said.[22] However, over the next month, with complaints about the Japanese coming from such diverse sources as congressmen, the American Legion, Walter Lippmann, Westbrook Pegler, the Hearst press, and the Los Angeles Chamber of Commerce, Biddle was forced to give up his opposition to the removal.[23] "Only a great outcry of protest on the highest moral grounds could have stopped the drift toward evacuation, and Biddle was neither temperamentally nor politically capable of it," said historian James MacGregor Burns.[24] After Roosevelt signed an executive order approving the evacuation, Biddle concluded that the removal's constitutional difficulties never bothered the president; but then "the Constitution has never greatly bothered any wartime President. That was a question of law, which ultimately the Supreme Court must decide."[25]

As a result of Biddle's reluctance to evacuate the Japanese, an assistant attorney general recalled that the public thought the Justice Department was made up of "incompetents."[26] Certainly that view was evident from a derisive term, "Biddling along," which was originated at the time by Californians to refer to anything ineffectual.[27] Such criticism, combined with Roosevelt's sudden emphatic demand to do something about seditionists, obviously put Biddle's job in jeopardy. The president wanted action, and he was determined to get it one way or another. Fortunately for Biddle, he had an extremely capable and politically astute aide in Assistant Attorney General James H. Rowe, Jr. It is not an exaggeration to say that Rowe may very well have been responsible for Biddle remaining attorney general in the troubled spring of 1942.

Like Biddle, Rowe was a Harvard alumnus who, following graduation, spent a year from 1934 to 1935 as the last secretary to Supreme Court Justice Holmes. After three more years in Washington in various governmental and Democratic Party posts, he was named an assistant in 1938 to James Roosevelt, who was serving as a secretary to his father at the White House. A year later, he became an administrative assistant and confidant to the President, a position he held until late 1941. At that time, Biddle's first assistant, Matthew F. McGuire, was appointed to a federal judgeship, and Biddle asked Rowe to join him at the Justice Department. Rowe, who had always wanted to be attorney general, accepted the offer eagerly. "I felt like I had been in the White House long enough," said Rowe, who recalled that Roosevelt tried to talk him into staying. "I felt like the White House was training me only to be president, and I knew I wouldn't be that. I knew I wasn't going to learn any more."[28]

When Rowe joined the department in December 1941, he found it somewhat in disarray and unable to cope with the war emergency. Indeed, "Biddling along" was an appropriate description. One problem was that the career men in the lower echelons were extremely capable and "pretty tough guys," but the majority of those with real power at the top were not tough enough and were not good trial lawyers. With Biddle's approval, Rowe immediately went about making changes to develop "a harder line." In addition, Biddle's liberal attitude, which was far more to the left than that of almost anyone else in the department, was rarely challenged by those under him because he was the attorney general. Rowe, however, was not awed by Biddle and not afraid to argue with him. "You have to remember that Biddle and I were great friends before I even joined the Justice Department. And I had an extra edge—he may have thought that Roosevelt was behind me. No, he wasn't, but I never discouraged that kind of thinking and Biddle never asked me," he recalled with a laugh.[29] Twenty years later, Biddle admitted that he prized Rowe not only for his political knowledge but because "he was aggressive, and could stand up and fight. . . . He was obstinate within reasonable bounds." Equally important, Biddle said that Rowe was "continually on the lookout to protect me from some inadvertent mistake."[30]

Rowe's outspokenness and protective attitude were particularly evident on March 23, only three days after Roosevelt lashed out at Biddle at the Cabinet meeting. Rowe agreed with the president that some of the seditionists should be silenced legally. After becoming a close friend of Roosevelt and seeing the press "kicking the hell" out of him, Rowe arrived at the Justice Department with the belief that the press needed "a good kick in the teeth."[31] However, the department's image, in the eyes of both the president and the public, was of more immediate concern to Rowe in late March. That was why Rowe wrote Biddle a three-page memorandum, "more as a friend than as a subordinate," in which he admitted he was "seriously disturbed about the Department both (1) from the short-range point of view and (2) from a long-range point of view." He continued:

There is instilled in the public mind a belief that you and the Department in general are "civil liberties boys" and "softies." . . . This public belief grew, first of all, from our handling of the alien enemy problem. We emphasized that most alien enemies are loyal. We soon found we had to change our tune, play down the loyalty of the many and emphasize how tough we were on the disloyal few. Unfortunately our change in tactics was "too little and too late."

There is constant "needling" going on: [Walter] Winchell has been doing it for weeks; last night he was much more vicious than usual. You must have seen Lippman [sic] the other day. I am convinced a great deal of it is planted by the Army. I am also convinced much of this is being presented exparte to the President. I don't know this to be a fact, but I spent enough years in "palace politics" to know that your enemies are taking advantage of this atmosphere. . . .

The question is what should be done immediately about it. . . . The hard, down to rock, fact is that we are at war and the entire Department of Justice is not equipped to fight a war. . . . I believe, Francis, that we are up against the gun! We had better get moving fast and set up some machinery that can move fast.[32]

Rowe suggested to Biddle that the department could improve its image immediately by moving quickly and publicly against some of the radical seditionists. In doing so, he said the actions should be dramatized in order to "jack up our public relations." "We must do this in a hurry," he stressed. "Otherwise the impression will be that we were reluctantly forced into action by adverse press criticism. Candidly, I think we may be in that position already."[33] More than forty years later, Rowe said that the department's disarray, particularly in terms of its mediocre trial lawyers, was why he suggested going after only extreme radicals. Other members of the press were simply too dangerous. "If you take the press on [in court], you had better be sure you're going to win at the end," he said. Thus, since the department was in no postion to "risk losing face in court," it limited itself to indictments that appeared to be sure victories.[34]

Biddle wasted little time in following Rowe's suggestions. For a man who had been avoiding action against seditionists for months, it would appear surprising that he could now proceed so rapidly. However, the long-vigilant and overzealous Hoover had more than enough information on radicals for the attorney general to move immediately. On March 25, Biddle held a press conference (which was suggested in Rowe's memorandum) to announce that sedition charges would be filed soon in three or four cases. Putting the department's lack of prosecutions in the most believable light, he claimed that he had moved slowly because he felt "we would get stronger cases—and we have." He also admitted that he finally had realized (it would have been more correct to say Roosevelt had made him realize) that written articles were more dangerous now than in World War I, and seditious utterances in the future might be considered the equivalent of seditious acts.[35] Biddle's announcement drew little attention from the press, which found far more newsworthy his statement about upcoming denaturalization cases against thirty to forty persons affiliated with subversive groups. But after months of apparent inactivity against seditionists, the reporters could not have known how rapidly the Justice Department was moving behind the scenes.

On March 27, the government's crackdown began in what *Newsweek* called a "real sensation."[36] George W. Christians of Chattanooga, organizer of the Fascist Crusader White Shirts, and Denver's Rudolph Fahl, a former high-school physical education teacher, were arrested and charged with sedition for distributing subversive material among army officers. Four days later, the Justice Department swooped down again, this time in Los Angeles, as it filed similar charges against Robert Noble and Ellis O. Jones, who had formed the Friends of Progress movement for National Socialism. Then, on April 4, federal agents completed a rapid nine-day roundup by arresting William Dudley Pelley and two aides, Lawrence A. Brown and Agnes Marion Henderson, who operated the Fellowship Press in Noblesville, Indiana. Pelley, leader of the pro-German Silver Shirts of America, was well known for publishing *The Galilean*, which had said after the bombing of Pearl Harbor that "the typical American . . . gloats when any of the Axis powers reports success abroad—even against our own forces." All were indicted by federal grand juries by June 9, and all were found guilty by August 5, except Fahl, who was acquitted.[37]

The Justice Department's sudden moves against seditionists, which continued throughout 1942 with about 150 persons arrested for utterances and publications by the end of the year, did not go unnoticed by the press.[38] However, in an example of the antilibertarian feeling lurking just below the surface in the press, Biddle was criticized mildly for waiting so long to act. *Time*, for example, noted that "milquetoast" had finally gotten "muscles."[39] A *Commonweal* editor, complaining bitterly about Biddle's "extreme forbearance with our poison-pen press" until the end of March, wished "more power to him" in the future. The article continued:

Winning the war is now the thing that chiefly counts. How deeply the acids of national dissolution have already eaten into the will-power and physical energy of our people with the aid of the conscious or unconscious pro-Axis press is alarmingly evident; and it is more than high time for the evil process to be ruthlessly checked. It will not do to sit idly by and wait for treasonable acts, clearly demonstrable results of this, that or the other specific utterances of this or that person. That would be fine for Hitler and the Japanese, and fine for the native anti-democratic forces that are well organized among us, and possess tremendous power, and who are out to take over this country's fate and line it up with the Axis "wave of the future"; but it would be national suicide for traditional America; and since traditional America is

now guarded by a government that enjoys the overwhelming
support of the majority of our people, that government should
employ the law of war and not the law of peacetime to protect
itself and the nation and all our hopes for a tolerable future.[40]

In the *Atlantic Monthly*, famed broadcaster and author William
L. Shirer expressed thankfulness that Biddle had not brought
back the witch hunts of the World War I period, but he also
criticized the government for being too "hesitant" about going
after fifth columnists. "Why can't a democracy be strong and
tough enough to squelch the little minority which is out to
destroy it?" he asked. "Is there anything undemocratic about
being strong and tough?"[41]

The press was not alone in putting pressure on Biddle to
return more sedition indictments. Roosevelt also remained re-
lentless. Biddle recalled that the president continued "to go
for me in the Cabinet" for four months after the March 20
meeting:

> His technique was always the same. When my turn came, as he
> went around the table, his habitual affability dropped. He did not
> ask me as usual, if I had anything to report. He looked at me,
> his face pulled tightly together. "When are you going to indict
> the seditionists?" he would ask; and the next week, and every
> week after that, until the indictment was found, he would repeat
> the same question. Of course I felt uncomfortable. I told him that
> there was an immense amount of evidence; that I wanted the
> indictment to stick when it was challenged; and that we could
> not indict these men for their naked writings and spoken words
> without showing what effect they had on the war effort. His way
> of listening made my explanation sound unreal. At the Cabinet
> meeting a day or two after the return of an indictment he said,
> now in his most conciliatory manner, "I was glad to see, Francis
> that the grand jury returned a true bill."[42]

But Roosevelt was not satisfied with getting his point across
to Biddle merely in Cabinet meetings. During April and May,
he kept hammering away at the attorney general in conferences

and memoranda. On April 22, for example, the president talked to Biddle about the "subversive mind" of Eleanor M. ("Cissy") Patterson, the publisher of the *Washington Times–Herald*, and suggested putting surveillances on her and her cousin, Joseph Patterson, the publisher of the *New York Daily News*. Obviously finding it politically necessary now to temper his libertarian views, Biddle promptly followed Roosevelt's instructions with no apparent qualms. His new attitude also was apparent publicly as he left the White House following his conference with the president. Biddle told newspapermen that a number of federal grand juries in large cities would begin immediate investigations into "dirty little sheets," such as *Social Justice*, to determine if they were seditious.[43] Eight days later, the president complained in a note to his press secretary about a United Press article on the Office of Price Administration that he felt was "partisan" rather than balanced. He suggested that the wire service should be telephoned or visited occasionally so it would know that it was being "watched."[44] It is likely that the Justice Department conducted that "open" surveillance, too.

Then, on May 7, the president sent Biddle a compilation of clippings from the *Chicago Tribune*, the *New York Daily News*, *Social Justice*, and the Hearst newspapers, all of which were antiadministration organs. The clippings were carefully selected to show how these publications promoted the Axis way of thinking, thus hurting the war effort. Roosevelt told the attorney general that he ought to consider charging them with sedition as well as publicizing what they were writing, "to let the whole country know the truth about these papers. The tie-in between the attitude of these papers and the Rome–Berlin broadcast is something far greater than mere coincidence." The Justice Department quickly conducted its own analysis of the editorials, columns, and letters and concluded that none of them followed the German propaganda line. Therefore, Biddle took no action, which was rather courageous considering Roosevelt's unhappiness with him.[45] In still another example of pressure, Roosevelt kept in close contact with Biddle in May while a compromise was worked out ending the publication of *Social Justice* but not resulting in any sedition charges against its nationally known publisher, Rev. Charles E. Coughlin.[46]

Roosevelt also kept the pressure on Biddle by occasionally reassuring the nation that seditionists would not be tolerated. In a "Fireside Chat" on April 28, 1942, he declared that "this great war effort . . . must not be impeded by a few bogus patriots who use the sacred freedom of the press to echo the sentiments of the propagandists in Tokyo and Berlin."[47] That statement worried Rowe, although only four days earlier Roosevelt had "commended" Biddle in a Cabinet meeting on his recent action against seditionists.[48] Rowe wrote Biddle the day after the president's "Fireside Chat" that "the signs are clear our actions are far from satisfactory to him." Therefore, he said he had met that day with the Justice Department attorneys who were working on the sedition cases and had needled them for two hours. "I yelled 'action, action, action,' " Rowe wrote, adding that now he felt the attorneys would work faster. "I can think of nothing more important at present for the Department of Justice than to get on top of, and perhaps a little ahead of, this situation in relation to the President," he concluded.[49] Again, Biddle followed Rowe's advice promptly. Two days later, at a Cabinet meeting, Biddle mentioned the sedition cases, although the president had not asked about them, and gave "a detailed report" on a dozen cases that were being investigated by the Justice Department. The attorney general also showed Roosevelt some press clippings to prove that the department was receiving favorable publicity. Biddle said this put the president "in excellent spirits."[50]

Shortly afterward, on May 22, the black press was discussed at a Cabinet meeting, possibly for the only time during the war.[51] It was included in a general discussion of the black situation, "which everybody seemed to think was rather acute," noted Biddle. The president suggested that both Biddle and Postmaster General Frank Walker should talk to some of the black editors "to see what could be done about preventing their subversive language."[52]

It is likely that Roosevelt merely wanted to frighten the black editors into toning down and never seriously considered supressing any of the black press. Blacks had played an important part in his reelection in 1940, and he would not have wanted to alienate them. At the same time, assigning Biddle and Walker to talk to the black editors was characteristic of the way Roosevelt dealt with blacks during most of his presidential career. There was more to it than efficiently spreading around the heavy wartime workload. He mainly had little contact with blacks while in office—for example, none of the black press was allowed to attend his press conferences until 1944—because he did not want to offend Southern voters. That did not mean, however, that he was a racist. Instead, historian Nathan Miller has observed that Roosevelt was a "gradualist" when it came to race affairs. "He believed that the rising living standards and broadened educational opportunities that were being provided by the New Deal for all Americans would also improve conditions for blacks," says Miller.[53] Burns, meanwhile, has summed up Roosevelt's position toward blacks as "a mixture of concern, realism and resignation."[54] Thus, while blacks took immense strides forward under Roosevelt, and he was responsible for many of the improvements, he preferred doing his work through others, who could take the blame if actions were unpopular. His wife, Eleanor, was one of those who worked closely with blacks. When asked if it was wise politically for his wife to do that, Roosevelt explained, "I can always say, 'Well, that's my wife; I can't do anything about her.' "[55]

The discussion of the black press on May 22, 1942, and Roosevelt's conclusion that it was "subversive," probably resulted from two special reports by the Office of Facts and Figures (OFF). On May 19, OFF's Extensive Surveys Division released a study of black attitudes toward the war, and three days later OFF's Bureau of Intelligence sent out a report on the black press.

The twenty-page, single-spaced report on May 22 examined five of the largest black weekly newspapers—the *Amsterdam Star-News* and the *People's Voice* (both in New York), the *Pittsburgh Courier*, the *Chicago Defender*, and the *Washington Afro-American*—as well as the white *New York Daily News*, for the period from April 18 to May 16. Noting that the *Courier's* Double V campaign had quickly spread to most of the black press, the report concluded that the "basic concern" of most articles and editorials in the black papers was discrimination against blacks and that this theme was hurting black morale. In addition, OFF pointed out that another survey of twenty-three black newspapers throughout the country in March and April had shown the same trend of continually playing up discrimination. "The militancy of the fight against it varied somewhat, but not much, from paper to paper," the report said.[56]

The OFF report was not the only black press information available to the president. Hoover zealously had been continuing his investigation, not only to gather information but also obviously as an unofficial form of censorship because of its semiopen nature. By the summer of 1942, FBI agents had visited a number of black newspapers, which they claimed were hurting the war effort with their hard-hitting and frequent articles on discrimination. In fact, P. B. Young, Sr., publisher of the *Norfolk Journal and Guide*, recalled that early in the war it was "a rare day" when the FBI did not visit a black paper.[57]

The first known wartime visit was in January 27, 1942, when an FBI agent visited columnist Cliff MacKay of the *Atlanta Daily World*. He was asked if the Orient News Service had sent any Japanese news releases to the paper, or if the Communist Party had tried to influence the paper editorially. MacKay, who was described by the agent as "very cooperative," said that neither had occurred.[58]

But two months later, the FBI was again interested in MacKay. This stemmed from a column on March 27 in which MacKay criticized Hoover for refusing to appoint blacks as FBI agents. Hoover complained to Emory O. Jackson, editor of the black

Birmingham World which used the column, that it was "grossly" inaccurate and constituted "a slander in my opinion upon the many loyal, patriotic Negro members of this Bureau." Jackson ran Hoover's letter in the *World* and said he would like to discuss the matter further when he was in Washington in late April. In a meeting on April 23, an FBI official criticized MacKay and told Jackson that "certain subversive forces were seeking to use the Negro press to stir up disunity." Perhaps out of fear, the editor agreed that the column should not have run and admitted that it was important for the country to "stick together" because of the war. After Jackson returned to Birmingham, Hoover thanked him for understanding the FBI's point of view and noted that he had instructed several local agents to "communicate" with him. This was obviously a ploy by which the FBI hoped to keep the *World* in line in the future.[59]

Then, on July 1, 1942, an FBI agent again visited MacKay at the Atlanta paper on an undisclosed matter. MacKay was so upset by the visit that he lashed out at the FBI in his column on July 10:

> One gathers after the conversation [with an agent] that some white people would like to read "sedition" and "subversive activity" into the determination of Negroes to achieve democracy here at the same time they are called upon to fight for its preservation abroad.
>
> Nothing could be further from the truth, as these FBI agents were told on both occasions of their visits. The Negro, in fact, is the most American of all Americans. He has proved this over and over again. He has no split loyalties, no ties with other countries, no relatives "across the pond." He is all American, first, last and always.[60]

MacKay's account of his visits from FBI agents was not the first time the black press had mentioned them. Such visits were revealed on March 14 when the *Pittsburgh Courier* lashed out editorially at the FBI for sending agents to the *California Eagle* in Los Angeles as well as to one of the other "largest" black papers, which was unnamed. "This sort of thing is an obvious effort to cow the Negro press into soft-pedaling its criticism and ending its forthright exposure of the outrageous discrimination to which Negroes have been subjected," wrote the *Courier*.[61] The unidentified paper may very well have been the *Courier* itself. Although it never admitted that it was visited by FBI agents, perhaps because it feared that such an admission would disturb readers and hurt circulation, the *Courier* was visited at least once during the war's first six and a half months. Forty-one years later, columnist Frank Bolden still recalled the visit:

> The investigation was a farce. They [the agents] never harassed anybody or threatened anybody. They just expressed their dissatisfaction at what we were doing. . . . They suggested that we protest in another way or wait until after the war. But to my knowledge, they never threatened to arrest anyone or told anyone they had to do something. . . .
>
> [Executive Editor Percival Prattis] just called them scared white people, Hoover's flunkies. We all said that. We just considered them Nazi strong men. We just ignored them. I guess you could call it comtempt. I understood why they came around. I thought it was a stupid waste of time and taxpayers' money, but I could put myself in the white man's shoes—he was saying, "We'd better investigate them niggers. The might be forming a Communist cell." But none of us feared them. When you're not guilty, you have no fear.[62]

It is indeed conceivable that the *Courier's* writers did not fear the FBI agents. The *Courier*, after all, was the largest black newspaper in the country, with a growing circulation of about 200,000 in the spring of 1942. Its reporters and columnists surely reasoned that the government would not dare to indict such a large publication under the Espionage Act. Even if it did, Bolden said those at the paper had faith that the courts would uphold freedom of the press. He recalled, however, that Prattis was understandably "nervous" about the *Courier's* criticism of the government in the first half of 1942. He was the paper's liaison with Washington, frequently meeting with government officials, and such criticism only made his job more difficult, said Bolden.[63] Others also were concerned. William O. Walker, publisher of the *Cleveland Call and Post*, revealed in May that a black newspaperman in Texas had written him that "the FBI has frightened all of the Negro editors in the southland." Just what the FBI was doing Walker did not say, but he suggested that "the papers in the northern and more liberal states are going to have to assist those in the South to resist intimidation."[64] Young of the *Norfolk Journal and Guide* also recalled in 1947 that early in the war the FBI often subscribed openly to black newspapers.[65] Such attention obviously could be intimidating.

It also could lead to paranoia about the government. That quickly became apparent in the black press's response to a nationally syndicated column by Westbrook Pegler on April 28. In a savage and unexpected attack Pegler blasted the *Pittsburgh Courier* and the *Chicago Defender*, calling them "reminiscent of Hearst at His Worst in their sensationalism, and in their obvious, inflammatory bias in the treatment of news they resemble such one-sided publications as the Communist Party's *Daily Worker* and Coughlin's *Social Justice*." He concluded that they were "dangerous . . . particularly in their appeal to colored soldiers whose loyalty is constantly bedeviled with doubts and with the race-angling of news."[66]

The black press, particularly the *Courier*, responded with a barrage of bitter editorials and columns over several months. Running consistently through the articles was the allegation that the government had been secretly behind Pegler, which was unlikely considering his hostility toward the administration. "Westbrook Pegler launches the anticipated drive against the Negro press as subversive," wrote George S. Schuyler, the *Courier's* outspoken and widely read columnist, on May 9. "Other attacks from other directions will probably follow. . . . Washington contemplates muzzling black editors. Pegler launched the buildup for the crack down."[67] On the same day, fellow columnist Marjorie McKenzie echoed the same line of reasoning: "It is foolish not to understand that his efforts are not unrelated to other moves under consideration for the suppression of Negro papers generally."[68] Then, a week later, an unsigned editorial in the *Courier* expressed concern that the government was moving toward suppressing all criticism of it. "To the Negro press and public this trend cannot be viewed with complacency," it said.[69] On May 23, the *Defender's* editors charged that Pegler's attack undoubtedly was "inspired" by unnamed persons in the Navy Department who wanted to "smear the Negro Press, and intimidate Negro editors."[70] Walter White, executive secretary of the NAACP, also became alarmed. He invited black editors to a Washington conference on May 30 to discuss a number of issues, including his concern that the government might crack down on the black press for being so outspoken. "It is my conviction," White wrote the editors, "that the possibility of some sort of pressure on Negro papers within the near future is far from beyond the range of possibility."[71]

In the midst of this swirling storm of indignation, paranoia, and fear, black journalists continued an effort begun in February of assuring the White House of the black press's loyalty. On March 31, 1942, for example, Moss Hyles Kendrix, the director of the National Negro Newspaper Week, sent some clippings on the recent observance (March 1 to 7) to Press Secretary Stephen Early. He pointed out that the week's themes stressed not only that the black press was attempting to upgrade the conditions of blacks in the country, but that it was eagerly supporting the war effort by encouraging the sale of Defense Bonds and Savings Stamps.[72] On June 1, the promotions manager of the black *Ohio State News* in Columbus wrote Roosevelt that his paper was pushing the sale of bonds and stamps because it had a "fervent desire to support the War effort with every resource at our command."[73] His message was followed several days later by a pledge of support from the Negro Newspaper Publishers Association. At its annual meeting, it unanimously adopted and sent to Roosevelt the following resolution:

Be it resolved: That the Negro Newspaper Publishers Association is unequivocal in its loyalty to the United States and to President Franklin D. Roosevelt, who is charting our national course in this hour of crisis. Freedom and Democracy must be saved for all the world. The spirit of the Constitution, especially the Bill of Rights, is an inheritance which we must pass on to future generations. To that course, we dedicate our newspapers.[74]

But black journalists' concern was indicated in far more than just letters and resolutions to the government. At the same time that Biddle and Walker were under orders from Roosevelt to talk to black editors, the editors were seeking out high government officials to discuss their growing apprehension over the possibility of suppression. Contributing to this concern were rumors, which were running rampant in the first half of 1942. For example, the *Pittsburgh Courier's* Billy Rowe, who worked in New York as the paper's theater editor, recalled not only hearing that some black papers might lose their second-class mailing permits but also that the government wanted to shut down some of the papers. He did not believe such talk. "The government was powerful enough that if it wanted to, it would have been able to do these things," he said. "But I didn't see any evidence of anything being done. So, I figured it was just rumors started by groups who hated blacks, like the Ku Klux Klan."[75]

The "nervous" Prattis was not so sure. On May 3, Roosevelt sent a note to Early, telling him that the *Courier's* executive editor was in Washington and wanted an appointment with the press secretary to discuss "disconcerting reports concerning their own newspaper—coming from various sources."[76] It is not known what those disconcerting reports were or if Prattis ever talked with Early.

Sengstacke definitely had a meeting, however. Over a month later, he was in Washington talking to one of the government's most influential blacks, Mary McLeod Bethune, who was Roosevelt's special adviser on minority affairs and director of the

Division of Negro Affairs for the National Youth Administration. Sengstacke told her the black publishers were worried that the government was going to try to shut down one or more papers. In fact, he said he had recently received word from Lucius Bates, publisher of the black *Arkansas State Journal* in Little Rock, that the government wanted to take action specifically against his paper.[77] As the founder and one of the leaders of the Negro Newspaper Publishers Association, Sengstacke told Bethune that he must see Biddle before the government moved against any of the black press, and he asked her to arrange an appointment. She did so promptly, but Sengstacke was disappointed. When he arrived, Biddle's assistant said that the attorney general could not see him immediately because of an urgent matter that had arisen unexpectedly. Sengstacke waited in vain for two hours and then left. After flying back to Chicago that day, he sent Biddle a telegram, saying that he was sorry they had not been able to meet and offering to return to Washington if another meeting could be arranged. Biddle wired back that he'd be glad to talk with him the next time Sengstacke was in the capital. That turned out to be sooner than the attorney general probably imagined. Sengstacke telephoned Biddle that he would be back the next day and returned to Washington for a meeting that he still recalled forty-one years later.[78] It was one of only two known meetings Biddle had with the black press during the war.

Sengstacke knew that Biddle would be tough, but he also felt that he would be fair. In Washington's strong Southern atmosphere, where discrimination was easily accepted and practiced, the attorney general was one of the high government officials most sympathetic to blacks.

Upon becoming solicitor general in January 1940, he immediately championed the work of the Justice Department's civil liberties unit. It was created in February 1939 by Attorney General Frank Murphy "as a warning that the might of the United States government was on the side of oppressed peoples" in their fight against such injustices as peonage and voting discrimination.[79] But what particularly impressed blacks was Biddle's role when black congressman Arthur W. Mitchell filed a complaint with the Interstate Commerce Commission. It stemmed from Mitchell being forced in 1937, under threat of arrest, to move from a Pullman car to a segregated coach when the train he was riding on passed into Arkansas. This was because of a state statute requiring "equal, but separate and sufficient accommodations" on trains. The case eventually went to the Supreme Court in 1941, and Mitchell won, with Biddle writing a memorandum supporting Mitchell's right of equal and nonseparate travel means.[80] It was not surprising, therefore, that a number of blacks backed him vigorously as "a friend of the colored people of America" when he was being considered for attorney general. When Biddle was sworn in, he recalled that he was proud of having shown "a decent respect for all human beings" and playing a part in the ongoing campaign for black rights.[81] As head of the Justice Department, he quickly continued that campaign, including prosecuting some whites in Detroit in 1942 for preventing blacks from moving into the federally supported Sojourner Truth housing project.[82]

Despite his reputation as a friend of blacks, Biddle immediately dispelled any thoughts Sengstacke might have had of a friendly, low-key chat at their mid-June meeting. When Sengstacke and Charles P. Browning of the *Defender's* Washington office were ushered into a Justice Department conference room, they found Biddle and a white assistant who dealt in black affairs. On the table in front of them were numerous black newspapers, including the *Defender*, the *Pittsburgh Courier*, and the *Baltimore Afro-American*. Each of the papers carried headlines about clashes in early April at Fort Dix in New Jersey and Tuskegee, Alabama, between black soldiers and whites, leaving three people dead and several more injured.[83] A friend once described Biddle, when under pressure, "as polite as hell—and as definite as hell," and he fit the description that day.[84] Without mincing words, he pointed out that such black press articles were a disservice to the war effort, and if the black papers did not change their tone soon, he was "going to shut them all up" for being seditious.[85] Then, turning specifically to the *Defender*, he complained about an article on nine black soldiers being transported through Alabama and having to wait twenty-two hours to eat because white restaurants in railroad stations would not feed them. Biddle said it would have been better if such an article had not appeared. In addition, he said a number of the paper's other articles "came very close to sedition," and the Justice Department was watching it closely "for seditious matter."[86]

Sengstacke, who was just as tough as Biddle and had a hard, withering, stare, was undaunted. As he boasted in 1983 when recalling his meeting with the attorney general, "I've never been afraid of anybody." Biddle quickly discovered that. "Attorney General," Sengstacke began, "I can understand what you're saying, but that isn't true [about the black press doing a disservice to the war effort]." He pointed out that Biddle evidently had never seen a black newspaper before the war because what the Little Rock paper and others were writing about discrimination was not new. In fact, he said, the black press had been fighting race prejudice for more than 100 years. Nor was the fight about to end now. Looking Biddle "straight in the eye" to show that he "wasn't kidding," Sengstacke took a hard line: "You have the power to close us down, so if you want to close us, go ahead and attempt it." However, Sengstacke continued, a compromise solution existed. The publisher recalled what he said next:

> "I've been trying to get an appointment to see Stimson [the secretary of war]. . . . I've been trying to get in touch with everybody else [in the government]. Nobody will talk with us. So, what do you expect us to publish? We don't want to publish the wrong information. . . . We want to cooperate with the war effort. . . . But if we can't get information from the heads of the various agencies, we have to do the best we can." So, he said, "Well, I didn't know that." I said, "That is correct." . . . He said, "Well,

look, I'll see if I can help you in that way. . . . And what I'll do is make arrangements for you to see some of these people." So, he called Secretary Knox [of the navy] and made an appointment for me to see him.

By this time, Sengstacke said it was obvious that Biddle "had changed his tune completely." That was apparent in what occurred at the end of the hour-long meeting. Biddle promised Sengstacke that the Justice Department would not indict any of the black publishers for sedition. Sengstacke, in turn, said that he could not promise that the black press would tone down its criticism in the future because he could not speak for the other publishers. But he repeated what he had said before: if the black papers were granted interviews with top government officials, they would be "glad" to cooperate with the war effort.[87]

Since Sengstacke's account of the meeting is the only one that exists, with the exception of a brief summary in a Post Office document, and because he was recalling something that occurred forty-one years before, it is possible that some of the details are inaccurate.[88] It also may never be known whether Biddle actually considered prosecuting some of the black publishers and had his mind changed by Sengstacke, or whether he was merely bluffing. Common sense suggests the latter, considering Biddle's libertarian beliefs and pride in helping blacks.

Documentary evidence supports this conclusion. From late March to late July 1942, Assistant Attorney General Wendell Berge, who was in charge of the Justice Department's criminal division, sent Biddle frequent memoranda updating the status of sedition cases. The black press did not appear in any of the memoranda, which indicated that it was not a target of the major investigations.[89] This was not surprising since there were already those in the department who had concluded that the black press was not seditious. That was shown by an in-house memorandum of May 8, 1942:

Mr. [Ralph] Boyd and I conferred with Mr. [Morris] Janowitz [a Justice Department examiner] who reported his opinion quite definitely to the effect that the Negro press is not disloyal or subversive; that it is quite true the Negro press hammers away consistently on discrimination against Negroes in the Army, Navy and industry, but that a campaign is directed not to impede the war effort but to promote the war effort, by giving Negroes a better chance to fight and work. Janowitz has prepared a report on this subject, which is due today. If that report supports his oral report to Boyd and me, it was our opinion that we should inform the Attorney General that we are of the opinion that there is no problem with the Negro press such as we had with other newspapers and mediums.[90]

Lawrence M. C. Smith, chief of the Justice Department's Special War Policies Unit, passed on Janowitz's views to Biddle on May 14 and May 15. In the initial memorandum, he stressed that a survey of "the most widely circulated and the most outspoken" black papers had shown that they did not present "any problem of disloyalty or subversiveness." Therefore, he cautioned against an open investigation of the press or a sedition prosecution because this could have negative, "far-reaching repercussions."

The Negro press is unanimous in its demands that discrimination be ended. Investigation of one newspaper or periodical would not provide any solution to the problem [the publishing of critical articles], and investigation or prosecution of all would probably lead to the charge that the Government and, particularly, the Department of Justice, is discriminating against the Negro press. At present the Negro press is favorable to the Department and has frequently lauded your efforts to end discrimination and to protect civil rights. Investigation or prosecution would lead to a reversal of that policy and a general condemnation of the Administration and the Government.[91]

A month later, Smith again urged Biddle not to prosecute any of the black newspapers because their tones had "improved considerably" in the previous two or three weeks. He credited the improvement to both the government's attempt to solve some of the black problems and "possibly" a leak that the Justice Department was paying close attention to some of the newspapers.[92] With these views from trusted associates in the department, it would have been surprising if Biddle was doing more than bluffing with Sengstacke.

Some historians have assumed that Roosevelt kept the black press from being indicted for sedition during the war. This is based almost entirely on Walter White's autobiography, *A Man Called White*, in which he recalled a meeting with the president in December 1942. Roosevelt told him that the government was being pressured to bring sedition indictments against black editors, and "some of the men high in government believed that convictions could be secured." After their meeting, White said that Roosevelt apparently "called in his advisers and ordered them to abandon the absurd and dangerous proposal to charge Negro editors with disloyalty."[93] It is unknown whether White misunderstood Roosevelt and thought the president was talking about the situation in December instead of during the previous spring and summer. However, the documentary evidence does not support White's contention that Roosevelt saved the black press. It is more likely that it was Biddle. Historian Lee Finkle also has stated that Roosevelt almost certainly "remained calm and took no action" against the black press in World War II because he had been present at the government's June 1918 meeting with black editors, where they were asked to tone down for the duration of the war. Finkle offers no evidence to support his statement, and it appears unlikely that the president's presence at one meeting almost a quarter of a century before had any far-reaching impact on decisions he made regarding the black press.[94]

Given his satisfaction over what had been accomplished with Biddle—and unquestionably it was a milestone for the black press—Sengstacke quickly spread the word to other black publishers that there would be no sedition indictments.[95] Bolden confirmed the black journalists knew this by the end of the summer of 1942. He said that Prattis told him confidentially in August that none of the papers would be shut down, although the government considered some of the writing "strong." Bolden was not surprised. "We didn't think we were doing anthing unconstitutional," he said. "Of course, that may have been debatable. But we had confidence in our government that it wouldn't do anything silly like shutting down the black press. There was just too much pressure on the government to do that."[96]

Biddle kept his promise to Sendstacke not to indict any black publishers for sedition, and the initial proof came only about a month after their meeting. Following four months of intensive Justice Department investigations, obviously speeded up by Roosevelt's Cabinet meeting attacks on Biddle, twenty-eight right-wing extremists were indicted by a Washington grand jury on July 21 for violating both the Espionage Act and the Smith Act. The motley group included James True, who claimed to have a patent for a "Kike killer," a short club which came in a smaller size for women; Joseph E. McWilliams, who called Roosevelt "the Jew King" and was head of the Christian Mobilizers; Lois de Lafayette Washburn, who founded the National Liberty Party and enjoyed giving Nazi salutes in public; and Gerald L. K. Smith, who would be the America First Party's presidential candidate in 1944. Three of the seven (Jones, Noble, and Pelley) who were arrested in the initial Justice Department crackdown in late March and early April were included.[97] According to a Justice Department spokesman, those indicted were specifically charged with forming "a nation-wide conspiracy to destroy the morale of our armed forces through systematic dissemination of sedition."[98] The Associated Press noted that fifteen of those charged had journalistic connections, either publishing or writing articles in thirty publications.[99]

The indictments were praised by the media. *Newsweek* said they were a warning that the Justice Department "was going to quit fooling" around:

Until they were handed up, Biddle had been pursuing an easy-going course to avoid a wave of hysteria which might start the witch hunts of the last war. But all the time he was waiting, confident that the real subversive forces would build up the then doubtful evidence against themselves if given enough rope. When the FBI accumulated what was considered conviction evidence, the roundup was on.[100]

The *New Republic* assumed that the indictments were a sign the government was starting cautiously to establish legal precedents and that "more powerful seditionists" would be the next target. While mildly criticizing Biddle for "moving too slowly," it also applauded him for not seeking more stringent sedition laws from Congress.[101]

In mid-August, the Justice Department moved again, this time against the *Chicago Tribune* for an article by war corre-spondent Stanley Johnston about the Battle of Midway. John-ston's story described the Japanese fleet in detail, revealing indirectly that the navy had broken the enemy's naval code. The government sought an Espionage Act indictment on the grounds that the paper had published a closely guarded military secret, but the grand jury refused to indict the *Tribune* because the Justice Department was unable to show what harm had been done. In fact, the government withheld evidence, fearing that its presentation would alert the Japanese that their code had been compromised. This turned out to be the only time during the war that the government sought a criminal indict-ment against one of the large antiadministration organs.[102]

At the same time that the Justice Department was moving publicly against seditionists, Hoover attempted quietly to take action behind the scenes against the *Oklahoma City Black Dis-patch*. Between July 7 and July 18, the FBI director sent Assistant Attorney General Berge four issues of the paper from June and July, inquiring whether they violated any federal statute. Hoo-ver specifically pointed out articles that complained about black soldiers riding twenty-four hours on trains without food and about the soldiers being fed in Oklahoma City in "dirty, filthy, Jim Crow" kitchens located at the rear of white restaurants. He also noted an editorial that concluded that all men should be equal instead of only one race being granted "special dispensation to inherit happiness." On July 25, Berge replied that none of the *Black Dispatch*'s issues had violated the Espionage Act.[103] That was Hoover's second such setback of the summer. He had received a similar rebuff from Berge when he had forwarded to him on May 30 ten March, April, and May issues of the *Baltimore Afro-American* which he considered seditious. In noting Berge's subsequent decision not to prosecute the *Afro-American*, Hoover encouraged his Baltimore agent on July 6 to continue sending in possibly seditious material from the paper because the Justice Department wanted to review it. Thus, even as Hoover's early wartime attempts to suppress the black press failed, the possibility existed that he might be successful in the future.[104]

Following that summer, none of Biddle's Cabinet notes or any other documents indicate that Roosevelt ever pressed him again to move against any publication. The president's forbearance was understandable. While he probably would have liked to have been tougher on the press, the spring and summer indictments indicated that the Justice Department was taking a firmer stance against sedition, which helped to restore public confidence in the department. That was enough to satisfy the president, particularly in wartime because he was so busy. He also knew that the attorney general was inundated with work. According to Biddle's annual report, the FBI and the Justice Department's Criminal Division handled more than 300,000 national security matters, including espionage, sabotage, sedition, and treason, in the fiscal year ending June 30, 1942.[105] Thus, both Roosevelt and the attorney general compromised on their original positions and came to an amicable agreement that each could accept. For Biddle, the compromise may have been painful (he never said), but he probably realized that it was necessary in order to remain in the administration. Quite simply, the importance to him of being attorney general cannot be minimized. It obviously was easier to protect civil liberties inside the government than outside it.[106]

The indictments also were a sign to the black press that it no longer had reason to be concerned about the Justice Department, although black publishers could not have been too complacent with the powerful Hoover lurking ominously in the background. But Hoover was not an immediate threat, as future events would show—it would be more than a year before he would mount his major wartime attack on the black press. Instead, the Post Office posed a new danger. Just as the resolution was being reached between Sengstacke and Biddle, the Post Office was starting to closely examine the black press. It was a formidable foe.

5

"Is the Negro Press Pro-Axis?"
(March–August 1942)

Francis Biddle's clash with President Roosevelt, the attorney general's climactic talk with John Sengstacke, and the absence of black journalists among those indicted for sedition in the summer were important events for the black press in the period from March to August of 1942. But they were not the only significant ones. In addition, the Office of Censorship suppressed a black publication for the first time during World War II, the Office of Facts and Figures studied the question of whether the black press was pro-Axis, and the army considered imposing massive suppressions. Even more noteworthy, however, was an internal rift in June and July between the Justice Department and the Post Office over the mailibility of the *Chicago World*. It was further proof of the Justice Department's determination to protect freedom of the press in wartime, for all but the most radical publications, by being a brake on other government agencies. Such a Justice Department stance was not to be ignored, as an angry but frustrated Post Office would demonstrate. Meanwhile, as the Justice Department struggled to define the hazy but acceptable boundaries of the Espionage Act, numerous pressures caused the black press to become subtly less outspoken about the federal government. By August, even the army, which was one of the black press's most persistent critics, noted the change in tone and predicted that further improvements were expected. Not everyone in the government agreed with that assessment.

Low black morale, among both civilians and military personnel, was the major reason why a number of government agencies focused on the black press in the spring of 1942. When the United States entered World War II, blacks assumed that many discriminatory barriers would disappear immediately in the patriotic push to win the war. But they were wrong. The marines and the coast guard still refused to accept blacks, the navy would allow them to enlist only as messboys, and the army turned away numerous black volunteers because of a lack of segregated facilities. In addition, the Red Cross followed the advice of the army and the navy and refused to accept blood from blacks. Under heavy black pressure, the Red Cross relented on January 21, 1942, and welcomed black donors, but their blood was segregated from whites. This infuriated blacks. "I bet the same person who would refuse a transfusion of Negro blood would gladly accept a monkey gland transplanted into his carcass to restore his manhood," a woman wrote to the *Pittsburgh Courier*. Still another problem was violence directed at blacks. On January 9, a riot erupted in Alexandria, Louisiana, after a white policeman struck a black soldier with a club, and twelve black soldiers were shot. That was followed on January 25 by a vicious killing in Sikeston, Missouri. A mob of about 600 whites stormed the jail and seized Cleo Wright, a black who was charged with attempting to rape a white woman. He was tied to a car, dragged at high speeds, and then hanged before being doused with gasoline and set on fire.[1] The black press was incensed. The *Baltimore Afro-American* ran an editorial cartoon showing Adolf Hitler and a Japanese soldier grinning from across an ocean as a white mob lynched Wright. The headline read: "Defending America Our Way."[2]

As a result of such incidents, plus continuing employment discrimination, it was not surprising that blacks quickly became bitter. Just how low morale had sunk became apparent on January 10, 1942, when William Hastie, a black civilian aide to the secretary of war, met with black leaders in New York to discuss the wartime role of blacks. Desiring to focus public attention on the morale issue, Hastie polled the group on whether blacks fully supported the war effort. The result was sobering. The black leaders agreed, thirty-six to five with fifteen abstentions, that blacks were not totally behind it.[3]

Hastie got his wish for publicity. The black press played up the controversial vote, while continuing to heatedly criticize numerous examples of discrimination against blacks. One of the most noteworthy attacks was by Emmett J. Scott, who had helped call the meeting during World War I in which black editors had agreed to tone down their demands until the war was over. Writing in the *Pittsburgh Courier* on January 24, Scott blasted "saboteurs of morale" who were "contributing to apathy and weakening national unity" by discriminating against blacks. He added that many of the saboteurs were government officials. "We need now, of all times," he concluded, "a completely unified effort to triumph over those who would destroy our government and its institutions."[4]

Two weeks later, the *Courier* began its famous Double V campaign, which pressed for victories over both totalitarian forces overseas and those at home who were denying equality to blacks. "We, as colored Americans, are determined to protect our country, our form of government, and the freedoms which we cherish for ourselves and for the rest of the world, therefore we adopted the Double 'V' War Cry . . . ," the *Courier* explained to readers on February 14. "WE HAVE A STAKE IN THIS FIGHT. . . . WE ARE AMERICANS, TOO!"[5] The campaign was an immediate hit with blacks, and the *Courier*, recognizing a chance to increase its ever-climbing circulation and to remain the country's dominant black newspaper, devoted immense amounts of space to it. On March 7, the paper ran 345¼ column inches of Double V material (8 percent of the available news space), and in the April 11 issue the total climbed to a campaign high of 568½ inches (13 percent).[6]

As the campaign gained momentum in the *Courier* and other

black papers began espousing its goals, government officials became nervous. They viewed the Double V crusade as possibly disloyal and quickly blamed the black press for black discontent. No distinctions were made between whether the black press was promoting discontent or merely reporting it. The war had to be won, and anything that made that goal more difficult could not be tolerated. Blacks and the black press were expected to abandon their demands, just as they had done during World War I, until after the victory was won.[7] But this time the press refused to back down, as *Courier* columnist Joseph D. Bibb noted on February 7 in an article titled "We Remember 1919." "We must and we will fight on for the Stars and Stripes, but we are no longer blindfolded," he said. "It is our duty to submit the injustices and hypocrisies of this nation to the conscience of the Republic. . . . We will remember Pearl Harbor and we will aid in avenging it, but we are not forgetting ourselves."[8]

The government's concern was apparent in the spring of 1942, when officials of the Office of Facts and Figures (OFF) met in Washington for five hours with about fifty black leaders to discuss how to improve black morale. Joining ministers, businessmen, educators, and labor leaders at the March 20 session were editors from the *Pittsburgh Courier*, the *Baltimore Afro-American*, the *Michigan Chronicle* (of Detroit), the *Norfolk Journal and Guide*, *The Crisis*, and the Associated Negro Press.[9] The blacks did not mince words. In an almost complete show of unanimity, they said that it would be difficult, if not impossible, to bolster black morale unless the government eliminated some of the discrimination. "The Negro has been psychologically demobilized in this war," Roy Wilkins, editor of *The Crisis*, told the officials.[10] The meeting ended with the blacks making no promises to tone down criticism until after the war.[11]

Four days later, OFF Director Archibald MacLeish wrote Carter Wesley, general manager of the black *Houston Informer*, to say that he felt the conference had achieved a "satisfactory" result.[12] He did not elaborate, but he was mistaken if he thought the black press would begin to tone down. It could not afford to

become less outspoken because of likely circulation losses. "It
is a plain fact that no Negro leader with a constituency can face
his members today and ask full support for the war in the light
of the atmosphere the government has created," Wilkins noted
on the same day that MacLeish wrote to Wesley.[13] In referring
to the government's atmosphere, Wilkins was speaking of federal discrimination.

In reflecting on the Washington meeting, some publications
were cautious. *The Crisis*, for example, assured the government
in April that the blacks' complaints to OFF should not be viewed
as an ultimatum of "either you give us what we want or we
won't support the war."[14] But the *Pittsburgh Courier* was more
unrestrained. On April 11, columnist George Schuyler noted
the growing concern in Washington over black morale and the
increasing tendency of government officials to blame the black
press. He argued, however, that the government was really the
one at fault. Blacks knew this, he said, and would continue to
be "bitter and complaining" until discrimination ended. "My
observation has been that the Negro newspapers are largely
following, not leading, the colored people," Schuyler concluded.[15] Three weeks later, the *Courier* returned to the theme
of blaming the black press for morale problems and raised the
specter of possible suppressions:

> The hysteria of Washington officialdom over Negro morale is at
> once an astonishing, amusing and shameful spectacle.
>
> It is astonishing to find supposedly informed persons in high
> positions so unfamiliar with the thought and feeling of one-tenth
> of the population. One would imagine they had been living on
> another planet, and yet every last one of them insists that he
> "knows the Negro."
>
> It is amusing to see these people so panicky over a situation which
> they have caused and which governmental policies maintain.
>
> It is shameful that the only "remedy" they are now able to put
> forward is jim crowism on a larger scale and suppression of the

Negro newspapers; i.e., further departure from the principles of democracy. . . .

If the Washington gentry are eager to see Negro morale take an upturn, they have only to abolish jim crowism and lower the color bar in every field and phase of American life.

Squelching the Negro newspapers will not make the Negro masses love insult, discrimination, exploitation and ostracism. It will only further depress their morale.[16]

Also commenting on black morale was Claude A. Barnett, director of the Associated Negro Press (ANP). In a letter to Vice-President Henry A. Wallace in mid-April, he suggested that morale could be improved dramatically and blacks would "be champing at the bit to fight" if the black press was given a chance to get the "truth" directly from government sources rather than having to rely on misinformation, such as rumors. To remedy the problem, he recommended stationing four or five "competent" ANP reporters with black troops and in industrial areas where more blacks were beginning to be hired. "The hope, the encouragement, the inspiration which will come from these factual stories of the real truth, distributed through an impartial organization not of the government itself, would absolutely reverse this situation," said Barnett. Wallace referred the letter to MacLeish, who assured Barnett in May that his suggestions would be considered.[17]

The black journalists might have been even more fearful of suppression if they had known how closely they were being watched by OFF and the Office of War Information (OWI), which took over OFF's duties on June 13, 1942. Neither agency depended solely on the March 20 meeting for information on black morale and the extent to which the black press affected black thinking and actions. Between March 16 and August 24, the black press appeared, sometimes extensively, in eight of the agencies' reports on blacks.[18] While most of the information merely described the press with examples of what it was publishing, occasional opinions crept into the reports. For example, in a March 16 survey a researcher concluded:

> While Negro newspapers can scarcely be considered representative of the thinking of the rank and file of the American Negro, they do, nevertheless, give expression to points of view held by some Negro leaders and by at least a portion of the better-educated colored people. And since the education level of Negroes is now rising sharply, their influence is by no means negligible.

The researcher added that the papers played up "the one dominant, swelling and poignant plaint of the Negroes everywhere . . . : 'If you want to win the war so badly, why don't you let us fight?' "[19]

Far more significant, however, were OFF's conclusions about whether the black press was an outlet for pro-Axis propaganda. This was not a new concern. From the early 1920s until World War II, both Military Intelligence and the FBI had been investigating Japanese efforts to develop black support. When the black press continued criticizing the government about discrimination and injustices following the bombing of Pearl Harbor, nervous government officials wondered if the Japanese propagandists might have succeeded. OFF addressed the issue initially on May 22, devoting only two sentences to it in a twenty-page report on what had appeared in black papers from March through May. After noting that the black press "on the whole" was encouraging blacks to support the war effort and saying that an Axis victory would worsen black conditions, the survey concluded that "Axis propaganda seems to make little headway." As an example, the survey noted a May 8 editorial, "Japan Is Enemy of Black Folk," in the *Kansas City Call*:

> There is a lot of loose talk going the rounds in colored America regarding the friendship of Japan for the darker races. Some Negroes seem stupid enough to believe that Japan is actually fighting in this war to bring worldwide freedom and happiness to the black man. Nothing is farther from the truth.[20]

On June 22, OWI's Special Services Division returned to the issue in a five-page memorandum titled "Is the Negro Press Pro-Axis?" OWI admitted it was "not difficult" to identify the black press as pro-Fascist because of its heavy and continual opposition to possibly discriminatory aspects of the war effort. The report pointed out, however, that the black press and Fascist publications differed in six important ways:

1. The Fascist press wanted to limit, and often abandon, civil liberties, while the black press wanted to increase them. "Since Negroes would be the chief beneficiaries of a more equal participation in the war program," the report said, "their only opposition to the conduct of the war (and to the present social order) is that there is too little democracy in it for Negroes."

2. Fascist publications opposed the war, claiming it was a mistake that had been foisted on the United States by Roosevelt and his Jewish advisers. The black press had never said that.

3. Pro-Fascists repeatedly sympathized with and approved of Nazi ideology and practices, something the black press had never done. Furthermore, rumors that the black press circulated Japanese propaganda were simply untrue. "As a matter of fact," the report continued, "the editor of the 'Chicago Defender,' which is as 'agitational' and 'inflammatory' as any of the Negro newspapers, wrote a lengthy editorial, arguing that there was no identification between Negroes and Japanese based on color."

4. While Fascist publications continually heckled Roosevelt and his administration, the black press was supportive of the president and the Democratic Party.

5. Most of the Fascist press only "came to life" immediately before the war, but only one "important" black publication, *The People's Voice* in New York, started at that time. Other influential black newspapers, and certainly those that were the most "inflammatory," had been publishing ten to thirty years before the U.S. entry into World War II.

6. The Fascist press obtained most of its income from subsidies, mail contributions, and "high-pressure street sales." In

contrast, the black press's income came from the traditional journalistic sources: advertising and circulation.

The report also attacked allegations of a close link between the Communist Party line and the black press's editorial policy. "The Negro press has never advocated the overthrow of the present form of government and has never upheld a philosophy or a policy alien to constitutional formulations of the American way of life," it pointed out.

After stressing that the "agitational" nature of the black press was necessary for it to sell newspapers, and that the papers with the largest circulations were "the most violent in support of Negro rights," the report concluded that it would be a mistake to suppress the most sensational black papers. It pointed out that suppressions would cut off blacks from much of the news about themselves, since no other media existed to fill the void, and the result would be resentment along with rumors and gossip. "Enemy propaganda would thrive in such an atmosphere and dampen Negro ardor for the war more completely than the native agitation of the Negro press could possibly do," the report predicted. Furthermore, it warned that if the black press was suppressed while other "divisionist" publications, such as the *Chicago Tribune*, were allowed to continue printing, blacks would conclude that their publications were suppressed because of racial considerations rather than for national security reasons.[21]

OWI endorsed that logic in the following month. In a "confidential" in-house memorandum in early July, the Special Services Division recommended that any statements about the black press being seditious, suggesting that it should be suppressed, ought to be "neutralized" if possible. "The facts do not support the allegation," it said. Instead, the division suggested that the black press should be used "constructively" by the government to emphasize race improvements in war industries and in the military. Such articles, it concluded, would have an effect on "the minds and hearts of the Negro population."[22]

While OFF and OWI were issuing their reports, MacLeish joined numerous others in suggesting that Attorney General Biddle should attempt to tone down the black press. At the encouragement of George A. Barnes, a top aide, MacLeish forwarded to Biddle two clippings from the *Washington Afro-American* on April 27 that he felt contained possible "seditious implications." "It might have a very useful preventive effect if your department could somehow call attention to the fact that the Negro press enjoys no immunity," MacLeish wrote.[23] When Biddle ignored the advice, Barnes went on May 8 to Ulric Bell, OFF's assistant director. He again urged the need for a statement by the attorney general as well as a warning that the black press was being watched closely by the Justice Department. As Barnes explained:

The Negro press is flagrantly abusing the privilege [of freedom of the press] every day. Much of the present unrest among the Negro population is due to the inflammatory and extremist tenor of the Negro papers. Much of the material they print violates every tenet of honest journalism.

As long as the Negro press is permitted to continue its present practices with impunity, we can expect very little improvement in morale of the Negro population.[24]

Documents do not show if Bell went to Biddle a second time, but the attorney general, on the advice of his staff, apparently never issued the statement that Barnes sought. "Until we get more definite evidence of subversive activities, as opposed to protests against discrimination, I would not be inclined to recommend that you issue any statement," Lawrence M. C. Smith, head of the Special Defense Unit of the Justice Department, wrote Biddle on May 15. ". . . We may develop a more definite basis on which some action would be justified, but at the present time there is a great deal of rumor and not much fact."[25]

Meanwhile, black editors attempted to improve their relations with OFF and OWI. For example, Sengstacke, publisher of the

Chicago Defender, wrote Bell on April 11 to assure him that his
paper wanted "to be of every possible cooperation to the government in doing whatever it can to improve and help maintain
American morale."[26] Less than two months later, Sengstacke
met with OFF officials, and Percival Prattis, executive editor of
the Pittsburgh Courier, had a similar meeting in late July.[27]

Sengstacke also visited the Office of Censorship. On April 6,
1942, he met with Director Byron Price to discuss how the
Defender and the Negro Newspaper Publishers Association could
assist in the agency's wartime press censorship program. He
assured Price that the black press wanted to help the war effort,
and he would see that black publications were informed of the
censorship guidelines. Less than two months later, he was again
in Washington for another meeting at the Office of Censorship.[28] The meetings apparently were successful; no documents
indicate that the agency ever criticized a black newspaper for
violating the voluntary censorship code, which forbade publishing information about such things as troop movements, the
strength of military units, and war contracts.[29]

Meanwhile, Price was also being pressured to help tone down
the black press. On March 11, aide Bill Steven complained to
him that the headlines in some black papers were increasing
race consciousness and an "under-dog feeling" among blacks.
He said that the headlines—which included "Red Cross Has
No Use for Negro Blood," "Supervisors Foster Segregation
Among Government Workers," and "Negro Air Raid Warden
Will Be Trained in Jim Crow Classes"—presented rich opportunities for enemy propagandists. While Steven acknowledged
that the Office of Censorship was not charged with shaping
opinion, he felt that the agency still had a duty "as Americans"
to create "some sense of achievement and pride" among blacks.[30]
Another complaint came from John H. Sorrells, assistant director of the agency. He sent Price in mid-April a Pittsburgh Courier
article that he felt was "calculated to drive a wedge between
US and Allies." He suggested that the Post Office might want
to take action if similar articles appeared consistently.[31]

Price also received a complaint about the black press from MacLeish. On March 12, the OFF director sent him a number of black newspapers, including three (which are unnamed in the document) that he particularly considered inflammatory. He called one of them "an extremely dangerous publication. . . . If it were being paid for by enemy money, it could not possibly be designed to be more disruptive or more conducive to violence." Therefore he recommended calling a meeting of the government's Censorship Policy Board, chaired by Postmaster General Frank Walker, to discuss the matter. Price replied that he was "concerned" too and was forwarding MacLeish's letter to Walker. Whether the board ever discussed the black press, however, is unknown.[32]

While Price undoubtedly revealed his concerns to Sengstacke at their meeting in early April, no transcripts are available to document their conversation. It is clear, though, that Price took advantage of every chance to encourage the black press to help the war effort. One opportunity occurred in mid-May, when William O. Walker, the president of the Negro Newspaper Publishers Association, invited Price to attend the Association's annual convention in Chicago on June 5 and 6. Walker said that the black press was concerned about press censorship and wanted to cooperate with Price's agency, but he warned, "We do not want to be intimidated." Price, who wrote back that he could not attend because of prior commitments, praised the black press for cooperating with the Office of Censorship, which he claimed was not trying to intimidate any publication. He then delivered a patriotic lecture:

The Negro press of the country has as great an interest as anyone else in keeping news of troop and ship movements and similar information from the enemy. I know of no time in our history when the members of your Association have had a greater opportunity than they have now. We are all in this together and the abuses and suffering which our enemies have imposed upon the conquered peoples of other lands provide conclusive evidence of what will happen to all of us if we lose.[33]

As the publishers knew, the Office of Censorship had limited power to legally punish a paper that wrote about military information that was potentially useful to the enemy. Since censorship was voluntary, the agency could do little more than criticize a publication that went too far if it was mailed within the United States.[34] Only the Justice Department and the Post Office could move legally in such a case. Under the War Powers Act of 1941, however, the Office of Censorship became extremely powerful if a publication was sent outside the country. Then any issue considered objectionable by the chief postal censor could be suppressed. The purpose was to halt the flow of useful information to the enemy and to gather information for the United States.[35]

Black press suppressions began with the February 1942 issue of the *New Negro World*. The district postal censor in Miami complained to Washington on March 9 that the last paragraph of an article, "Let's Face the Truth," was "distinctly subversive." The article, which noted that whites were killing blacks around the country, concluded: "If my nation cannot outlaw lynching, if the uniform [of the army] will not bring me the respect of the people that I serve, if the freedom of America will not protect me as a human being when I cry in the wilderness of ingratitude; then I declare before both GOD and man . . . TO HELL WITH PEARL HARBOR." The chief postal censor agreed that this went too far and refused to allow that issue of the *New Negro World* to be mailed outside the country.[36]

Almost the same thing happened at the end of March to an issue of the *Pittsburgh Courier* addressed to Baranof, Alaska. An examiner complained about two sentences in Ira F. Lewis's front-page column: "Between the JAPANESE and the CHINESE, the NEGROES much prefer the JAPANESE. The CHINESE are the worst 'UNCLE TOMS' and stooges that the white man has ever had." The examiner felt those sentences "cast a slur" upon the Chinese, who were an ally, and at the same time accord left-handed praise to the JAPANESE, our enemy. The context of the column is such that there appeared no need the paragraph be written; it stood alone, unrelated to preceding or following comment. As such it can only be regarded as a detriment to racial accord and harmony at a time, when such accord and harmony is a valuable adjunct to the war effort.[37]

However, he still allowed the paper to be mailed. Further problems occurred in August. The July issue of the *New Negro World* and the August 1 and August 22 issues of the *Pittsburgh Courier* were held up while a district examiner sent "objectionable" material to Washington. This included "scathing criticism" of Britain's North African campaign, details of lynchings and mutilations of blacks, and advice that blacks should stop being patient and resort to "mass action" and a "bloodless revolt." It is unknown if these publications eventually were mailed.[38]

During the spring and summer of 1942, the *Chicago Defender* apparently was the only black publication to complain to the Office of Censorship about suppression. The complaint resulted from a *Defender* vendor in Havana receiving the April 11 issue of the paper cut up "until only the border remained." In addition, Sengstacke said that the paper had received other reports from vendors in the Caribbean and South America about issues never arriving. "We would like to know the objectionable feature of the paper in order that we might prevent future loss," Sengstacke wrote Price, enclosing a copy of the April 11 *Defender* so that he could point out what concerned the government. If Price offered an explanation to Sengstacke, it does not appear in the records.[39]

The army was potentially more dangerous. "The military found it easier to clamp down on everything than to exercise the difficult practice of judgment [during World War II]," Attorney General Biddle recalled seventeen years after the war.[40] When the "clamp down" began is unclear. In March 1941, the *Pittsburgh Courier* reported that a *New York Post* staff member claimed he had seen a War Department order banning *Opportunity* magazine, which was published by blacks in New York City, as well as several other publications from government-owned but privately operated canteens in army camps. The War Department denied that such an order existed. The *Courier* pointed out that it was believable, however, since *Opportunity* was "more vehement in its denunciation of their [the army's] racial policies" than any other publication.[41]

Shortly afterward the army unquestionably began suppressing books and publications on posts. On June 24, 1941, the adjutant general ordered army libraries to examine all donations of reading material to prevent the introduction of "any subversive literature, or literature that is derogatory to the morale of the men in the camps." Objectionable material was to be turned over to the post intelligence officer "for necessary action," but the donors were not to be informed.[42] In May 1942, the army broadened its order. "Any reading material found in camps, which in the opinion of commanding officers is unsuitable for soldier use from the standpoint of being subversive, obscene, or otherwise improper, may be destroyed," the army said in a pamphlet for special service officers.[43] A month later, paralleling what had occurred during World War I, the adjutant general's office ordered the establishment of a "confidential black list" of publications "deemed subversive or otherwise undesirable." Any publications on the list were to be destroyed.[44] While no document can be located showing all of the publications that were affected, at least two magazines, *The Cross and the Flag* and *National Defense*, were blacklisted within the first ten days of the order.[45]

Although the black press was unaware of the suppression orders and the blacklist, it definitely was concerned about the army in the spring of 1942. Secretary of War Henry L. Stimson attempted to allay those fears at a press conference on May 21 when he said that there would be no suppression of the black press "or any other class or group press as a whole."[46] The black press played up Stimson's words without noting how carefully he had chosen them. The black journalists apparently thought Stimson meant that the army would not suppress any of the black press, but all he really promised was that the entire black press would not be suppressed. Such a statement was consistent with Stimson's view of the black press, as outlined by McGeorge Bundy in an autobiography he wrote with Stimson in 1947. He said that during the war the secretary found "the attitudes and opinions advanced by most Negro newspapers . . . shockingly biased and unreliable; as little as their white opponents would the Negro editors look for the mote in their own eye." What irritated Stimson about much of the black press was its insistence that blacks should achieve total equality with whites during the war. Bundy noted that while Stimson was "a northern conservative born in the abolitionist tradition," which resulted in his belief that blacks should have full political and economic freedom, he still felt "social intermixture" was undesirable. "The deliberate use of the war emergency [by the black press as well as some black leaders] to stir unrest and force new policies for which the Negroes themselves were unprepared seemed to Stimson blind folly," wrote Bundy.[47]

Many in the army agreed with Stimson that the black press was "biased and unreliable," making it detrimental, even dangerous, to the war effort. One of those who was critical of black publications was Assistant Secretary of War John J. McCloy. He complained to Biddle on March 24 that the black press had an insatiable appetite for writing about discrimination. "The discrimination note has gotten such momentum in the Negro press," he said, "that one demand granted leads only to another and you do not bury any issue permanently by the concession." He noted that MacLeish believed constant complaints about discrimination aided Axis propaganda, which was trying to convince blacks that this was a war "in which the colored races should be on the other side." But instead of suggesting that the black press be suppressed, McCloy called for "vigorous counter-propaganda" to check "the many extravagant statements."[48]

Meanwhile, Military Intelligence (G-2) was continuing an extensive investigation of the black press—and, as usual, it was not pleased with what it found. For example, it complained that a "secret ace reporter" from the *People's Voice* in New York had sneaked into a barracks at Fort Dix in New Jersey on April 3 to cover a gun battle between white military police and black soldiers. The reporter understandably angered the army further by not only predicting in his article that the riot was a sign of things to come but also by scoffing at an official statement that the shooting was not racially motivated.[49] In the same month, G-2 compiled a twenty-two-page report on "Japanese Racial Agitation among American Negroes," in which it noted that some unidentified black publications were encouraging black troops to be subversive. While expressing doubt that the black press was working directly with Japanese agents, the report pointed out that the inflammatory articles "by various Negro organs of suspected Communist Party affiliation" were being exploited by the Japanese. It concluded by listing the various forms of racial discrimination identified by the black press, without commenting on whether the complaints were justified.[50] It was another example of the army's attitude paralleling Roosevelt's: the press should not strive for race gains until after victory was won.

The black press's drive against discrimination did not end, however, and neither did the army's investigation. In May 1942, the Justice Department was asked by the army to investigate the financial backing of "anti-war Negro papers" circulating in army camps. The army presumably believed, or at least hoped, that enemy backers would be discovered, allowing the government to suppress the papers. But the investigation apparently turned up no link with enemy agents.[51] Later in the month, a Military Intelligence report concluded that one of the main reasons for problems with black troops in the South was the black press playing up discrimination "under the guise" of blacks patriotically wanting to contribute to the war effort. The report said the most radical publications included the *Pittsburgh Cour-*

ier, the *Baltimore Afro-American,* the *Detroit Tribune,* and the *Chicago Defender.*[52]

In mid-June, however, Military Intelligence admitted in another report on "The Negro Problem in the Army" that it was impossible to blame the black press for any of the "racial disturbances" at or near army installations in the previous ten months. The posts where black soldiers had been involved in racial incidents, and sometimes riots, were Fort Bragg and Camp Davis in North Carolina, Fort Benning in Georgia, Fort Dix in New Jersey, and Mitchel Field in New York. Problems also had occurred in Alexandria, Louisiana, which was near Camp Livingston, Camp Claiborne, and Camp Beauregard. Both blacks and whites had come into conflict at each location, except at Camp Davis, where about 300 black soldiers and black civilians had a "free-for-all" at a beer parlor after a bartender refused to serve a soldier. Even if such disturbances were not the fault of the black press, continued the report, articles in some publications about specific racial incidents in army camps as well as general service problems were "beyond the normal agitational behavior of the press" and did nothing to increase black soldiers' allegiance to the army. Compounding the problem was the influence of several papers. The report noted that a survey of almost 500 black troops had shown that 76 percent of them read one of the five papers in the *Afro-American* chain and 56 percent read the *Pittsburgh Courier.* "As long as these papers carry on their efforts for the purpose of racial betterment they cannot be termed as subversive organs," the report said. "They do, however, at times appear to achieve the same result as outright subversive publications."[53]

Although black editors were unaware of the Military Intelligence reports, they probably suspected their existence and certainly recognized that the army represented a major threat. Their concern was evident in a series of letters in April and May between Roy Wilkins of *The Crisis* and two black army officials, William Hastie and Truman K. Gibson, Jr., acting civilian aide to the secretary of war.

On April 10, Gibson noted that a majority of black newspapers had been running troop movement information not cleared by army censors, and he cautioned Wilkins that the black press must be careful to avoid "a crack-down." He added ominously that numerous people in the War Department would welcome a chance to suppress some of the black papers, but he said that would not happen if reporters followed the censorship rules.[54] It is unclear why Wilkins did not reply until May 7, when he said that army suppression of the black press appeared imminent. He based this conclusion on the fact that the black press had been attacked by Westbrook Pegler and others in the mainstream press, and he felt the War Department was behind the attacks. "It is my belief that the whole business is building up to a great mess which will do nobody any good," said Wilkins. "I wish very much that someone in the War Department would exhibit a little give-and-take instead of the traditional brass hat stubborness [sic]. If that would come to pass, I am certain the Negro press would come more than half way."[55]

Gibson showed Wilkins's letter to Hastie, who agreed on May 11 that a "crack-down" was a possibility. He told Wilkins that the papers were to blame by making themselves "vulnerable" with sensational, inaccurate, and irresponsible reporting, and he warned that only one or two more "outrageous stories" could lead to censorship. "We are trying to forewarn the editors," said Hastie. ". . . I hope that we shall be able to work the matter out without an explosion which would injure everyone concerned."[56] Gibson also wrote Wilkins a critical letter on May 22, the day after Stimson's comments about the black press. He castigated the black press for "flagrant disregard" of the army's censorship rules as well as ignoring the "principles" of responsible reporting (he did not say what he felt those principles were). As a result, he said the army was developing "an increasingly critical attitude" toward black newspapers. "It would serve a very useful purpose if those of us interested in continuing effective criticism through the media of the press would insist that all rules, good and bad, be rigidly adhered to," counseled Gibson. If that was done, he said the black press had nothing to fear.[57]

In a June 30 memorandum, Hastie criticized McCloy for apparently believing that blacks should not attempt to eliminate discrimination during wartime because this resulted in more harm than good. Hastie argued on the contrary that segregation resulted in "wasted time and effort," and he enclosed editorials from the *Chicago Defender* and the *Philadelphia Tribune* which stressed that point. McCloy replied that Hastie had misunderstood him:

> Of course, there is no group in the country that should not agitate for the elimination of undemocratic practices. Like sin, everyone is against undemocratic practices. What I urge upon the Negro press is to lessen their emphasis upon discriminatory acts and Color incidents irrespective of whether the White or the Colored man is responsible for starting them. Frankly, I do not think that the basic issues of this war are involved in the question of whether Colored troops serve in segregated units or in mixed units and I doubt whether you can convince the people of the United States that the basic issues of freedom are involved in such a question. In its policy of playing up the incident of which I speak, I believe that papers like the *Pittsburgh Courier* and, perhaps, some others, serve to take the mind of the Negro soldier and the Negroes generally off what you term the basic issues of this war [freedom both at home and abroad]. If the United States does not win this war, the lot of the Negro is going to be far, far worse than it is today. Yet, there is, it seems to me, an alarmingly large percentage of Negroes in and out of the Army who do not seem to be vitally concerned about winning the war. This, to my mind, indicates that some forces are at work misleading the Negroes. I bespeak greater emphasis on the necessity for greater out and out support of the war, particularly by the Negro press, and I feel certain that the objects for which you aim will come much closer to achievement if the existing emphasis is shifted than if it is not.[58]

About a week later, McCloy met with Sengstacke and probably repeated some of the same views. Sengstacke said he was pleased to hear that the army's Bureau of Public Relations (BPR) might create a black press section, apparently feeling that it would ease the tension between the army and the black press. He added that the *Defender* "stands ready to be of every possible assistance in the broad progressive program of the War Department."[59]

The BPR, which had sent a representative to the annual meeting of the Negro Newspaper Publishers Association in June 1942, did in fact add a special section that summer to serve black publications. Black reporters gradually began visiting it regularly to get news, and BPR officials started making trips to black papers. The section not only arranged for black reporters to observe black troops on maneuvers, but sent out material especially written for black papers, and encouraged public relations officers in the field to aid black reporters. In addition, it began a weekly analysis of trends in the black press, sorting out articles according to their favorableness toward the army.[60]

The BPR mainly focused on increasing the accuracy of the black press's articles about black troops, emphasizing favorable racial aspects of the army while attempting to get black reporters to tone down critical or controversial stories and editorials. By August 31, the BPR noted that coverage of the army in the black press had improved markedly in recent months and probably would continue that trend. It cited the *Pittsburgh Courier's* August 22 issue as an example. Thirty-five articles attacked racial discrimination, and only eight of those dealt with the army, which was considered an improvement over past coverage. In addition, all twenty-three general news articles concerning blacks in the army were favorable. "It should be borne in mind, in analyzing such trends," the report concluded, "that the preponderant effect is not that of editorial opinion, but rather of the news headlines and pictures which are published. These latter reveal a still more definite improvement, both in quality and quantity."[61]

The army's immediate interest in the black press from the beginning of the war represented an extreme position. At the other end of the spectrum were agencies such as the Justice

Department and the Post Office, neither of which moved quickly in 1942, for different reasons. At the Justice Department, Attorney General Biddle's concern with civil liberties slowed all action. The Post Office, meanwhile, gave first priority to the foreign-language press and English-language publications directed at foreign nationalities, particularly Germans, Japanese, and Italians, and then it moved against pro-Axis and pro-Fascist publications. Not until the late spring and early summer of 1942 did the Post Office begin to concern itself with the black press. The trail that eventually led to the black press began in March. At that time, Postmaster General Frank Walker was deliberately proceeding slowly. A longtime personal friend and political ally of Roosevelt, he was not outspoken about civil liberties. In fact, he was not outspoken about anything. Walker was "as tight-lipped as an earthworm," according to one journalist. He rarely made speeches, held press conferences, or allowed interviews, feeling that no publicity was the best publicity.[62] This was a marked contrast from Biddle, who one reporter noted "does not object to publicity and (what is rare) makes no pretense to objecting to it."[63] On two occasions, however, both less than three months before the bombing of Pearl Harbor, Walker commented publicly about the importance of a free press. On September 20, 1941, in a speech to the Democratic Editorial Association of Indiana which was carried by the National Broadcasting Company, Walker praised newspapers:

> They furnish the information, they impart the knowledge, upon which intelligent judgment must be founded. They furnish a platform for public discussion, for an interchange of opinion, for the expression of opposing views. To interfere with this function, to inhibit it in any way, to intimidate the security of its freedom by any kind of pressure, would be to undermine one of the bulwarks of the democracy of this nation.[64]

Five days later, in New York, Walker spoke at a celebration of the 150th anniversary of the Bill of Rights and called freedom of speech "worthy of any sacrifice."[65] Although such public statements were similar to those made about the same time by Biddle, there was a basic difference. Time would show that Biddle believed fervently in freedom of the press, while Walker was merely uttering politically valuable but empty words. It was not a cause for which he believed in fighting and risking his job.

After the United States entered World War II, Walker remained in the background, waiting for public opinion to demand that his department move against radical publications. It was safer politically that way. The Post Office did object strongly to the January issue of William Pelley's *The Galilean*, which commented favorably on the Japanese attack on Pearl Harbor as well as the German and Italian declarations of war. But that was an easy target and easy glory, and the Post Office's protest and Pelley's suspension of the publication in March produced favorable publicity for the department.[66]

As the conservative mainstream press began increasingly to demand government action against seditionists, Walker must have enjoyed seeing Biddle and the Justice Department become the lightning rods for criticism. As a result, the Post Office was virtually ignored. It was busy behind the scenes, however, gathering information on possible seditious publications while waiting for an appropriate public atmosphere before it moved. On April 13, 1942, for example, *Life* ran an eleven-page article, "Voices of Defeat," which attacked individuals, groups, and publications that "sow lies and hate inside our lines." *Life* said it had written the article "not to frighten Americans with bugaboos, but to make them mad enough to see to it that their officials take the necessary action." What it did not tell readers was that the Post Office had "obtained and passed along" some of the article's information.[67]

When the president tired of inactivity and demanded at the March 20 Cabinet meeting that Biddle move against "subversive sheets," Walker joined with the rest of the Cabinet in agreeing that vigorous action had to be taken. At the same time, he protected himself. He shifted the initiative to Biddle by saying that he would take away the mailing privileges of any news-paper suggested by the Justice Department.[68] The maneuver earned Walker five and a half more weeks of delay. By late April, however, the Justice Department was clearly moving against subversive publications, although more slowly than the president would have liked, and Roosevelt wanted action from the Post Office as well. In a private meeting with Walker, he proved that their close friendship had limits when he lashed out at the postmaster general, demanding movement against seditionists.[69]

The Post Office took immediate steps on the basis of infor-mation and documents about subversive publications supplied by the Justice Department. By May 8, three weekly newspa-pers—the *Philadelphia Herold*, *X-Ray* (of Muncie, Indiana), and *Publicity* (of Wichita, Kansas)—had been barred temporarily from the mail until hearings could be held on their second-class mailing permits. All three lost their permits by June 8.[70] In revoking the permit of *X-Ray*, Walker released an eleven-page decision which discussed the right of the press to use the mails during wartime. After noting that this right was a "privilege" that was not constitutionally "unrestricted," Walker concluded that loyal publishers had nothing to fear from the Post Office:

> No publisher need have difficulty in conforming to the injunctions of the Espionage Act in time of war. If he has doubt whether an utterance may violate the law, then his good conscience, his sin-cere regard for the Nation, for the Constitution and for his fellow-countrymen will invariably lead him to resolve the doubt in favor of the United States. Such a self-imposed and self-chosen restraint would in no way be restrictive of the boldness of the press in thought and speech.[71]

In addition to the three weekly papers, Rev. Charles E. Cough-lin voluntarily ceased publication of his controversial *Social Jus-tice* after being summoned to Washington for a May 4 hearing. As a precaution, the Post Office revoked his permit anyway.[72]

The publications that the Post Office moved against represented less than a third of the fourteen mentioned in the *Life* article in April. Furthermore, well-known broadcaster William L. Shirer, writing in *Atlantic Monthly* in May, stated that there were ninety-five pro-Axis publications circulating through the mail, reaching several million readers. He complained that the government was "hesitant" to take action.[73] But the person who counted—Roosevelt—was apparently satisfied. No documents indicate that he ever complained again to Walker about seditious publications.

In his annual report on June 30, Walker said that the Post Office was examining several hundred books, magazines, newspapers, and circulars each month to determine their mailability under the Espionage Act. He summarized what the Post Office could ban:

> The law renders nonmailable false reports or false statements intended to interfere with the operation or success of the military or naval forces of the United States or to promote the success of its enemies. It also renders nonmailable written or printed material which causes, or attempts to cause, insubordination, disloyalty, mutiny, or refusal of duty in the military or naval forces, or obstructs the recruiting or enlistment services of the United States. [The law also] renders nonmailable writings, pictures, etc., containing any matter advocating or urging treason, insurrection, or forcible resistance to any law of the United States.[74]

Under these guidelines, a few black publications were examined in the war's first nine months. Even before the Cabinet meeting of May 22, where Roosevelt ordered Biddle and Walker to talk to some black editors "about preventing their subversive language," the Post Office had begun looking at the *Pittsburgh Courier*.[75]

The examination began in early May after the Post Office in Washington received a complaint that the paper's May 2 issue was "subversive." "The complainant stated that prior issues of this publication have contained even worse material," the solicitor told an examiner.[76] The examiner concluded, in a five-page, single-spaced letter, that the May 2 issue was unmailable. He cited numerous passages from the *Courier*, including the editorial which discussed low black morale and the possibility of black newspapers being suppressed; an article on a speech by Rev. Adam Clayton Powell, Jr., in which he emphasized that American blacks were being subjected to the same evils spread by Germany and the Gestapo; and a story about how Jim Crowism in America was hurting unity among countries in the Western Hemisphere. The examiner concluded:

> The various articles . . . are designed to cause insubordination, disloyalty, mutiny or refusal of duty in the military or naval forces of the United States among Negroes. Furthermore, it will obstruct the recruiting or enlistment service of the United States by such persons. In addition this type of reading matter tends to cause persons of the colored race to advocate [resistance] or forcibly resist the laws of the United States and induces insurrection amongst those people. The affect [sic] upon Negro readers of this newspaper coincides with the German propaganda ideas of "Divide and Conquer" since it creates racial enmity between the Negroes and whites of the United States. The undermining of the morale of Negro citizens of this country (represented as being 13,000,000 or $\frac{1}{10}$ of our national population) is playing into the hands of Hitler's propaganda artists. During these perilous war times there is no place in our national program for papers of this type.

The examiner suggested that other issues also should be examined to determine if the paper's second-class mailing permit should be revoked.[77]

The report prompted the Post Office to look at the April 4, 11, and 18 issues of the *Courier*. The April 4 and 18 issues were declared "borderline" mailable, but the April 11 issue was considered unmailable because it contained a large amount of the same type of objectionable material found in the May 2 issue. In looking at the four issues together, the Post Office examiner concluded that some of the paper's statements were "inadvisable" because they did not result in the "full cooperation and complete harmony of everyone" toward winning the war.

Nevertheless, the examiner admitted that the "continuous policy" of the *Courier* did not appear to be the publishing of subversive material. It was recommended, therefore, that the April 11 and May 2 issues should not be mailed (a meaningless decision because it was not made until May 29) and that the Post Office should continue to examine future issues while taking no other action against the paper at that time.[78]

Surprisingly, this did not result in an immediate increase in the Post Office's investigation of the black press. During the summer of 1942, the Post Office only examined one issue each of the *Chicago Bee* and the *New Negro World* and two issues each of the *Chicago Defender* and the *Chicago World*.[79] The *Bee*, the *Defender*, and the *New Negro World* were declared mailable although the Post Office found objectionable material in all of them.

Of the three, the *New Negro World* came the closest to being suppressed. An examination of its July issue occurred after the Justice Department forwarded a nine-page report on July 22 to the Post Office's assistant solicitor, Calvin W. Hassell. The report was on the publication as well as the organization that published it, the Universal Negro Improvement Association of Cleveland. Noting that the magazine contained "a large quantity of material which is seditious" and might cause mutiny and disloyalty among blacks in the armed forces, the Justice Department stressed that the Post Office should watch the *New Negro World* closely. Therefore, further mailing of the July issue was held up immediately by the Cleveland postmaster pending a decision from Washington. An examiner found that the publication bordered on being seditious with articles such as an appeal for blacks to arm themselves and retake their African homelands, an attack on British rule in India, and criticism of the conduct and attitude of American whites toward blacks. However, the examiner considered none of this "sufficiently inflammatory or lurid" to bar the magazine from the mails, and the Justice Department concurred that it did not violate the Espionage Act. On August 20, after almost a month's delay, the Cleveland postmaster was told to resume mailing the *New Negro World* and also to exercise what amounted to informal censorship:

> You should advise the publisher that he must accept full responsibility for depositing any matter in the mails in violation of the law, and that the dispatch of matter deposited by him in the mails constitutes no guarantee of its mailability.
>
> The contents of a single issue or a single dispatch are not necessarily controlling on whether or not the publication has violated the law.[80]

No document indicates the publisher's reaction when he was told this, but obviously such words were threatening. Nonetheless, as time would show, the publisher of the *New Negro World* refused to be intimidated or to tone down the magazine.

The Post Office's examination of the *Chicago World* turned out to have the most far-reaching and significant consequences. It caused an unexpected disagreement between the Post Office and the Justice Department which resulted in the Post Office not suppressing any black publications during the war.

The *World* was an unlikely candidate to occupy a pivotal position in the government–press struggle over libertarianism during World War II. Established in 1917, it had become one of the country's ten largest black newspapers by 1942, with a weekly circulation of 28,000.[81] However, unlike the *Pittsburgh Courier*, the *Baltimore Afro-American*, the *Amsterdam Star–News*, and the *Chicago Defender*, it was virtually ignored by the government both before and during the war. It simply was not considered one of the country's leading black newspapers.

According to government documents, the only time it was examined was in June 1942, when two issues were sent in by the Chicago postmaster, who considered them unmailable. A Post Office examiner agreed. He found that the May 23 issue contained "highly inflammatory news articles and editorial matter alleging injustice and discrimination against the colored race in the Army and Navy." Examples cited included articles about the navy only allowing blacks to be messboys and black soldiers being refused lunch and dinner while riding in a train across Alabama and Kentucky. The examiner agreed that such comments about discrimination ordinarily were acceptable, but, as Justice Holmes had noted in the *Schenck* case following World War I, press freedom shrank in wartime. "When a nation is at war many things that might be said in time of peace are such a hindrance to its effort that their utterance will not be endured so long as men fight and no Court could regard them as protected by any constitutional right," Holmes had written. The May 16 issue was considered equally objectionable because of articles with headlines playing up racial intolerance, such as "Let the Federal Government Investigate the Condition of Negro in the White South." That article included the following:

> What is tyranny in one imperium should not be a blessing in another. If segregation is the curse of Hitlerism then segregation is the curse of any nation that indulges in it. We should not substitute the brown complexion for the star of David; we should not create Negro ghettoes and deny Negroes complete vocational opportunities to establish a false racial supremacy. If we do so we are no better than the enemies we fight.[82]

As a result of such material, the Post Office asked the Justice Department on June 10 if it agreed that the May 16 issue was unmailable.[83] Such a request was standard procedure. The Post Office was hesitant to move against any publication without the approval of the government's legal experts. To do so and then be challenged and lose in court was a disaster that had to be avoided, particularly with Walker as head of the department.

The Justice Department's reply on June 30 deserves close examination because it demonstrates the department's liberal attitude toward wartime dissent. It is unknown whether this approach to the *Chicago World* was influenced by Biddle's promise to Sengstacke only days before not to prosecute any of the black press for sedition. What is clear, however, is that the Justice Department's attitude disappointed the Post Office.

After admitting that it had no information in its files on either the paper or its owners, the Justice Department declared the May 16 issue "unobjectionable." It said "the essence of the problem" was whether a publication legally could project an attitude, as the *World* clearly did, that combined support for an "all-out united" war effort with denunciations of discrimination against blacks, thus bringing into disrepute certain parts of the government. In examining such published "stigmatizations," the Justice Department said it relied generally on a statement by legal expert Zechariah Chafee, Jr., in his book, *Free Speech in the United States*. He had written that "in our anxiety to protect ourselves from foreign tyrants," the country should not "imitate some of their worst acts, and sacrifice in the process of national defense the very liberties which we are defending." The Justice Department also cited three other statements. One was by Justice Holmes. "We do not lose our right to condemn either measures or men because the Country is at war," he declared in his 1919 decision in *Frohwerk* v. *United States*. A year later, in *Schaefer* v. *United States*, Justice Louis D. Brandeis said in a dissent (which Holmes joined) that "the nature and possible effect of a writing cannot be properly determined by culling here and there a sentence and presenting it separated from the context. In making such determination, it should be read as a whole; at least if it is short like these news items and editorials." The Justice Department also noted that Chafee had pointed out in his book, "You cannot limit free speech to polite criticism, because the greater a grievance the more likely men are to get excited about it, and the more urgent the need of hearing what they have to say."

Applying these "general principles" to the *World*, the Justice Department concluded that the May 16 issue was "basically, neither defeatist nor obstructionist nor divisionist." In reporting on discriminatory acts against blacks, the newspaper was merely pointing out what blacks considered unjust treatment. Fur-

thermore, no evidence demonstrated that the paper was deliberately distributed to men subject to the draft. "If such utterances [as in the *World*] do not fall within the traditional
constitutional immunities for freedom of speech," the Justice
Department report declared, "categories long established will
have to be formulated anew."[84]

The Justice Department's disagreement with the Post Office,
and particularly the overwhelming finality of its last statement,
stung George Breen, the Post Office examiner who had prepared
the department's report on the *Chicago World*. Presumably feeling that his integrity had been questioned, as well as his understanding of the law, he "respectfully submitted" a five-page
response a week later to his superior. It also must be examined
closely to appreciate the widening gulf between the two government agencies.

Breen began by noting that numerous peacetime liberties had
to be sacrificed temporarily during wartime. Furthermore, he
pointed out that it was difficult to build up the country's military
forces, of which blacks obviously were an important part, while
a black newspaper was playing up discrimination and injustices.
To say that such a publication did not meet Holmes's famous
criterion of a "clear and present danger" was "unconvincing,"
according to Breen.

He attacked the Justice Department report point by point.
For example, he noted that the *World* contained numerous inflammatory headlines—including "Missouri Hill-Billy Calls
Woman 'Nigger,' " "White South Starves Colored Soldiers,"
and "Knox Opposes Giving Medal to Negro"—which obviously
were "obstructionist" and "divisionist" and certainly were not
culled "here and there." Turning to the argument that the paper
was not distributed deliberately to try to affect the draft, Breen
countered that all the paper had to do to violate the law was
publish articles having a tendency to accomplish the evil. It was
not necessary to show an actual effect. Nor, he said, was it
"unreasonable" to believe that a paper with a circulation of
28,000 "will not only tend to interfere with their [blacks'] in-

duction, but will incite them after induction to mutiny, disloyalty, and insubordination, to the injury of the service of the
United States." Breen concluded by quoting a passage in the
Frohwerk decision of 1919 that he felt was "far more applicable"
than the one chosen by the Justice Department: "But we must
take the case on the record as it is, and on that record it is
impossible to say that it might not have been found that the
circulation of the paper was in quarters where a little breath
would be enough to kindle a flame and that the fact was known
and relied upon by those who sent the paper out."[85]

It is unclear why Breen's memorandum apparently was never
sent to the Justice Department. However, with the Justice Department still cooperating closely with the Post Office on numerous investigations of publications and individuals, the latter
probably did not want to jeopardize such valuable assistance.
But a short-lived trend had developed. On June 13 and 16, the
Justice Department had sent reports to the Post Office, similar
to the one about the *Chicago World*, disagreeing about the unmailability of *National Defense* and *The Malist*, respectively.[86] Such
momentary differences of opinion obviously did not justify a
major break between government agencies. But what the Post
Office did not realize was that those three reports would be the
last in-depth ones it would receive from the Justice Department
on the question of mailability during World War II.

The Post Office, however, was not totally dependent upon
the Justice Department for action. It might balk at moving legally against seditious publications without any backing, but it
needed no encouragement in instituting informal censorship
measures. The *Chicago Defender* and the *Amsterdam Star–News*
discovered that in June, at the same time that the fate of the
World hung in the balance, when each paper had disturbing
meetings with Post Office officials.

It is unclear which meeting occurred first, since the exact date
of the conference with the publisher and editors of the New
York paper does not show in the records. The date is irrelevant,
however, since the two meetings were similar. In talking to the

Star–News, Post Office officials pointed out that the paper's articles about Jim Crowism could harm the war effort. The Post Office's account of the meeting added that the editors were told that the "benefits of citizenship entail certain duties, and that in time of war it was the duty of Negro publishers not to 'play up' isolated and rare instances in such a fashion as to obstruct recruiting and in other ways hamper the war effort."[87]

The *Defender* already was wary of the Post Office before its meeting on June 26. A month before, in a front-page column, Lucius C. Harper had discussed the *Chicago Tribune's* "almost seditious" criticism of Roosevelt for setting Communist Earl Browder free after he had served only fourteen months of a four-year sentence in an Atlanta prison. Harper had said that if the *Tribune* were not so powerful "it would be paid a visit from the postmaster general and told to tone down considerably or find some other way to circulate the paper otherwise than through the U.S. mails." He speculated that was what would happen to the *Defender* if it mounted a similar attack against Secretary of the Navy Frank Knox for not allowing blacks and whites to fight together in that branch of the service.[88]

At the meeting in late June, Hassell rather than Walker played the major role. Walker called Hassell to his office, introduced him to Sengstacke and Charles P. Browning, who worked in the *Defender's* Washington office, and told him and F. A. Ironside to talk with the newspapermen. Evidently, Walker felt he had fulfilled his obligation to talk to black editors, as he had been ordered to do by Roosevelt a month before, by having a short, polite conversation. He was quite content to let others in the department deal more directly with the controversial topic of possible sedition in the black press.

After describing their recent conversation with Attorney General Biddle, according to the Post Office memorandum on the meeting, the blacks pointed out that the black press was in a difficult position:

Their very reason for existence in addition to the white press is to emphasize and play up discriminations against the negro which are usually played down in the white press; that this condition obtained long before the entry of the United States into the war and it is not their intention in emphasizing these discriminations at this time to hamper or in any way obstruct the war effort; that while they are certain that we do not have democracy in this country in that the negro has many grievances, they also know down in the bottom of their hearts that they do not want the Axis powers to win this war. They stated that they had been seeking from the Attorney General and the Postmaster General and from any other source open to them a statement of policy which would indicate just where the line can and should be drawn.

Ironside conceded that the blacks had a problem. He added, however, that "the benefits of citizenship entail certain duties," and one of those in time of war was not to do anything that the Espionage Act considered harmful to the country. Noting that the Post Office and the Justice Department were working together closely on espionage matters, he concluded by cautioning them "in general terms against maintaining a publication systematically devoted to the dissemination of matter" forbidden by law. While such remarks may have frightened the journalists, or even been resented, they thanked Hassell and Ironside upon leaving, saying they were "fully satisfied" with the discussion.[89] Sengstacke wrote Walker after returning to Chicago, also expressing appreciation for the meeting. He claimed that he now better understood the government's position, which he said had been misunderstood widely by the black press.[90] It is unlikely, of course, that there ever was any misunderstanding. Instead, Sengstacke's statement probably was designed to please the Post Office officials.

Faced with threats from the Justice Department, the FBI, and the Post Office, as well as other government agencies, it would have been surprising if the black press had not changed its tone by the summer of 1942. In fact, as the army noted, it did become less critical. A study of the *Pittsburgh Courier*, the country's

leading black publication, shows that the space devoted to the
Double V campaign declined by half between April and August,
and by the end of the year the campaign was virtually dead.
Furthermore, the paper subtly switched the target of most of
its criticism by the end of the summer from the federal government and the military to state and municipal governments
as well as private businesses. A more positive tone also began
creeping into articles and picture cutlines.[91] A cutline on May
23 was representative of the *Courier*'s new tone:

> These black men [in the defense plants] realize that they have as
> much, or more, at stake than any other group of people. They
> know that democracy is their only hope. And, because they are
> conscious of these things, they have rolled up their sleeves and
> are enthusiastically helping in the development of America's might.
> "America first, last and always!" is their song as they work in
> the arsenals of democracy.[92]

But to attribute the new tone solely to government pressure
would be misleading. Other equally pressing concerns weighed
on black publishers, making them amenable to change. One
was black morale; everyone agreed it was low, however much
they may have disagreed about the reasons. It had to be improved. Equally apparent were a number of black gains. Among
the most noteworthy in the first eight months of 1942 were
black men being commissioned for the first time in the air corps,
marines, and coast guard, and their status being upgraded in
the army and navy; black women being accepted for the Wom-
en's Army Auxiliary Corps; and blacks being hired in large
numbers at defense plants, largely because of government pressure on employers. Not to become less critical of the government in the face of such improvements would have placed black
publishers in a largely indefensible position.

The basic conservatism of black publishers also contributed
to the changing tone of their papers.[93] They had to be concerned
that it would hurt the black cause if they remained strident as

the country's war fortunes began improving in 1942 and the United States went on the offensive militarily. The change began with important naval victories in the Coral Sea and at Midway in May and June, respectively, and continued with the landing at Guadalcanal in August. Black publishers would not have wanted to appear unenthusiastic as the wartime tide turned.

There were also economic reasons to tone down. Until 1942, black newspapers always had depended basically on circulation to earn a profit and remain in business. Unlike their white counterparts, they made little money from advertising because virtually none of the white-owned corporations advertised to a black audience. But in the spring and summer of 1942 the situation changed. Faced with a new federal excess profits tax, American companies slowly but understandably began advertising in the black media instead of merely giving surplus income to the government in the form of taxes.[94] By the end of the summer, Philip Morris, Pepsi-Cola, Pabst Blue Ribbon, and Esso were advertising regularly in some of the larger black papers. Old Gold, Chesterfield, and Seagram's 5 Crown Whiskey followed this trend by the end of the year.[95] With a lucrative new source of income, it would have been surprising if black newspapers had not toned down to avoid jeopardizing the opportunity of obtaining still more advertising accounts. More than one researcher pointed out the effect of increased profits on the editorial content of the black press. "Negro publishers are apt to be primarily business men whose interest in race welfare is secondary to their interest in selling newspapers," Thomas Sancton wrote in April 1943.[96] Five years later, Vishnu V. Oak noted basically the same thing. "Many [black] newspapers seem quite willing to sell their pages to anyone who is willing to pay the proper price," he found.[97]

Sengstacke claimed in 1983 that still another reason for the change in tone was that government leaders agreed to talk with black journalists. After the conference with Biddle in June 1942, black publishers and editors began meeting with other top

Washington officials. Sengstacke said that was why the black press became more factual and less sensational in its articles about the government.[98]

The black press was far from content, however, in August 1942. Despite its increasing cooperativeness in supporting the war effort, it faced constant reminders of the government's distrust, if not outright distaste. For example, Sengstacke wrote Roosevelt on July 29 that the *Chicago Defender* was sponsoring a Victory Week and was planning a special edition to promote "inter-racial unity and good will." He asked the president for a statement that he could use in the paper. On August 4, Press Secretary Stephen Early replied curtly, turning down the request. He said the president had already made many appeals for "inter-racial good will," and it was impossible for him to single out one newspaper for a special message. Sengstacke finally got a letter from Roosevelt a month later, however, after OWI Director Elmer Davis noted that the *Defender* was "very influential" with blacks and that such a statement might be "very useful." The president's letter on September 9 stressed that everyone in the country had to fight and work together to win the war. "In helping to strengthen the sense of unity among our people," Roosevelt wrote, "you are helping to create the power to crush tyranny and secure freedom for ourselves and all the world."[99]

Early's initial denial was unimportant, but it was the type of thing that nettled black publishers, especially when such slights occurred again and again. By August 31, Sengstacke was despondent about the future of the black press, as he revealed in a letter to Gibson, the acting civilian aide to the secretary of war:

> I have had several conferences with [government] officials, all of whom promised their cooperation and felt that my suggestions [about how to get blacks more involved in the war effort] would produce the results desired, but so far no constructive action has been taken. I feel very definitely that the greatest force we have

today to do the job the government wants done has been grossly mishandled and little attention given to it along positive lines. That force, the Negro Press, has been given little or no recognition in comparison to what has been done with the large, metropolitan dailies. . . .

I have shown in every way possible my willingness to extend the facilities of the *Chicago Defender* toward raising the morale of the Negro people, as well as assisting government officials in their program for national unity. The nature of cooperation given by administrative officials in Washington to date is far from being encouraging. I am beginning to wonder whether the government really wants sincere cooperation or whether there are clandestine forces working against the interest of a section of the Negro Press.[100]

Just whom Sengstacke was referring to when he mentioned "clandestine forces" is unclear. But there were a number of possibilities. Both the Post Office and the army were actively conducting massive, secret investigations which would continue over the next year. The former would not move against the black press; the latter would. The War Production Board also may have entered the picture for a brief but apparently significant period. Blacks would claim after the war that the agency had illegally cut back on newsprint supplies to some black newspapers. Meanwhile, other agencies would grind on with their investigations, adding to the government's already vast amount of information. Such a federal fixation on the black press might have made Sengstacke even more despondent if he had known what was coming.

6

"It Is Not Believed That Such Critical Matter Is Conducive of Unity During These War Times"

(September 1942–August 1943)

Washington reporters enjoyed a full news day on December 1, 1942. During that Tuesday, Secretary of the Interior Harold L. Ickes conferred with President Roosevelt at the White House about becoming secretary of labor; the American Federation of Labor and the Congress of Industrial Organizations met for the first time in three years to discuss combining into one organization; a House Ways and Means subcommittee unanimously approved a new war powers bill; the State Department announced that the United States and Canada had agreed to lower trade barriers and to increase exchange of goods following the war; the government's Joint Economy Committee unanimously called for the Senate to investigate the massive number of federal forms being filled out by businessmen; and the president announced that a compromise had been worked out between the military and the War Production Board over control of production scheduling.

In the midst of such activity, overburdened reporters could not be blamed for ignoring an afternoon meeting of six Justice Department and Post Office officials. In fact, it is unlikely they even knew about the meeting. Neither Attorney General Francis Biddle nor Postmaster General Frank Walker, both of whom might have drawn notice from the capital's many journalists, were present. If reporters had known what took place, however, they definitely would have been interested because it directly concerned freedom of the press. Over the past six months, the Post Office slowly had realized that the Justice Department was unlikely to support any unmailability decision, particularly concerning the black press. The two departments, therefore, confronted each other on that December 1 in a showdown over seditious writing. The result virtually guaranteed an end to all Post Office suppressions for the remainder of the war.

The disagreement between the Justice Department and the Post Office was the most significant governmental event involving the black press between September 1942 and August 1943, if not throughout the war. But these were not the only government agencies concerned about the black press at this time, and this concern was evident in a variety of activity, much of it behind the scenes. Roosevelt warned the black press through an official of the NAACP of the possibility of Espionage Act indictments, the War Production Board may have limited or cut off newsprint supplies illegally to several black newspapers, the army continued its steady investigation with suppressions taking place at several camps, and the Office of Censorship "condemned" several more issues of black publications being mailed outside the country. It was further proof that not everyone in the government shared Biddle's belief in the value of wartime dissent.

Certainly that was true in the Post Office, where examiners struggled in determining whether the black press was seditious. Their examinations were the initial step in a process that could lead to a departmental hearing, where a publication's second-class mailing permit could be revoked if it was shown that seditious material had been printed. Strongly suspecting the existence of such material, the Post Office continued to examine a small number of black publications in the autumn and early winter of 1942. The investigation included an October issue of the *Oklahoma City Black Dispatch*, September and November issues of the *New Negro World*, five issues of the *Amsterdam Star–News* in October and November, and seventeen issues of the *Pittsburgh Courier* from October to January.[1] Apparently the Post

Office did not examine more publications simply because it felt that most black newspapers were identical. This attitude was evident in an examiner's remark in November when he found the *Black Dispatch* mailable. "It is typical of other Negro newspapers and contains the usual critical remarks concerning alleged discrimination against Negroes in America," W. C. O'Brien wrote. "As stated in similar cases, it is not believed that such critical matter is conducive of unity during these war times, but the same is not considered violative of the Espionage Statutes."[2]

The lengthy examinations of the *Star–News* and the *Courier* resulted mainly from each paper's application for a new second-class mailing permit. The former had to obtain a new permit after continual printing problems forced it to move from Trenton to Ridgewood in New Jersey. The *Courier*, meanwhile, needed a permit for a new Florida edition it had begun that fall.

The Post Office's investigation of the *Star–News* began with the October 3 issue. An examiner, confronted with stories containing headlines such as "U.S. 'Forces' Britain to Jim Crow Troops," concluded that the paper's articles were "capable of accomplishing the incitement of racial hatred, and the obstruction of recruiting and enlistment." Therefore, he recommended studying further issues before making a decision about the mailing permit.[3] In examining four more issues of the *Star–News*, he noted that the paper avidly attacked the South in articles that had few factual details and little reportorial objectivity. Front-page headlines included "Hell to Break Loose in South if Anti-Poll Tax Bill Passes" and "Negroes Are Told to Get Out of Dixie." Feeling that such material was "capable of inflaming the minds of the average Negro reader to the point of hatred of the whites," he labeled the *Star–News* "a hate mongering, vicious instrument of propaganda" that could incite race riots in the South. Thus, he recommended on December 2 that its application for a second-class permit be denied if the Justice Department concurred. The Justice Department replied a month later, however, that all the issues were mailable.[4]

The Post Office also did not hesitate in going to the Justice Department concerning the *Pittsburgh Courier*. Between October 21 and December 29, 1942, Assistant Solicitor Calvin W. Hassell of the Post Office wrote to the Justice Department six times requesting opinions on the mailability of the newspaper.[5] On five of the issues, the Post Office was merely making routine checks to see if the Justice Department agreed they were mailable. But the Post Office's view regarding the October 3 issue was different; the examiner felt it was unmailable. That opinion was rendered by George Breen, who had declared the *Chicago World* unmailable in the summer and then had become irritated when the Justice Department did not agree with him. In a five-page memorandum on October 14, Breen claimed that the *Courier* of October 3 created "a clear and present danger of causing the subversive results intended to be prevented by the Espionage Act." As evidence, he noted that the "entire" paper contained material designed to pit blacks against whites, aiding the Axis's "divide and conquer" program. Examples included articles about the American Bar Association refusing to admit blacks to membership and an Arizona restaurant owner who supposedly said that he would rather serve Hitler than black army officers. He concluded, as he did in his opinion on the *World*, by citing court decisions to bolster his argument that the paper was unmailable. Again, the Justice Department disagreed.[6]

This was Breen's final examination of the *Courier* during the war, and it quickly became apparent that most Post Office examiners did not share his view about the paper's unmailability. One of the principal reasons was a feeling that the *Courier*'s tone was gradually improving. "It may be stated that since the publishers of this newspaper have learned of the fact that the *Pittsburgh Courier* is being subjected to government scrutiny, the vigorness [sic] of its complaints have been considerably modified," examiner Ralph Manherz wrote on November 6, 1942. On December 31 and February 4, he noted further improvements in tone.[7]

At the same time, signs began to creep into examiners' reports indicating the Post Office's awareness of nonsupport of its mailability decisions by the Justice Department. "According to previous information furnished by the Department of Justice," an examiner noted on November 13 in an opinion on the *Pittsburgh Courier*, "such matter does not constitute violation of the Espionage Statutes."[8] Without such support, the Post Office had no intention of revoking a publication's mailing permit.

After the summer disagreement over the mailability of the *Chicago World*, it probably would have surprised the Post Office to discover in late October that the Justice Department still was struggling with what constituted seditious writing in the black press. As a result of a letter from Hassell inquiring about the legality of the *Courier's* October 3 and 10 issues, the Justice Department took an in-depth look at the paper. Coral Sadler, a Justice Department analyst in the Sedition Section, concluded:

> In the opinion of the analyst, the paper has been reporting honest and legitimate complaints. *The Pittsburgh Courier* and other large Negro newspapers express the existing unrest of 10% of the total population of the U.S., rather than create it. The question of sedition and mailability of Negro newspapers cannot be considered apart from the Negro problem. In other words, it is the grievances themselves that discourage recruiting and enlistment rather than the reporting of them by the Negro press.
>
> A policy of declaring Negro newspapers unmailable or of considering prosecution on charges of sedition—particularly a paper as prominent and as respected by the Negro population as *The Pittsburgh Courier*—could only result in aggravating further unrest and possibly arouse a spirit of defeatism among the Negro population.[9]

The Justice Department adopted Sadler's line of reasoning for the remainder of the war. Documents show that not once did it agree with the Post Office about the unmailability of a black publication. Sadler's superior, D. Newcomb Barco, Jr., concurred with his analysis. On October 29, he advised Lawrence M. C. Smith, the chief of the Special War Policies Unit of the War Division and the person who corresponded with the Post Office on sedition matters, that the Justice Department should "proceed cautiously" unless a black publication was "clearly seditious." However, he did not define what constituted "clearly seditious" writing, probably because he was unsure. Barco also suggested that the department should draw up an "established policy" concerning the black press, but it is unclear if this was ever done.[10]

Post Office officials unquestionably would have been interested in Sadler's memorandum. However, except for the Justice Department's June 1942 analysis of why it considered the *Chicago World* mailable, the Post Office never received a wartime explanation of how the Justice Department arrived at its black press decisions. Instead, Smith sent Hassell virtual form letters of two paragraphs. The first paragraph would mention the publication that had been examined, and a typical second paragraph would read, "Consideration has been given to these issues of *The Pittsburgh Courier* and it is concluded that they should not be declared nonmailable."[11]

Such curt, evasive replies were partly the result of Justice Department contempt for Post Office officials. Herbert Wechsler, who was a special assistant to the attorney general from 1940 to 1944 and an assistant attorney general for the following two years, recalled vividly the feeling in the Justice Department as repeated requests were received from the Post Office regarding mailability:

The people in the Post Office were just terrible. We had no respect for them. They had no sense for the law, no sense for the Constitution. They were not good lawyers. They had to be smacked down steadily [by the Justice Department]. They were examples of how people without standards can exploit the whole system tremendously. They continually sent us material because they were compiling a paper record for themselves so they would look good. That was a pattern of the people they had on deck there. They never got anywhere with us because of Biddle and his assistants. [12]

Furthermore, because Biddle's desire for extremely limited wartime suppressions was well known, lengthy explanations for nonsuppression decisions simply were unnecessary. Finally, as James H. Rowe, Jr., noted, the department was anxious at this time to avoid court cases that it might lose, particularly involving the press, because of a desire to build public confidence in the agency. Short replies intentionally frustrated the Post Office and strongly discouraged it from making mailability decisions that might end up in court.

The Justice Department's brief answers irritated Post Office officials. Not only were they rebuffed concerning the *Pittsburgh Courier*, but they had received similar treatment from the Justice Department when they suggested that the August–September issue of the *New Negro World* was unmailable. Breen found that the publication pitted "race against race, ally against ally," as in an article about British soldiers massacring Hindus. In Breen's estimation, this made the publisher an "agent of the Axis." It was "immaterial" whether such material was used deliberately, he said, nor did it matter that the magazine had pledged "full and complete support to the war effort." [13] The Justice Department did not agree. [14]

On November 24, the Post Office finally could contain its anger no longer, as Hassell went to Smith with what he considered a valid complaint. Hassell pointed out in a letter that the Post Office always submitted the detailed reports of its examiner when asking the Justice Department for an opinion on a publication's mailability. However, the Justice Department had refused since June to give the Post Office anything more than two-paragraph statements. Hassell noted that he had asked several times in vain for the reasoning behind the Justice Department decisions and demanded to know why such information was not being supplied. "I am unable to discover any reason why this practice of your furnishing memoranda by members of your staff should not be followed in all cases where there is a disagreement between members of our staff and yours with respect to questions of mailability," said Hassell.[15]

Hassell's letter resulted in a conference at the Post Office on December 1 at which he and O'Brien met with Smith and three others from the Justice Department. From the Post Office's viewpoint, the meeting was unproductive. "They [the Justice Department officials] proved themselves just about as evasive and nimble in concealing their views as a carnival rigger in concealing a pea," O'Brien complained.[16]

Both Smith and Eugene F. Roth, chief of the Sedition Section, were "particularly emphatic," according to O'Brien, about not furnishing additional information to the Post Office to explain how the Justice Department arrived at mailability decisions. They argued that the Post Office received all that was necessary and that to render a "formal," in-depth opinion listing the reasons for every decision would be impossible because the Justice Department did not have the manpower and time to do so. O'Brien found such a stance "inconsistent with the position of the Attorney General who advises Government officials through opinions which state the basis for the advice given." Hassell and O'Brien complained to no avail that the Post Office had been "blindly following" the Justice Department's advice about mailability, which possibly resulted in seditious material being mailed. Furthermore, they pointed out that the Post Office, not the Justice Department, would be liable if a suit was filed over a revocation of a publication's second-class mailing permit or if the Senate launched an investigation. If either of those events occurred, the Post Office would be in a vulnerable position because of the unavailability of the reasoning behind the Justice Department's decisions. The Justice Department officials replied that their two-paragraph opinions provided "sufficient protection" for the Post Office, and any investigatory body needing further information could examine the Justice Department files.

In an attempt to ease the tension, Smith suggested that occasional conferences might be held at which Justice Department officials could explain the reasoning behind their decisions. But when Hassell countered that such reasons should be dictated formally to a stenographer, Smith disagreed, "taking the position that no one would be competent to frame such a conclusion." This irritated Hassell. "After hearing their views," he said, "I have reached the conclusion that such conferences are going to be entirely fruitless."[17]

Whether any such conferences were held is unknown. There is no question, however, that the obstinacy of the Justice Department at the December 1 meeting had an impact on the Post Office, particularly in its investigation of the black press. In January 1943, for example, the Post Office felt that the November 1942 issue of the *New Negro World* was objectionable because it was "devoted in the main to an attack upon alleged unjust treatment of Negroes by whites." Breen noted numerous examples of what he considered seditious material, including the following editorial statement:

> What is meant by Subversive and pro-axis activities, when a Negro can be arrested for evading the draft and the same Government has no right to interfere with a white civilian in Louisiana who shoots down a Negro after he becomes a soldier? If the Axis shoot him down, he died in service of his country, if a Cracker shoots him down no harm is done.[18]

However, the Post Office took no action against the magazine and did not consult with the Justice Department, apparently feeling that such an attempt would be futile.

Just as the black press was allowed to continue using the mails, so were most other publications. By 1943, it was clear that there would be no repetition of the massive World War I clampdown by postal authorities. Some observers took this as a sign of inactivity, not realizing that the Post Office indeed was vigilant but reluctant to act because of the impasse with the Justice Department. For example, Democratic Representative Samuel Dickstein of New York introduced a bill in March 1943 barring anything from the mail causing "racial or religious hatred, bigotry or intolerance." "While our boys are risking their lives to defeat the forces of fascism and reaction abroad," said Dickstein, "these people—in a very subtle way—are trying to break ground for these dark forces in our own country. The Post Office Department, in permitting this type of propaganda to be distributed through the mails, unwittingly becomes a party to this conspiracy." The House, recognizing that the mood of the country was against a return to "witch hunts," buried the bill in a committee.[19]

Seeking to dispel the image of his department's apparent inactivity, Postmaster General Walker noted in his 1943 annual report that the Post Office had inspected 5398 publications between July 1, 1942, and June 30, 1943, to see if they violated the Espionage Act.[20] The figure was misleading, however. Post Office records show that only two publications—the *Boise Valley Herald* of Middleton, Idaho, and *The Militant* of New York—had their second-class permits revoked during this period.[21] Furthermore, according to the American Civil Liberties Union, only "a slightly larger number of individual issues" were barred from the mail between June 1, 1942, and May 31, 1943.[22] This trend became even more dramatic in the final two years of the war. The Post Office examined 10,532 publications during that time, and not only did it find none to be seditious, but in the first five months of 1944 it restored the second-class mailing permits of the *Herald* and *The Militant*.[23] Thus, only four publications did not have their permits reinstated during the war.

Even as the postmaster general's upbeat annual report appeared in the summer of 1943, Post Office officials were still steaming privately over the Justice Department's lack of cooperation. O'Brien held a meeting with six attorneys of the Post Office's Espionage Section on July 16, and all agreed that the Justice Department was responsible for seditious material continuing to move through the mails. Among the publications mentioned as possibly seditious was the *Pittsburgh Courier*.

O'Brien pointed out that he recently had complained to Ralph Boyd of the Justice Department's War Policies Unit about his department taking "too narrow" a view of publications. "I suggested . . . that they don't seem to appreciate the effect upon the reader as far as creating at least an impression or state of mind that is favorable to discord and to following the agitator and breaking down the home front," he told the attorneys. "I pointed out, for example, that some of these publications may have advocated forcible resistance to some law of the United States." O'Brien said that Boyd surprised him by admitting that the Justice Department was concerned only with those parts of the Espionage Act that made it illegal to give aid to the enemy and to interfere with enlistment and recruiting. Meanwhile, it was ignoring the illegality of material advocating treason, insurrection, or resistance to laws, as well as any material that might incite arson, murder, or assassination. O'Brien called that "a keyhole view" and accused the Justice Department of deliberately seeking reasons to find publications mailable, although he offered no explanation for such action. Therefore, he suggested that the attorneys should gather examples of the most seditious material moving through the mail in preparation for a "showdown" conference with the Justice Department. He also noted that it might be time to involve both the attorney general and the postmaster general in the controversy.[24] There is no indication that such a conference was ever held, but even if it did occur the absence of Post Office suppressions throughout the remainder of the war indicates that the Justice Department stood firm.

While the Post Office and the Justice Department were moving toward an impasse, the White House also was showing concern about the black press. A number of historians, for example, have noted Walter White's conversation with Roosevelt at the White House in December 1942.[25] As a result of this meeting, as well as continued criticism of black publications by the mainstream press, White called a conference of editors at the NAACP's New York office on January 23, 1943. He explained his purpose in a letter to Carter Wesley of the *Houston Informer*:

> The government and the powers that be who run this country know that they cannot deny the truth of ninety-eight per cent of the complaints of Negroes as voiced by the Negro press. They are unwilling to do anything fundamental about correcting these complaints. Therefore this campaign is launched and will inevitably grow to create the impression that the "racial tension" is caused by Negroes themselves and in particular the Negro press.
>
> None of us can deny that in some respects we are vulnerable. The idea of the conference is to pool our thinking and attempt to work out some sort of strategy to meet the storm that seems to be approaching. . . . The situation seems so critical that we will need to move fast.[26]

Among those attending were editors from the *Amsterdam Star–News*, the *Baltimore Afro-American*, the *Chicago Defender*, the *Kansas City Call*, the *Michigan Chronicle* (Detroit), the *New York Age*, the *Norfolk Journal and Guide*, the *Oklahoma City Black Dispatch*, the *People's Voice* (New York), the *Pittsburgh Courier*, and the Associated Negro Press.[27]

White told the editors what had been said in his meeting with Roosevelt and urged them to tone down their publications in order to avoid government prosecution. This was not the first time he had cautioned the black press about the possibility of government suppression; he had issued a similar warning in an article in the *California Eagle* in May 1942.[28] So the warning was not unexpected, but what must have surprised the editors in January was White's ignorance of the situation. They had known since the previous June, when Sengstacke had met with Biddle, that there would be no sedition prosecutions of the black press during the war. Although White may have misunderstood Roosevelt's comments about sedition indictments, it was more likely that the president was using the NAACP official, without his knowledge, to warn the black press once again that it was under close government surveillance. Whichever, White's warning infuriated Sengstacke. He was not about to take advice from someone he felt knew virtually nothing about journalism. Turning to the *Afro-American*'s Carl Murphy, who was sitting next to him, Sengstacke recalled saying, "Carl, this is the first and last time I will attend a meeting called by Walter White to tell us what to do." When White concluded his remarks, Sengstacke informed him that he would never again come to such a meeting and walked out.[29] It must have been a blow to White because of Sengstacke's prestige as one of the country's principal black publishers.

The other editors apparently remained to discuss the situation, and a code of journalistic ethics was drawn up. White, in his autobiography, claimed that the conference produced "almost immediate results," including less sensationalism in news articles "with little loss of militancy in attacking discrimination" and a decrease of racial "hypersensitiveness" which resulted in longer and more prominent accounts about whites who constructively fought discrimination.[30] White's claims almost surely were designed to enhance his reputation because they contained little truth. The black press already had toned down considerably by the end of the previous summer, as the army in particular had noticed. The readers knew it, too. In the Febrary 1943 issue of *Negro Digest*, a poll disclosed that a number of those who were interviewed said they recognized that the black papers had become less critical in their editorials because they feared censorship "if they took a stronger stand."[31]

White and Sengstacke also figured prominently in an episode supposedly involving the black press and the War Production Board (WPB), which allocated newsprint from January 1943 until the end of the war. Even today, more than forty years later, the facts are in doubt. White claimed in his autobiography that shortly after his meeting with Roosevelt in December 1942 the government began sharply limiting or totally cutting off newsprint to black papers that exposed or attacked discrimination. Such a move would have hurt the black press especially because of its rapid circulation increases since the beginning of the war. White said he gathered the facts and presented them to Roosevelt, who promptly "squelched" the WPB's illegal attempt to tone down the papers.[32]

The only confirmation of the cutbacks comes from Sengstacke. In a 1983 interview, he said that when he found out about them he contacted the *Chicago Tribune*, which immediately sold him some excess Sunday magazine newsprint stock. This stock was sent initially to the *Pittsburgh Courier*, but Sengstacke said that the paper declined to buy the newsprint after some hesitation. Presumably, the *Courier's* decision was predicated on pride; it probably did not want to be indebted to the *Defender*, which was a major competitor. Sengstacke then shipped the newsprint to the *Amsterdam Star–News* and several other black papers. He said the shipment enabled them to continue publishing until the government ended the illegal cutbacks a short time later.[33]

The *Chicago Tribune*, however, can locate no documentation showing that it sold newsprint to the *Chicago Defender* or to Sengstacke at that time.[34] In addition, the WPB vehemently denied on a number of occasions in 1943, 1944, and 1945 that it was involved in illegal cutbacks. For example, the WPB reviewed its wartime regulations of newsprint in October 1945 and said:

> Our Division, from the very start of scarcities, contended that our job involved equitable distribution of scarce materials, and we were not intended to set ourselves up as censors, to determine what kind of periodicals or printed data the American public should or should not read. The press, it was emphasized, is the only industry in the United States privileged [to have] a freedom which is specifically guaranteed by the Constitution.
>
> As Donald M. Nelson, WPB Chairman, declared in a statement presented to the Truman Committee [the Senate's Special Committee to Investigate the National Defense Program], printing paper is not a commodity (such as steel or textiles) but the free speech medium. Our Division felt that it is an indispensible vehicle of intelligence, a conveyor and moulder of public opinion,

a major weapon of democracy. Unhampered freedom of speech is essential, even in wartime, if a free people are to remain free.[35]

While such a statement may have overstated the WPB's love of freedom of speech, no evidence can be located to show that the agency discriminated illegally in its newsprint allocations to any publication. The agency admitted to the Truman Committee in 1944 that there was an "insinuation" of "other than honest and fair administration" of newsprint allotments.[36] However, in the absence of evidence to back up such rumors, it can only be assumed that they were started by individuals who disliked the WPB's allocations.

But the most telling evidence refuting illegal cutbacks by the WPB was the lack of complaints from the black press. The *Pittsburgh Courier*, the *Chicago Defender*, and the *Amsterdam Star–News*, which knew about the illegal cutbacks according to Sengstacke, never mentioned them. If the WPB had been cutting back newsprint illegally to the black press, it is inconceivable that these three papers, which were among the most outspoken in the country and the quickest to attack discrimination, would not have written about it. The absence of complaints throws doubt on the White and Sengstacke accounts, although the latter still insists that his story is correct.[37]

While questions remain about the WPB's treatment of the black press, considerably more is known about the activities of the army, which continued its steady investigation during this period. For example, on November 9, 1942, Military Intelligence (G-2) looked at "The Negro Problem and Its Factors" and concluded that black newspapers "can hardly be disregarded as a major factor of Negro unrest." However, G-2 admitted that it could find "little evidence" of seditious motives, and it noted that the black press's tone had continued to improve. It pointed out that a survey of articles in thirty-one black newspapers in mid-September had shown that 67 percent of the stories had a patriotic tone.[38]

In the army camps, however, not everyone shared G-2's view

that the black press was improving. The commanding officer at Camp Lee in Virginia complained to the adjutant general in late December and again in mid-January about the *Baltimore Afro-American* and the *Norfolk Journal and Guide.* Both papers had run articles about two black soldiers at Camp Lee who were demoted from master sergeant to private after joining a delegation which demanded that the camp's commanding officer grant "full and equal" rights to black soldiers at the camp and in a nearby community. The commanding officer claimed they were demoted for destroying "valuable papers" and "abusing newly inducted soldiers," but the mother of one of the men contended that they had been "framed."[39] When the articles appeared, the commanding officer criticized both papers for "false and subversive" statements that hurt the "soldierly mood and attitude" of both blacks and whites. He added that neither paper, nor the Associated Negro Press, had sought a statement or information from the camp's headquarters. He recommended, therefore, that such articles should be halted immediately or that the War Department should make an official investigation of the complaints contained in the articles. The camp commander's superior agreed that some type of action was necessary. He requested either a "prompt modification" of the papers' tones or the suppression of both papers and the prosecution of their editors.[40]

The complaint went to the War Department's Advisory Committee on Negro Troop Policies. Formed in August 1942 to deal with racial questions, the seven-man committee was headed by Assistant Secretary of War John J. McCloy.[41] It decided in March 1943 that legal action was inadvisable although a number of black papers unquestionably were hurting troop morale. Instead, the commitee recommended that the army's Bureau of Public Relations should increase its efforts to assist black reporters as well as to furnish them with additional "constructive" news articles and pictures. It also ordered public relations officers in the camps to be more attentive to the black press.[42]

Still more black press problems surfaced in April, and, unlike the Camp Lee incident, the army notified the publications that were involved. During the January 1943 court-martial of a black soldier who was convicted of sedition and sentenced to twenty years of hard labor, the defendant claimed that he had been influenced by articles in the *Afro-American* and the *Pittsburgh Courier*. Some army officials wanted to widely publicize the soldier's statement, but Maj. Gen. A. D. Surles of the Bureau of Public Relations refused to allow that. He did have a conference with Percival Prattis, executive editor of the *Courier*, on April 8 to inform him of what the soldier had said. On the following day, the *Courier*'s president, Ira F. Lewis, wrote Surles to thank him for his "liberal attitude" in not publicizing the soldier's testimony. He assured the general that the paper supported the government "100%" in the war and was telling blacks that they would lose all they held "dear" if the Axis won. After adding that the *Courier* was the only newspaper in western Pennsylvania where every employee had purchased War Bonds, he concluded:

> I am quite sure that there is much justification for the Negro newspapers to fight against segregation, discrimination and the one million insults that are daily hurled at citizens of color. At the same time, I realize that we are in a war and the War Department cannot become a laboratory for an analysis of social ills. The *Pittsburgh Courier* is as much interested in the United States winning the war as the War Department itself. Surely, I cannot make it any stronger.[43]

Lewis's statement about the War Department not being a laboratory for an analysis of social ills presumably was chosen carefully to impress Surles. It was a subtle reference to a talk by Col. Eugene R. Householder, who had told black editors at an army conference on December 8, 1941, that "the Army is not a sociological laboratory."[44] For a top official at the country's largest and most influential black newspaper to concede that point, even if it took almost a year and a half, indicated how much the black press had changed since the war had begun.

But the army remained concerned. Only a month after Lewis's letter to Surles, a quiet investigation was conducted at Camp Patrick Henry in Virginia to determine if the *Courier* was causing dissension among black soldiers. The investigator was unable to turn up any evidence that the paper was causing "a state of unrest." He recommended, therefore, not banning it or trying to talk soldiers into canceling their subscriptions, fearing that the paper would find out and criticize the army for opposing freedom of the press. He did, however, encourage curtailing the *Courier's* availability as much as possible. "[A] special effort should be made on the part of the officer in charge to get rid of the paper as soon as it is left laying [sic] around the orderly room," said D. P. Ludwig.[45]

Then, after racial disturbances in the Alexandria and New Orleans areas of Louisiana, the War Department's inspector general had a survey conducted in June and July of 1943 of about 350 white and black soldiers. The findings included the now familiar charge that the black press was one of the major reasons for racial problems because of its "highly inflammatory and exaggerated articles printed under glaring headlines." While the survey turned up no evidence that the newspapers were tied in with enemy agents, it concluded that the black press was "interfering with the war effort" and recommended informing publishers of this. Furthermore, if patriotic and public welfare appeals failed to bring about changes, the report suggested taking "drastic steps," although it did not say what these were. It also agreed with the War Department's Advisory Committee on Negro Troop Policies that camp public relations officers should work more closely with the black press. Finally, the report said that commanding officers should be reminded of a War Department Training Circular of February 16, 1943, which authorized them to censor mail, including newspapers, in order to control racial unrest. "It is obvious that the utmost care and secrecy should be exercised in this matter," urged the report. The recommendations were forwarded to McCloy, but it is unknown whether they were sent out to camp officers.[46]

Considering the number of army complaints about black newspapers, it is not surprising that actual suppressions occurred in the summer of 1943. In fact, the only surprise is that they did not begin ealier. In late July, the *Chicago Defender* reported that its newsboys at Camp Rucker in Alabama had been seized, their papers had been confiscated, and they had been "chased" away. The camp's soldiers never received that issue, and the army offered no explanation of why the action had been taken. The *Defender* told readers that distribution of it and the *Pittsburgh Courier* also had been halted at several Mississippi camps, which had emboldened Southern white civilians to move against the black papers. In Carthage, a young boy had his papers destroyed by a group of white men, who gave him a "light whipping" and warned that something worse would occur if he was caught selling any more black papers. Police in Hattiesburg not only told newsboys that they could no longer sell Northern black newspapers in the town, but they jailed one of the blacks, beat him badly, and threatened to kill him if he sold any more of the papers. In Brandon, a *Courier* columnist was "called into question" by some of the town's prominent white citizens, while a *Courier* newsboy in Gulfport was arrested for selling the paper. Following the latter incident, a local *Defender* agent was advised by a white lawyer to stop selling the paper. "I shall probably send for more [papers] in a couple of weeks," John A. Coleman wrote the *Defender*. "I hate this very much as it was the only way our boys at the Navy base had to find out what was going on in their home towns."[47]

These were not the first wartime actions by Southern white civilians against black papers. In the late summer and early fall of 1942, the *Pittsburgh Courier* complained to the Justice Department that its newsboys had been threatened or it had been suppressed in nine towns in Alabama, Arkansas, Georgia, and Mississippi. This resulted in an extensive FBI investigation to see if the newsboys' rights had been violated under the Fourteenth Amendment. Frank Bolden, a columnist on the *Courier*, recalled that the paper was told the government "could only see that the papers reached a certain destination, and then they couldn't guarantee that the papers would be distributed from that point." However, what the black press did not know was that the Justice Department went beyond the investigatory stage with two Georgia towns, Thomaston and Tennille, which suppressed the *Courier* by claiming its sale violated city ordinances. Assistant Attorney General Wendell Berge instructed the U.S. attorney in Macon in February 1943 to have an "informal conference" with officials in each town. They were told that the ordinances were illegal and that they might be prosecuted if they continued to apply them to the selling of black newspapers. Apparently the ordinances were not used again against the black press. The Justice Department investigated still more complaints of suppressions in the summer of 1943 in four locations in Alabama, Mississippi, and Texas.[48]

The confiscations of black newspapers brought an angry retort in August 1943 from S. I. Hayakawa, a *Defender* columnist and professor at the Illinois Institute of Technology who would become a U.S. senator from California in the mid-1970s. He called them "about the most direct abridgements of the freedom of the press that can be imagined, short of shooting the editors or dynamiting the printing plant." Thus, he wondered why there were no complaints from Roy Howard, William Randolph Hearst, and Col. Robert R. McCormick. After all, he noted, they were "so anxious about the freedom of the press that they leap into action every time a government official wiggles an eyelash."[49]

At about the same time, problems also occurred at the antiaircraft training center at Fort Bliss in Texas. Following racial disturbances, the commanding general banned black papers from the post because they were of "such an agitational nature as to be prejudicial to military discipline within the training center." Therefore, the camp's postal officer began confiscating "objectionable newspapers" before mail was delivered to black battalions. When the Antiaircraft Command contacted the War

Department in August about the legality of the Fort Bliss suppressions, the army immediately ordered them to cease. Camp commanders were told that they could halt an occasional issue, but doing so permanently "would only serve to supply ammunition for agitation to colored papers."[50]

In the midst of such suppressions, top army officials continued to complain about the black press. For example, McCloy wrote to Eleanor Roosevelt on July 26, 1943, that the black press had been careless repeatedly in reporting instances of alleged injustices. He admitted, however, that it was only partly to blame for racial unrest in the service. "There is room for great improvement in our handling of the Negro in the Army," he said.[51]

Another exchange of letters also occurred that summer between Truman K. Gibson, Jr., the black acting civilian aide to the secretary of war and a supporter of the black press, and Carter Wesley, president of the *Houston Informer.* Following a race riot at Camp Stewart in Georgia, Gibson sent a memorandum to black editors, cautioning them to be more careful in their reporting because of errors in recent articles about the army. When Wesley complained about the memorandum, Gibson wrote back, complimenting the black press on how much it was helping black soldiers. He said that was why he wanted to avoid having the War Department take action against black newspapers for distorted and untrue articles. "All of my efforts have been directed at bringing the War Department and the Negro press together," said Gibson. "At no time have I requested in any way that justifiable criticisms be not published. That would be an inexcusable position . . . for a man of our race." In a lengthy response, Wesley said he still was unsatisfied and once more criticized Gibson's memorandum:

> I know that in some instances I published stories in the beginning [of the war] which were not thoroughly checked, and which could have done harm to the morale of the Army. I never tried to shirk responsibility for having done that. But once it was called to my

attention, I have never failed to try to get both sides of stories and to check every story to make sure that there is fire under the smoke. I believe that all of the responsible publishers have taken that attitude. . . . Most of us want to play ball with you and to recognize the fact that you have a delicate position. But you ought to reciprocate by being most tactful in your expression, so that you don't seem to make an attack on us when you are not intending one.[52]

Whether other black editors also attacked Gibson because of the memorandum is unknown.

The Post Office, the War Production Board, and the army were not the only threats to the black press during the period from September 1942 to August 1943. The Office of Censorship was also dangerous. On the surface, Director Byron Price maintained good relationships with black editors. When Moss Hyles Kendrix, for example, asked Price in February 1943 for a comment about the upcoming fifth annual National Negro Newspaper Week, Price complimented the plans and noted that the black press had "an unparalleled opportunity" to help defeat the enemy by stressing the need for worldwide unity among minorities. He said that such unity would ensure victory.[53]

That encouragement was for public consumption. Behind the scenes, however, the agency's postal censors wielded immense suppressive power in determining what mail would be allowed outside the country, and they exercised this option almost ruthlessly. The censors could afford to be that way because of the secrecy under which they worked; they were not required to make any public accounting for their decisions.[54] The *Chicago Defender*, which had some issues suppressed in 1942 by the Office of Censorship, had more problems with the agency early in 1943.[55] The February 6, 13, and 27 issues of the paper, mailed to Cuban subscribers, were "condemned" and sent to the Post Office's dead letter office. But, because of a bureaucratic error, they were then returned to the *Defender*. When the paper discovered the "condemned" stickers, it immediately asked the district postal censor for an explanation. It did not get one. The chief postal censor said he could not disclose any information because of the "confidential nature" of the censorship operations. "You can appreciate that considerations of National Security alone dictate this policy," he wrote the *Defender*, which had no recourse but to give up attempting to find out what was objectionable in the banned issues.[56]

In still other examples of censorship, the *Pittsburgh Courier* of October 3, 1942, and the *Racial Digest* of April 1943 were "condemned." Copies of the *Courier* mailed to the Canal Zone were confiscated because of news stories and editorials criticizing "race discrimination in the war effort," according to an examiner. Among the groups criticized in articles were the army, the rubber industry, and bus companies.[57] Action was taken against the *Racial Digest* after the Office of War Information (OWI) requested permission to place a copy in its London library. The Office of Censorship's district postal censor, however, noted that the magazine contained "inflammatory racial material which has frequently been condemned by this Station."[58] Included in the *Racial Digest* was an article that claimed blacks were not first-class citizens and another one that said black conditions had worsened since the bombing of Pearl Harbor.[59] Still another example noted that "politically, socially and certainly economically the Negro is still a slave." That article continued:

There are defense industries operating today at full speed whose top salary for the Negro regardless of his experience, proficiency and skill (the so-called criteria for advancement) is fixed . . . and fixed lower than the salary of the unskilled white worker in the same plant. Then, of course, there are plants that flatly refuse to hire Negroes at all; while a universal cry rings for speedier production to every Allied Base in the world.

Does a bullet made by a Negro have less penetrating element as compared with the bullet of a white worker?

Do the Negro-made parts of a P 38 fail to assemble with the parts made by the white machinist?

> Do the tanks and jeeps constructed by Negro Labor operate with
> less efficiency that [sic] those constructed by white workers? . . .
>
> The Negro is tired of this willful discrimination; he is fed up with
> this medley of contradictions upon which our Democracy rests.
> . . . Life is not so sweet and Peace is not so dear that the black
> man must bow and acquiesce to continued injustices.[60]

Faced with such articles, the district postal censor asked for
advice. The chief postal censor admitted that the *Racial Digest*
posed a "difficult" problem. He pointed out, after all, that none
of the articles by themselves would be enough to condemn
large publications such as the *New York Times* or *Newsweek* if
they had used them. "However, since Racial Digest is a publication of limited circulation, our condemnation of it may not
be entirely in vain," he advised. "Certainly there can be no
good reason why it should go to a library in London." Therefore, OWI's request was rejected.[61]

By the summer of 1943, the Office of Censorship felt that a
more thorough examination of black newspapers was necessary. On July 27, district postal censors were ordered to forward
to Washington for approval all black papers being mailed out
of the country.[62] It is unclear why such an order was issued at
this time, but it would remain in effect for almost seven months
and would result in some newspapers being held up for months
before being delivered.

While black publishers were unaware of the Office of Censorship's new order, enough was known about the activity of
other government agencies to make them concerned. Investigations continued, and suppression remained a constant threat.
Meanwhile, the publishers' only assurance was that the Department of Justice would not move against them. Complicating
the situation and making it more dangerous were simmering
racial tensions; disturbances broke out in a number of cities
before the end of the summer, which did not bode well for
unity between blacks and whites. Obviously, something more
was needed to bring the black press and the government closer

together than the steady stream of letters from black journalists to top government officials.[63]

Sengstacke of the *Chicago Defender* recognized the urgency of the situation. In the summer of 1943, when he was elected president of the Negro Newspaper Publishers Association (NNPA), the organization he had founded in 1940, he announced that one of his goals would be "to promote an understanding of the problems of the Negro press among officials of government for protection of the interests of Negro publishers."[64] On July 16 and 17, eleven members of the NNPA's executive commitee met with government officials in Washington. They represented the *Atlanta Daily World*, the *Baltimore Afro-American*, the *Chicago Bee*, the *Chicago Defender*, the *Cleveland Call and Post*, the *Houston Informer*, the *Louisville Defender*, the *Pittsburgh Courier*, the *St. Louis Argus*, and the *Washington Tribune*.

In a series of meetings with Vice-President Henry Wallace, Biddle, War Manpower Commission Chairman Paul McNutt, and McCloy, as well as officials from the navy, the War Production Board, the Selective Service, and the Office of War Information, the blacks discussed discrimination and morale problems. They also zeroed in on black press concerns: how to obtain more government advertising, how to increase newsprint allotments, how to get draft deferments for employees, how to improve news coverage of black servicemen, and how to gain admission to Secretary of the Navy Frank Knox's press conferences, which were closed to black reporters.[65] Carter Wesley of the *Houston Informer* was particularly impressed with Biddle, who talked with the group because Roosevelt was unavailable. Upon returning to Houston, Wesley told his readers:

This was the capstone of all of our conferences. Naturally, it was off the record, but this baby talked not only to the point, but to a series of points that were as sharp, frank, clear, concise and unequivocal as anything I've heard yet. . . . Everybody in our group realized that the baby had a mind, a heart, a conscience and the courage to combine them. Mr. Biddle had the most touchy problem of all with all those publishers shooting at him in lieu of the President and he made the highest rating of all of those we met.[66]

In actual gains, the publishers did not get everything they sought from the government. For example, the WPB promised to study the problem of inadequate newsprint allotments, but no changes were forthcoming. In October 1943, after several months of waiting, the NNPA petitioned the WPB's Newspaper Industry Advisory Committee, which considered complaints about newsprint. It asked for "special consideration" in obtaining more newsprint, citing several justifications: the black press printed news unavailable elsewhere of interest to 10 percent of the population, the migration of black workers to war plants had increased demands for black papers in cities, and the black press already was "effecting numerous economies in the use of paper." The committee rejected the plea on the grounds that the black press had created its own problem. It pointed out that most black papers had doubled their prices from five to ten cents in early 1942, justifying the step by "substantially" increasing the number of pages they printed. When the government on January 1, 1943, had instituted newsprint allotments which were based on paper consumption in 1941, many black papers suddenly had been faced with having to cut back either on circulation or on size. Since either choice would have irritated readers, who were the lifeblood of black papers because of the importance of circulation, nothing had been done. The committee expressed "sympathetic interest" but refused to make allocation changes.[67]

The publishers were more successful with the Selective Service. In a meeting with Director Lewis B. Hershey, they stressed that black newspapers could be crippled, even destroyed, unless their employees were treated fairly by draft boards.[68] C. A. Scott, general manager of the *Atlanta Daily World*, complained in particular about the drafting of A. C. Searles, editor of the *Southwest Georgian* in Albany. After Searles ran an article on February 6, 1943, about the abduction and lynching of a

Newton man, claiming that a sheriff and two deputies were responsible, he was reclassified from 3-A to 1-A in six days and not allowed to appeal the reclassification. When he was inducted on June 19, he wrote a signed article in the paper, saying that he did not mind serving in the army but resented being treated unfairly by the board. Within a week, the new editor was ordered to appear before the local draft board and bring a copy of the paper with him. The editor was so frightened that he ceased publication, leaving blacks in Albany with no news outlet. "This type of action is a serious threat to the Negro press," said Scott. "[The black press] is essential to our war effort by printing news of interest to Negroes and thereby keeping up their morale." Scott and others on the executive committee contended that Searles should have been deferred under Selective Service Occupational Directive No. 29, which made newspaper managing editors as well as other essential employees eligible for deferment. As a result of the complaint, the Selective Service ordered an investigation in August of the Albany draft board. There is no indication that Searles was released from the army, but black papers triumphantly played up the investigation.[69] Lee Finkle has noted that this was the only apparent attempt by a draft board during the war to put a black newspaper out of business. Numerous other papers had employees drafted, which produced hardships, but they continued publishing.[70]

The NNPA's meeting with McCloy also paid dividends, although it was not evident at the time. In July, Chief of Staff George C. Marshall wrote to him regarding disturbances among black troops and asked if some black editors should be called to Washington for "a frank talk." Less than a week after he talked with the NNPA, McCloy responded that it would be "inappropriate" to have further talks at that time because the publishers had just "evidenced a disposition to take a different line." However, he said that if "inflammatory articles" continued, "I would call them in and dress them down." He also suggested making further improvements in the way the Negro

Section of the Bureau of Public Relations worked with the black press.[71]

On August 5, McCloy wrote Sengstacke, answering in detail the various questions that the executive committee posed about the army on July 16. He concluded by pointing out that the War Department was interested in being fair to the black press, which in turn was expected to cooperate with the army:

> The influence of the negro press among colored soldiers and their families is very strong and there continues to be evidence that the negro press unduly plays up alleged discrimination in the Army, inflamatory [sic] incidents and the like. The indications are that this type of press contributes greatly to the conditions which have brought about some of the recent disturbances in the camps and elsewhere. Negro soldiers are prepared to believe the wildest rumors, and do. I am aware that all the fault cannot be ascribed to the Negro press, but it is a fact, in my judgment, that the negro press can have a very important effect on the opinion of the negro soldier by putting greater emphasis than it has in the past upon the very good aspects of Army life.[72]

Sengstacke thanked McCloy, saying that he believed "some good results in understanding and action" already had come from the July meeting.[73]

The black publishers also made headway with the Office of War Information. Throughout the previous year the agency had continued its investigation of the black press.[74] This led to the belief in some government quarters that OWI somehow could change the black press's tone. In both January and March of 1943, for example, the Justice Department complained to OWI about articles appearing in the *Pittsburgh Courier*. It specifically noted that columnist George Schuyler had labeled the past year disillusioning. "Aframericans . . . have little hope left of future national existence characterized by liberty, equality and fraternity," wrote Schuyler in January 1943. "The Negrophobic philosophy, originating in the South and aided by the indifference or acquiescence of white people in the North, and Negro opportunists everywhere, has now become the official policy of the government." Schuyler concluded that he personally was not disillusioned, however, "because I expected no improvement." The Justice Department suggested that OWI might want to take "action" to tone down such criticism in the *Courier*, but there is no evidence that the agency did anything.[75] Even so, the black press was unhappy with OWI. Claude A. Barnett, director of the Associated Negro Press, accused OWI in November 1942 of giving black newspapers "large doses of pure propaganda designed to lull colored people to sleep and make them forget the discrimination and mistreatment accorded Negro soldiers and civilians, instead of grappling realistically with the problems involved." He said that blacks immediately recognized such "paternalistic pap" for what is was.[76]

By the summer of 1943, however, such complaints were no longer heard, if not forgotten. When he took over as president of the NNPA, Sengstacke declared that he wanted the NNPA represented "on all publishers' committees appointed by the government to work out the war-time problems of the industry."[77] Although it is unclear how much success Sengstacke had, he did get quick action from OWI. At the publishers' Washington meeting in mid-July, the blacks stressed that OWI should present their race's war role in such a way as to add to "the effectiveness of the Negro's contribution to the government's effort."[78] A month later, OWI named a black-press committee to advise it "on the problems of war information." It included Sengstacke, Howard Murphy of the *Baltimore Afro-American*, William O. Walker of the *Cleveland Call and Post*, C. A. Scott of the *Atlanta Daily World*, and Carter Wesley of the *Houston Informer*.[79]

The committee represented another indication of how much had changed since the bombing of Pearl Harbor. By mid-1943, it was apparent that both the black press and the government were willing to grant concessions in order to strengthen and improve their relationship. The government remained wary of the black press, but suppressions were largely over. Not everyone in the government was pleased, however. At the Post Office, a bitter feeling remained until the end of the war over the Justice Department's stubborn refusal to approve mailing permit revocations of possibly seditious publications. Meanwhile, the army and the Office of Censorship continued to move against black publications, but time would show that their actions were relatively minor. Only one significant threat remained—the FBI. In September 1943, J. Edgar Hoover launched a major attack against the black press. It was the last serious threat during the war, but neither the president nor the Justice Department was impressed by Hoover's continued insistence that the black press was seditious and therefore dangerous. It was the final indication, and certainly a powerful one, that the black press had indeed survived the perils of World War II.

7

"Edgar Hoover Is Busy Again"
(September 1943–August 1945)

In 1947, publisher P. B. Young, Sr., of the *Norfolk Journal and Guide*, one of the country's major black newspapers, recalled the FBI's examination of the black press during World War II. He boasted of the result:

> The fact that years of watching and distilling of every line, every word printed in the Negro press that could by any process of reasoning have been classified as treasonable brought not one single arrest, nor one single act of suppression, constituted irrefutable proof of the undiminished patriotism of the American Negro at a time when efforts to sabotage our war effort were quite general in other circles.[1]

Young was only partially correct. Certainly the loyalty of black journalists played a role in their lack of arrests and the non-suppression of their publications by the FBI. After all, they began stressing their patriotism when the United States entered the war, and most black publications soon became less critical of the government. That did not go unnoticed by concerned government officials. But the deciding factor for the FBI, regarding arrests and suppressions, was the unwavering constitutional views of Attorney General Francis Biddle. He had to approve any indictments and thus could control the FBI's court actions, if not its investigations. The final major test of Biddle's resolve not to prosecute the black press for sedition, a decision he had announced to John Sengstacke in the summer of 1942, came more than a year later in September 1943. FBI Director J. Edgar Hoover compiled a 714-page report on blacks in the United States which solidly linked a number of black publications and black journalists with the Communist Party. Hoover did not ask specifically for any sedition indictments, because associating with Communists was not against the law, but the report's implication was that such associations were seditious. It was his chief wartime thunderbolt against the black press, a group that had convinced him in 1919 that it was dangerous because of its influence. But Biddle held firm, and no evidence shows that he even contemplated any action against the black press, demonstrating that he still could control the spymaster who had become so powerful and so feared. It was not a defeat that Hoover accepted easily. He continued to seek sedition indictments of the black press into 1945.

Meanwhile, three other government agencies were involved actively—and significantly—with the black press. The army was pleased over its ever-improving relations with black journalists. Nevertheless, this relationship was threatened by escalating censorship at army camps in the fall of 1943. The War Department moved to halt this trend in November, but some suppressions continued, mostly in the South, until the late summer of 1944. At the Post Office, examinations of black publications occurred until the end of the war although most inspections were cursory, almost routine. The Justice Department's nonsupport left Post Office examiners bitter but virtually helpless to move against any publications, and this futility was reflected in their reports. The Office of Censorship also halted mandatory black press inspections in Washington in early 1944. Even so, several issues being mailed out of the country were condemned, and at least one issue was held up four and a half months before being delivered. The thread running throughout these agencies was a cautious, frequently reluctant spirit of acceptance by government officials. There was even occasional outright cordiality. The black press had weathered the storm, and the ultimate proof came from the White House. Not only did both Franklin D. Roosevelt and Harry S Truman meet with the Negro Newspaper Publishers Association, but early 1944 saw the first black installed as a White House correspondent. Considering the developments as a whole, it was obvious that both the black press and the government had modified their positions, making possible immense strides since the bombing of Pearl Harbor.

The FBI's 1943 survey, whose critical comments about the black press resembled what appeared in the attorney general's reports to Congress in 1919 and 1920, resulted from Roosevelt and Congress granting Hoover mammoth but ill-defined investigatory powers in the years immediately preceding the U.S. entry into World War II. Such grants of power were not unnecessary or harmful in themselves; they were designed to protect the country's security as war became imminent. The problem was the unclearness about whether the FBI was limited to investigating violations of the law when collecting domestic intelligence. In 1936, the president secretly ordered Hoover to gather information on communist activities and two years later broadened his mandate to include an investigation of all "activities of either a subversive or a so-called intelligence type."[2] Both orders, given orally, obviously authorized surveillance of noncriminals, a Senate committee concluded in 1976, and apparently the orders were understood that way by Hoover. Then, in September 1939, Roosevelt announced that the FBI was to "take charge of investigative work in matters relating to espionage, sabotage, and violations of the neutrality regulations."[3] Domestic intelligence investigations of subversives were not mentioned then or in January 1943, when Roosevelt repeated his order.[4] "Nevertheless, the President clearly knew of and approved informally the broad investigations of 'subversive activities' carried out by the FBI," the Senate committee said.[5]

Congress also played a role at this time in legitimizing domestic intelligence operations. In 1938, the Foreign Agents Registration Act required the registration of all foreign agents disseminating propaganda in the United States. That narrowly drawn act was broadened over the next three years. In 1940, the Smith Act made it illegal to propose military insubordination or to advocate overthrowing the government violently, and the Voorhis Act of 1941 required the registration of any "subversive" organizations having foreign links and advocating the government's overthrow. In 1976, the Senate noted the significance of the 1940 and 1941 acts:

> In other words, the danger to domestic security was understood as including American citizens whose political activities might lead them to serve the interests of opposing nations. Attorney General Jackson used the term "Fifth Column" in 1940 to characterize "that portion of our population which is ready to give assistance or encouragement in any form to invading or opposing ideologies." He told a conference of state officials that the FBI's intelligence mission involved "steady surveillance over individuals and groups within the United States who are so sympathetic with the systems or designs of foreign dictators as to make them a likely source of federal law violation."
>
> The assumption that such persons and organizations posed a direct and immediate threat to the nation's security was not seriously questioned. . . . In his effort to discourage prosecutions and to persuade the nation that FBI intelligence could handle any threats, Attorney General Jackson failed to acknowledge the risks to individual rights from unregulated federal surveillance. With no clear legislative or executive standards to keep it within the intended bounds, the FBI (and military intelligence in its sphere) had almost complete discretion to decide how far domestic intelligence investigations could extend.[6]

The FBI eagerly used—and in some cases abused—the newly granted investigatory powers both before and during World War II. In looking at groups with German, Italian, Japanese, or communist links or sympathies, investigations included such diverse organizations as the NAACP, the Ku Klux Klan, and the German–American Bund.[7] Many government officials, who knew of the breadth of the investigations, were shocked but helpless to stop them. As Kenneth O'Reilly has noted, the

Roosevelt administration quickly lost control of "resourceful and highly motivated FBI officials who sought far different and more conservative political objectives."[8] A revealing glimpse of the way FBI agents viewed constitutional liberties and communism occurred in November 1942, when the special agent in charge in Oklahoma City complained about the *Oklahoma City Black Dispatch*. He noted that the September 19 issue of the paper "is of a rather biased nature and is sprinkled with such well-known Communistic phrases as 'Civil Liberties,' 'Inalienable Rights,' and 'Freedom of Speech and of the Press.' "[9]

The agents, of course, were mere reflections of their strong-willed leader. And if there was one thing that Hoover disliked passionately, it was communism. He had become convinced of communism's danger in the "Red Scare" days of 1919 to 1921, and by World War II Biddle found that this concern had become an "obsession," driving Hoover to pursue "fish that are hardly worth catching."[10] He continually played up the communist threat, doling out inside information to authenticate his public statements. This approach, according to former American Civil Liberties Union Director Frank Donner, "conjured up in the minds of his followers a patient midnight review and evaluation of untold numbers of informants' reports." But Hoover assured the nation that his own hard work was not enough. Although the FBI had stymied communism so far, he claimed, the country had experienced a narrow escape, and in the future "everyone [would have] to join in fighting the menace."[11] Considerable disagreement has arisen about whether Hoover exaggerated the dangers of communism and even whether his statements were sincere. Donner felt the danger was a "myth," which Hoover exploited "to free himself and his agency from official control."[12] And William C. Sullivan, a former assistant to Hoover, claimed that the director emphasized communism's threat merely to pry appropriations out of Congress.[13] But John P. Mohr, the number four man in the FBI for many years, disagreed. "Sure, it [the Communist Party] was a weak organization," he recalled in the 1970s, "but Hoover's contention was that, by God, with Communists you don't need to have a great big organization, that they're still a threat even when they're small, and that's true."[14]

Such disagreements notwithstanding, Hoover's distaste for foreign ideologies, particularly communism, guaranteed that blacks and the black press would be watched closely during World War II. The investigations began in the "Red Scare" days, when Hoover became convinced that blacks were an easy target for bolshevik propaganda, and the black press was considered extremely dangerous because of its influence with readers. Therefore, it was unlikely that the FBI stopped investigating blacks in the years between the wars, when both the Communists and the Japanese made vigorous attempts to curry black favor, and it was no surprise when blacks were investigated heavily by the Bureau during World War II.[15] William P. Rogers, a former attorney general, felt that Hoover overreacted throughout his career to communism's appeal to blacks:

> To some extent I think there was a greater fear of the Communist Party than was justified. . . . One of the reasons I don't think the fear was justified was because the blacks in this country just didn't fall for it. Logically, they might well have. I mean, they were underprivileged, they did not have their constitutional rights, they were neglected and all the other things that would give rise to the feeling of "Why don't we try something else?" Communism might seem to be a viable alternative from the standpoint of people in that position in our society. So to me the remarkable thing was that they did not.[16]

But an even more basic reason existed for the investigations: Hoover was a well-known racist. "J. Edgar Hoover, who has steadfastly refused to include Negroes among his 4,800 special agents, has a long record of hostility to Negroes," *The Nation* noted in July 1943.[17] Calling him hostile to blacks may have been an overstatement, but Sullivan found in his years in the FBI that Hoover definitely "disliked" blacks.[18] Historian Sanford J. Ungar labeled him "prejudiced and narrow-minded, overtly biased against black people," and said this resulted from Hoover's Old South attitude.[19] Still another historian, David J. Garrow, pointed out in 1981 that Hoover's racism was "widely documented."[20]

Hoover's racism and his distrust of communism were not issues, however, when the FBI's wartime investigations resulted in some black arrests and convictions for sedition and draft evasion. In September 1942, for example, sixty-three members of the Temple of Islam (Black Muslims), including their leader, Elijah Muhammad, were arrested in Chicago. Although the Muslims openly sympathized with the Japanese because they were dark-skinned, the government's sedition case failed, and instead they were found guilty of draft evasion. Muhammad received a five-year sentence, and the other defendants were given three years each. In the same month, five members of New York's Ethiopian Pacific Movement, including Robert O. Jordan, who was known as the "Black Hitler" because of his pro-Axis leanings, were indicted for sedition. They were accused of "urging soldiers and others to resist service in the armed forces of the United States and to support Japan, holding that Japan was going to liberate the darker races." They were found guilty, and their sentences ranged from four to ten years in jail, with Jordan also being fined $10,000. In St. Louis, two black members of the Pacific Movement of the Eastern World were convicted of both sedition and draft evasion and received two- and four-year jail terms. Still other convictions, mostly for draft evasion, occurred in Newark (New Jersey), San Diego, and Chicago.[21] Historian Neil A. Wynn noted that the draft evasion convictions usually resulted from the government finding it difficult to prove a sedition charge:

> It is apparent that the mixtures of religious and racial consciousness made the line between draft evasion and sedition a difficult one to distinguish. The F.B.I. attempted to relate such beliefs to Japanese agents and propaganda. . . . However, the fact that sedition charges were generally dropped, and that little, if any, connection was found linking these groups with the Japanese in subversive activities, makes it seem likely that, as the American

Civil Liberties Union saw it, "the defendants were the victims of over-zealous race consciousness, while others were religious zealots."[22]

The black press condemned those arrested for sedition and draft evasion. That was not surprising because it had been stressing the loyalty of blacks since the beginning of the war. On January 17, 1942, for example, the *Pittsburgh Courier* pointed out that blacks had nothing in common with any foreign group. "The Japanese, Germans, Italians and their Axis stooges know that it is futile to seek spies, saboteurs or Fifth Columnists among American Negroes," it said. "Every attempt in that direction has been a miserable failure."[23] In another typical comment, *Courier* columnist Joseph D. Bibb said in mid-May, "There is no intention or purpose of sedition underlying his [the black's] thinking." Instead, Bibb continued, blacks wanted only "Democracy, Christianity and Freedom."[24]

The *Courier's* outrage at those blacks who were arrested was predictable. More than being traitors to their country, they were considered traitors to their race. The paper labeled them "fools and fanatics" and said there was less danger of blacks being alienated by foreign propaganda than by "anti-Negro propaganda and practices of some of the Negro's white fellow citizens."[25] In still another editorial in August 1942, the *Courier* declared that foreign ideologists, including Communists, did not understand that blacks put America first and had less foreign ties than any other group in the country. "He [a black] does not believe that anybody is going to treat him any better than the American white man, so he has no desire to incur the enmity of his white neighbor in working against his interest in any international set-up," it stated.[26]

Other black publications echoed this theme. A. Philip Randolph, the fiery journalist who had been denounced by Hoover in the period from 1919 to 1921 for his work on *The Messenger*, wrote in *The Black Worker* in September 1942 that he found it "almost inconceivable that a Negro in his right mind would advocate the victory of the Japanese over his own country in the present war or any war." He concluded that those arrested were "people on the lunatic fringe" who were either fanatics or hopeful of making some quick money.[27] Louis Martin, editor of the *Michigan Chronicle*, said in *Opportunity* in December 1942 that most of those charged with sedition were "well known crack pots and starry-eyed cultists who are without influence or intelligence. . . . The Jap propagandist might find them easy victims of his new world visions, but that they could sway any important faction of the Negro people is simply ridiculous." He predicted, however, that numerous whites, particularly in the South, would conclude that all blacks were seditious simply because of the few who had been arrested.[28]

Such declarations of loyalty did not satisfy Hoover. The black press also was expected to give up its demands for full black rights until the end of the war. That was emphasized by FBI agents, who openly visited black newspapers. Frank Bolden, a war correspondent for the *Pittsburgh Courier*, recalled hearing of one such visit in the latter half of 1942. "Edgar Hoover is busy again," Executive Editor Percival Prattis wired Bolden. "We had another visit last week. They stayed an hour. The usual rah-rah."[29] The FBI's investigations resulted in the black press defending its right to criticize discrimination and injustices. "The government is eager for Negro newsmen and editors to do more to lift Negro morale, and I am personally willing to do my part," wrote *Courier* columnist George Schuyler in October 1942. "But we need help from the government, and we are not getting it. How can we make Negroes feel good when the government does nothing to lessen or eliminate practices that make them feel bad?"[30] *PEP: Negro Publisher, Editor and Printer* pursued another common theme in September 1943, when it claimed that the black press only "mildly reflects the attitude of Negro citizens who are tired of squalor, filth, dirt, and the crumbs of democracy."[31] In *Opportunity*, the *Michigan Chronicle*'s Martin addressed the government directly in December 1942 under the subhead, "A Guide for Fifth Column Investigators":

> The loyalty of the American Negro is being demonstrated on every battle front and his eagerness to participate in the war effort at home belies the suspicion which is gaining ground today. The simple truth is that the Negro people are human beings who have been nurtured on the principles and precepts of democracy; they know no other faith. To them democracy means freedom, equality of opportunity, the rights of man. They believe that true democracy must be achieved in America and that it should be defended against all enemies at home and abroad.
>
> The investigator of the fifth column among Negroes must understand this and he must in the beginning seek to distinguish between legitimate resentment of the Negro over his basic grievances here, where the abuse of democratic principles is widespread, and such activity as can be directly traced to agents of the enemy.[32]

As if its complaints about equality were not enough to ensure the FBI's attention, the black press waved the red flag in front of the FBI by openly praising Russia both before and during the war and by showing no fear of communism. In October 1941, for example, columnist Ralph Matthews of the *Baltimore Afro-American* criticized the United States and England for getting rich by exploiting their citizens as well as the rest of the world, "especially the darker races." In contrast, he pointed out that Russia had tried to "perfect a way of life for her own people which will spread out the good things of life to the greatest number instead of to a chosen few."[33] Other publications praising Russia for supposedly solving its problems with minorities included the *Pittsburgh Courier*, the *Chicago Defender*, the *People's Voice* (New York), and the *California Eagle* (Los Angeles). The *Eagle* went so far in July 1945 as to call Russia the only country with no racial discrimination.[34]

Equally harmful were the continual contacts between black

journalists and Communists. Ironically, these often were unavoidable. Two former *Pittsburgh Courier* reporters—Bolden, who
was a columnist in Pittsburgh before becoming a war correspondent, and Billy Rowe, who worked in New York—said
Communist press agents constantly sought out black journalists
at the time. Rowe recalled how the agents operated:

> They were always wanting us to do something for a worthy cause,
> to help the family of someone who had been lynched or to help
> someone who needed money. It was never as blatant as doing it
> for the Communist Party. They didn't announce they were Com-
> munists, but you found out after awhile.[35]

Bolden had the same experience, although he said the Communists more actively sought the help of black journalists in
New York and Los Angeles than in Pittsburgh. He said one of
the Communist press agents' favorite ruses was to mail material
to papers using a fake name, but editors caught on to this
quickly.[36] Sometimes the appeal was more direct. A black newspaper editor in the Minneapolis–St. Paul area told the FBI that
both Trotskyites and Communists had sent him their publications, *The Militant* and the *Daily Worker*, and had come into the
office "in an attempt to influence him." A representative of the
Daily Worker also approached the editor of the black *Western
Ideal* in Pueblo, Colorado, about running Communist Party material but was turned down. The same editor burnt some pro-
Japanese material he received.[37]

Despite such associations, Rowe, Bolden, and John Sengstacke, publisher of the *Chicago Defender*, denied vehemently
that the black press was Communist-influenced or spreading
Communist propaganda.[38] Bolden termed such charges a "farce":

> Sure, the *Daily Worker* and the Communists jumped on the band-
> wagon when we started something. And we'd accept their help.
> We'd take any friends we could get, but we didn't side with
> them. It would have been very difficult for the black press to side
> with the Communist Party. It didn't offer what the blacks wanted—

power. All the Communists offered was a chance for a white man
and a black to sit down together and talk. But they didn't offer
any hope of getting that economic yoke off of his neck. They only
offered social comfort. And that wasn't enough.

As a result, according to Bolden, most of the black journalists
he knew felt communism was a "joke" and a "stupid movement."[39] But some disagreed. While not actually advocating
that blacks should become Communists, they did express ad-
miration for the party's goals of equal rights for all persons.
The *Baltimore Afro-American*'s Carl Murphy, one of the country's
leading black editors, felt that way when he was interviewed
by a reporter for *PEP: Negro Publisher, Editor and Printer* in November 1943:

> He [Murphy] admitted that he still believed that so far as the
> solving of racial problems is concerned, the spirit of the Com-
> munists was greatly needed. They represent, he thought, the
> spirit of the abolitionists which seemed to abate after the seventies
> and was supplanted by an era of condescension. A militant ap-
> proach to the race problem is needed, he believes, and the Com-
> munists are the only one who have the courage to carry on this
> type of struggle.[40]

Looking back forty years later, Rowe said he sympathized with
that attitude, although he had reservations. "I know one thing
for sure—they [Communists] were leaning more toward democracy than many whites," he said. ". . . But I really wondered
how much they cared for us. I suspected they cared more for
themselves."[41]

Thus, the black press supplied Hoover with more than enough
reasons for investigations. As Sengstacke admitted in 1983, "We
were just calling the shots as we saw them," and that was
guaranteed to draw the FBI's attention.[42] The black journalists
knew that. "Any time a black man pushes his protest too hard,
he's accused of being a Communist," said Bolden. "That's the
only defense of the white majority."[43]

Certainly, Hoover was more than willing to believe that the black press was a propaganda pipeline for the Communist Party because it gave him another reason to press the Justice Department for a sedition indictment. In April 1943, for example, he sent Assistant Attorney General Wendell Berge the March 13 issue of the *People's Voice*, a paper that the FBI's special agent in New York claimed was willing to follow the communist "line." Hoover noted that the paper said it supported the administration and the war effort, but it constantly ran critical articles that contributed to "the breach and extreme feeling between white and colored races." He particularly wondered about the legality of an editorial cartoon that showed a black soldier, who represented 450,000 black servicemen, with heavy chains on his wrists symbolizing the way blacks were hampered from fighting in the war. Berge replied that the cartoon did not violate the Espionage Act. However, he also noted that the Justice Department's Special War Policies Unit would appreciate any additional information that the FBI had on the *People's Voice* to add to a black press study begun several months before.

With such encouragement, it was not surprising that Hoover again went to Berge about the *People's Voice* on July 1, 1943. This time he inquired about the legality of a letter that appeared in the paper on May 29 from a black army corporal in Africa. The letter complained about discrimination against black army personnel, citing a number of alleged instances, and called for a government investigation. "I might be court-martialed for writing this but it is okay with me," concluded the soldier. "I am willing to die for justice and equality." Again, Berge declined to prosecute the paper but noted that the department's special investigation of the black press was continuing.[44] Hoover also went to Berge four times between November 1942 and June 1943 about possibly seditious material in the *Afro-American* chain of newspapers and in May 1943 about the *Pittsburgh Courier*. On each occasion, the Justice Department refused to approve an indictment.[45]

Finally, in September 1943, Hoover mounted his major wartime attack on the black press, and blacks in general, in a 714-page "Survey of Racial Conditions in the United States." The survey, which apparently was unknown to the black press, consisted of information gathered over more than two years from fifty-three FBI field offices in the United States, Alaska, Hawaii, and Puerto Rico. The material was accumulated, according to the report, "to determine why particular Negroes or groups of Negroes or Negro organizations have evidenced sentiments for other 'dark races' (mainly Japanese) or by what forces they were influenced to adopt in certain instances un-American ideologies."[46] The timing for the issuance of the survey was propitious. Between May and August, the country had been shaken by race riots in Mobile, Detroit, Beaumont, Los Angeles, and New York, leaving forty persons dead and about 1200 injured.[47] In sending the survey to the White House, Hoover emphasized that it contained information not only on "un-American" forces but also on the social, economic, and political factors causing "racial unrest and tension in various areas in this country."[48] The report's introduction elaborated on this theme:

> The information contained in . . . this study does not, nor is it meant to, give rise to an inference that Negroes as a whole or the Negro people in a particular area are subversive or are influenced by anti-American forces. At the same time, it must be pointed out that a number of Negroes and Negro groups have been the subjects of concentrated investigation made on the basis that they have reportedly acted or have exhibited sentiments in a manner inimical to the Nation's war effort.[49]

The report stressed that the FBI felt some black publications were among the groups hurting the country. Of the survey's hundred selectively chosen publications from thirty-three states and the District of Columbia, forty-three were criticized for causing black discontent and problems with inflammatory, sensational articles and headlines in the previous two years. Thirteen of those publications had alleged Communists on their editorial staffs or employees who maintained contacts with Communists, according to the FBI, or they ran articles that followed the Communist Party line. The publications included the *Baltimore Afro-American,* the *California Eagle* (Los Angeles), the *Chicago Defender,* the *Colorado Statesman* (Denver), *The Crisis* (New York), the *Denver Star,* the *Kansas City Call,* the *Los Angeles Sentinel,* the *Michigan Chronicle* (Detroit), the *Oklahoma City Black Dispatch, Opportunity* (New York), the *People's Voice* (New York), and *Racial Digest* (Detroit). In addition, five black publications— the *Cincinnati Union, The Crisis,* the *Moorish Voice* (Prince George, Virginia), the *Pacific Topics* (Chicago), and the *Pittsburgh Courier*—were cited for running pro-Japanese material.[50]

Although the report was basically critical, the FBI made occasional references to what it considered responsible journalism. For example, it praised Seattle's *Northwest Enterprise,* the only black paper in Washington, for attacking discrimination "in a manner that does not give offense" and for occasionally running articles warning blacks against "being used by others for purely subversive ends."[51] Other black newspapers that were commended included the *Iowa Observer* (Des Moines), which fought for equal rights but supported the government and opposed "ideals inimical to its [the government's] best interests"; the *San Antonio Register,* which ran material "liberally" on winning the war; and three Ohio papers—the *Dayton Forum,* the *Butler County American* (Hamilton), and the *Ohio State News* (Columbus)—which urged blacks to participate fully in the war effort.[52]

In contrast, the FBI noted what it considered objectionable:

> Sources of information have volunteered the opinion that the Negro press is a strong provocator of discontent among Negroes. It is claimed that its general tone is not at all, in many instances, informative or helpful to its own race. It is said that more space is devoted to alleged instances of discrimination or mistreatment of Negroes than there is to matters which are educational or helpful. The claim is that the sensational is foremost while true reportorial material is sidetracked.[53]

With this viewpoint, it is not surprising that the FBI devoted thirty pages of the report solely to the black press, looking specifically at seven newspapers that it claimed had "the largest circulations in this country." That statement was inaccurate. One of the seven, the *Oklahoma City Black Dispatch*, only had a circulation of 14,000 in 1943, making it considerably smaller than three papers that were excluded—the *Norfolk Journal and Guide*, the *New Jersey Guardian* (Newark) and the *Chicago World*.[54] Nevertheless, the FBI included the *Oklahoma City Black Dispatch*, despite admitting that it did not know the paper's circulation.[55] It probably did so in order to emphasize the *Black Dispatch*'s strong communist ties in a section of the report that would draw particular attention.

The information on the seven papers foreshadows what would become commonplace ten years later in the McCarthy era. The report did not claim that any illegal activity had taken place. All the FBI suggested was that six of the papers were causing massive discontent among blacks and, in numerous instances, had communist connections or were running pro-communist propaganda. This implied that the black papers were un-American and possibly should be suppressed, although the report did not say that. Of course, the survey may have been inaccurate or misleading. Knowing that Hoover had been concerned about Communists and blacks since 1919, some FBI agents may have reported only what they felt would please him. Furthermore, the report's information may have been selected from the FBI's Washington files with the intention of making certain black publications appear seditious. Unfortunately, in 1943 as today, outsiders did not have access to the FBI's files, and the survey's objectivity may never be determined.[56]

The material on the seven newspapers included the following.

Baltimore Afro-Amiercan. The FBI noted that the paper had numerous "Communist connections." A former staff member, for example, recently had been named the administrative secretary of the National Negro Congress, "a Communist influenced organization." In addition, the Communist Party and the Young Communist League had run an announcement on September 19, 1942, congratulating the paper on its fiftieth anniversary. Then, a week later, the *Afro-American* had carried an article about a radio program on the Communist Party's push for a second front. The paper's city editor also had expressed appreciation for the Communist Party's campaign to allow blacks to become telephone operators and bus drivers in the Baltimore area. "The city editor made it clear that in the future the *Afro-American* newspaper would be glad to print any other information concerning these or related programs which the Communist Party might sponsor," the report continued. It also noted numerous supposedly provocative articles and headlines, such as "Minister Beaten Because He Touched White Woman," "War Called Blessing for Dark Races," and "Some Nasty Situations Colored Actors Must Face Touring Democratic America."[57]

Amsterdam Star–News. The only one of the seven newspapers that was not criticized, it was included to show the difference between its editorial practices and those of the *People's Voice*, which competed with it for New York's black circulation. The FBI noted that the *Star–News* was "comparatively conservative" and had criticized communism several times. "In this regard, the newspaper has opposed the Communist Party line relative to the Harlem Section of New York, especially the crime wave there," said the report. "The *Amsterdam Star–News* has expressed itself editorially in a manner which is said to be descriptive of the law-abiding people in Harlem. It ran . . . a campaign to clean up Harlem and to rid it of the criminal element."[58]

People's Voice. In contrast, the FBI described this paper as "a very helpful transmission belt for the Communist Party." Not only were its editorials and articles considered pro-communist, but the FBI said its well-known publisher, Adam Clayton Powell, had been "affiliated" with numerous pro-communist individuals and groups. Furthermore, the FBI pointed out that Max

Yergan, who was prominent in several communist groups, recently had contributed at least $3000 to the paper, resulting in his name being carried in its "publication block."[59]

Oklahoma City Black Dispatch. Editor Roscoe Dungee, while not a Communist, was reported to be "sympathetic with the Communist cause to such an extent that he has allowed his name to be used by many Communist front organizations and is said to have used his talent as a speaker in appearing at meetings of these groups." The FBI also pointed out that the paper apparently did "considerable" printing for the state's Communist Party and had carried a pro-communist editorial on October 10, 1942. "We shall have to report that we personally do have Communistic leaning," the *Black Dispatch* had said. " . . . Communism believes in social equality and so does this writer." The FBI added that Dungee favored interracial marriage as well as "free association between Negroes and white people" and had boasted a number of times of associating with whites.[60]

Chicago Defender. The FBI reported that two of the paper's employees had been attending local Communist Party meetings, where they sat on the platform and made speeches. Numerous people with communist connections also had written articles for the paper. One of these, William L. Patterson, who was a member of the National Committee of the Communist Party, praised Russia for addressing the problem of racial and minority discrimination. The FBI admitted that the paper's editorials strongly supported the war effort but added that they also militantly attacked inequality. For example, on April 4, 1942, the paper reported that some black soldiers had been killed in Little Rock. The *Defender* said this proved "that in the South the uniform of the United States has no respect if the wearer is a Negro." In another article on August 8, 1942, the paper pointed out that a black military policeman had been shot by local police in Beaumont, Texas, because he refused to "acquiesce to the humiliation of a Jim Crow motor bus."[61]

Michigan Chronicle. According to the FBI, the paper's editor (whose name is blacked out in the document) was active in the

National Student League, a communist-front organization, during his years at the University of Michigan. Since then he had not joined any similar group, feeling that it might hurt the paper's reputation. However, sources said he still believed "sincerely" in communism, and they emphasized that the *Chronicle*'s editorials for years had followed the Communist Party line. Furthermore, the editor had attended the Communist Party's state convention in March 1943. The FBI also noted that a number of other editors and columnists at the paper had belonged to communist organizations in the past or currently were members. The report pointed out, too, that the *Chronicle* prominently played up discrimination and violence, frequently blaming the latter on the Ku Klux Klan. "Scandal, shootings, murders, divorces, lawsuits, family trouble have all been given front-page attention," it said.[62]

Pittsburgh Courier. Besides noting the Double V campaign, the FBI devoted more than four pages to listing articles and headlines that had appeared in the paper. Although no communist connections were noted, the report stressed the frequent use of both pro-Japanese and anti-Japanese articles. On January 10, 1942, columnist George Schuyler had written that blacks would not be worse off if the Japanese won. Then, on March 28, 1942, he praised the Japanese for "their cleanliness, their courtesy, their ingenuity, and their efficiency." The FBI specifically pointed out that this column contained no anti-Japanese material. In contrast, however, Executive Editor Percival Prattis wrote on May 16, 1942, that he preferred white Southerners to the Japanese. Other *Courier* articles were highly critical of discrimination, said the FBI. One example was a column by J. A. Rogers on February 20, 1943. "I am not half so scared about the Hitlers, Mussolinis, and Tojos thousands of miles across the seas as I am of the Hitlers, Mussolinis, and Tojos right here at home," Rogers wrote. " . . . And as for what Hitler has said about Negroes I could quote you worse and in far greater volume from the Congressional Record."[63]

* * *

If Hoover hoped that such revelations would result in black press indictments and suppressions, as he probably did, he was disappointed. No documents show that Roosevelt urged any action on the basis of the report, if indeed he even read it, and his failure to respond was predictable. As previously noted, the president rarely became involved in black problems because of the political risks.

Without the president's support, Hoover must have realized that there would be no black press suppressions. The only other person who could approve such action was Attorney General Biddle, and no evidence indicates that he commented on the survey either. That would not have been surprising in view of his well-known sympathy for blacks. As Herbert Wechsler, a special assistant to the attorney general from 1941 to 1944, noted, Biddle was "an almost passionate" black supporter.[64] Not only had he pushed for equal rights before the war, but he maintained that position even after the bombing of Pearl Harbor, when the national crisis made it easier to overlook injustices. For example, in an article in *Collier's* magazine in March 1942, Biddle noted that the United States was not as racially integrated as England. "But our brand of democracy will come through unscathed," Biddle insisted. "We can do it if we keep insisting on freedom and order and fairness to everyone."[65] He set a personal example in the Justice Department. When a new cafeteria was built, the plans called for blacks to eat in one corner, but Biddle had the arrangement changed so that they could sit anywhere. Furthermore, he instructed division heads to increase the number of black lawyers in the department, which resulted in some additions although well-trained blacks were difficult to find. In still another example, he threatened to resign as an honorary member of the Federal Bar Association if blacks were excluded. His stand resulted in the policy being changed.[66] He also voluntarily played a major role in May 1943 in restructuring and strengthening the Fair Employment Practice Committee (FEPC), which had been established to curtail discriminatory practices in defense industries.

Considering Washington's Southern atmosphere, Biddle's actions were surprising. After all, no white public restaurant, except at Union Station, served blacks at that time, and blacks could not stay at any of the leading hotels.[67] That made Biddle's drive against discrimination hardly conventional. "It is not a casual matter for a white official to take an open interest in Negro affairs," noted Malcolm Ross, who became the FEPC's chairman in October 1943, praising Biddle's courage. " . . . Most other white officials wonder what sort of political porridge So-and-so thinks he's cooking by his support of Negro interests."[68]

In addition, Biddle kept hammering away at the necessity for freedom of speech and of the press during wartime. "Subversive doctrines cannot flourish on free speech," he wrote early in the war, and his view never changed.[69] "The sedition laws have been vindicated in appropriate cases," he declared in his annual report in the summer of 1943, "though the Department has been guided by the broadest conception of freedom of speech and freedom of the press ever embraced by the Government in time of war."[70] Furthermore, Biddle admired the black press. "The Negro press throughout the country, although they very properly protest, and passionately, against the wrongs done to members of their race, are loyal to their government and are all out for the war," he said in a speech in Philadelphia on February 12, 1943.[71] That may have been his only public statement as attorney general about the black press, but it would have been more than enough to convince Hoover of the reception his report would receive.

Furthermore, the Supreme Court's decision in the first Smith Act case, *Dunne* v. *United States* on November 22, 1943, eliminated any faint hopes of success still harbored by Hoover. The case involved eighteen Minneapolis Trotskyites, who had published, sold, and distributed leaflets, pamphlets, newspapers, magazines, and books advocating a violent overthrow of the government. Biddle, believing that sedition statutes were "unnecessary and harmful," had approved the federal prosecution to test the constitutionality of the Smith Act. He had done so reluctantly, feeling that the 3000-member Trotskyite group "by no conceivable stretch of the liberal imagination could have been said to constitute any 'clear and present danger' to the government." However, he was confident that the Supreme Court would overturn the convictions. When the Court refused to hear the case, letting the convictions stand, Biddle was not only shocked, but he was criticized heavily by the American Civil Liberties Union and his liberal friends.[72] In such an atmosphere, it would have been inconceivable for him to have approved a black press indictment.

Hoover may not have recognized the irony of the situation. Just as he had used the unforeseen outbreak of race riots as a pretext to go after Communists and the black press, so another unforeseen event (the Supreme Court's decision in the *Dunne* case) had undermined any faint hopes he had for sedition prosecutions. At the same time, Hoover was rebuffed once again when he sought to attack a specific black paper. On October 11, 1943, he complained to Assistant Attorney General Tom C. Clark about a *Chicago Defender* column of June 19 which had been critical of the treatment blacks were receiving in army camps. "Mainly, their [the black soldiers'] bitterness adds up to—'I [would] just as soon die fightin' for democracy right here in Georgia, as go all the way to Africa or Australia. Kill a cracker in Mississippi or in Germany, what's the difference!' " Charley Cherokee wrote. Noting that the column apparently referred to racial tension and a gun battle between black and white soldiers at two Georgia camps, Hoover asked if such material violated the Espionage Act. Clark replied that the column was legal. Also in the fall of 1943, the Justice Department delivered yet another blow when it disbanded its Special War Policies Unit and discontinued weekly summaries of the contents of black newspapers. This was a definite sign to Hoover that the unit's study of the black press had concluded that sedition prosecutions were inadvisable.[73]

Nevertheless, Hoover tenaciously continued to collect what

he considered damaging information on the black press and used it to push futilely for an indictment. In February 1944, for example, he sent Clark a seventeen-page report on what the *Afro-American* chain of newspapers had written in November and December. The report emphasized articles "describing alleged brutal treatment of Negro soldiers in U.S. Army camps" and noted headlines such as "Germany Superior to U.S. in Treatment of Soldiers," "Army Can Protect Soldiers from Civilian Violence—Why Doesn't It?" and "White Officer Who Stabbed Soldier in Texas 'Reprimanded.'" Three months later, Hoover attacked the *Pittsburgh Courier* for a column by Schuyler which criticized Roosevelt and other government officials for allowing segregation and discrimination to continue in the armed services. "Indeed, one sometimes asks whether they [government officials] are not fighting the Negro harder than they are fighting the Germans and the Japanese," wrote Schuyler. "Certainly many German and Japanese prisoners are being treated better than some of the Negroes wearing the uniform of Uncle Sam." On both occasions, Clark refused to allow a prosecution.[74]

If Hoover still had any hopes of obtaining a black press sedition indictment, they abruptly ended on December 9, 1944. Ten days before he had forwarded to Clark a twenty-four-page report which pointed out that critical articles about the armed services were continuing in the *Afro-American* chain. He asked the assistant attorney general if the FBI's extensive investigation of the chain, which had begun in 1941, should continue. Clark began with the standard reply that none of the material violated federal statutes. But then he went further and said the investigation should be discontinued because of the Supreme Court's ruling on June 12 in a sedition case. It involved Elmer Hartzel, who had been convicted in a lower court of violating the Espionage Act by writing and distributing three pamphlets to about 600 persons in 1942. The pamphlets not only called upon the country to abandon its allies and to turn the war into a racial conflict, but they questioned the integrity and patriotism of Roosevelt. In reversing the decision, Supreme Court Justice Frank Murphy noted that there had been insufficient evidence for a jury to determine "beyond a reasonable doubt" that Hartzel had meant to bring about what was prohibited by the law, such as insubordination, disloyalty, or mutiny in the armed services. "An American citizen has the right to discuss these matters either by temperate reasoning or by immoderate and vicious invective without running afoul of the Espionage Act of 1917," said Murphy.[75]

Following Clark's reference to the *Hartzel* case, Hoover only sought one more wartime indictment of the black press. That occurred on February 22, 1945, when he complained to Clark about three issues of the *Courier* earlier in the month. Hoover said three officials of the federal War Manpower Commission had pointed out to the FBI that the *Courier* had used "confidential" agency information to attack the WMC for supposedly "condoning" black discrimination by some Pittsburgh-area companies with defense contracts. "The War Manpower Commission representatives expressed deep concern over this situation," said Hoover, "inasmuch as the data given to the interviewers is only received after plant officials have been assured that it will be handled in the strictest of confidence." Since the articles consisted of confidential material concerning a national defense matter, Hoover wondered if the newspaper could be charged with espionage. Clark was not sympathetic. He told Hoover on March 1 that "prosecutive action for violation of the Espionage Statute, or any other Federal statute, . . . is not warranted."[76] Thus despite all his information, Hoover was effectively controlled.

Meanwhile, as Hoover's major wartime thrust failed, other government agencies were rapidly resolving their relations with the black press. The army was an excellent example. On October 23, 1943, Truman K. Gibson, Jr., the black civilian aide to the secretary of war, pointed out to Assistant Secretary of War John J. McCloy that the chain of five *Afro-American* newspapers (Baltimore, Newark, Philadelphia, Richmond, and Washington) had run a recent editorial saying that relations between the War Department and the black press had never been better. Gibson agreed:

> I believe that a genuine understanding of the many problems involved is developing on both sides of the fence. This is not to say that the papers do not and will not continue carrying unfavorable items about the War Department. The accounts, however, show a reduction in the use of distortions and misstatements of fact.

Gibson added that the army's Bureau of Public Relations was sending "more and better material" on black soldiers to black papers, which were using nearly all of the publicity despite newsprint shortages and other wartime problems.[77]

Two months later, Gibson wrote McCloy again, praising the black press for developing an even better relationship with the army. He pointed out that the Negro Newspaper Publishers Association (NNPA) had recently begun a campaign, which several black papers had adopted, urging black soldiers that all would be lost if they did not perform up to their capabilities. The NNPA added that blacks had to be "good soldiers in spite of the many things that they hear about and see." Gibson was ecstatic. "Their new line will materially simplify the task of the Army," he predicted.[78]

The NNPA's campaign was particularly laudable because of the continuing animosity toward black papers on the part of some army officials. For example, the army became so irritated at the black press playing up military discrimination that at one point it considered publishing its own paper for blacks in order to counter the charges. It reportedly had both the money and the printing facilities for the project, but the plan apparently folded when the army was unable to find a qualified black editor who was willing to "take orders."[79]

The black press did not learn of the project until the summer of 1945, long after it had been abandoned, but it was aware in 1943 of black papers being banned on army posts. In some cases, the bans remained in effect, despite the BPR's attempt to halt them, because they were enforced by post intelligence officers acting without formal orders from post commanders. Therefore, the BPR was unaware of the censorship unless a black publication pointed it out.[80] Such complaints continued to surface in the fall of 1943. The Associated Negro Press, for example, notified the army in October that newsboys at Camp Rucker in Alabama were ordered in early September to stop selling the *Baltimore Afro-American*, the *Pittsburgh Courier*, and the *Amsterdam Star–News* because they "spread hatred among the troops."[81] In addition, the *Pittsburgh Courier*, the *Washington Afro-American*, and several other large black papers were banned at Camp Forrest in Tennessee. The BPR, in the midst of negotiations with the NNPA to start its campaign encouraging black soldiers, was appalled by the "hasty and ill considered action" in Tennessee. It moved quickly in November to issue an order that no publications could be banned without War Department approval, and the NNPA was informed of this.[82]

A misunderstanding about the order led to a further complaint from the *Chicago Defender*. The black press incorrectly announced on November 13 that the order had gone into effect.[83] All the black editors had been told, however, was that such a policy would be instituted, and a delay in sending it through army channels resulted in the order not being forwarded to post commanders until November 29.[84] Meanwhile, a soldier at Camp Forrest asked the *Defender* on November 13 to cancel his battalion's subscription to the paper because the camp's "internal security policy" would not allow it in the day rooms. The *Defender*, believing this violated the army's new order, which in fact had not been sent out yet, complained angrily to both Gibson and Secretary of War Henry L. Stimson. Calling such censorship "grossly un-American," Editor-in-Chief Metz T. P. Lochard said in his December 1 letter to Stimson:

We are at a loss to determine why the internal security policy of any Army Post would deny the privilege of colored troops reading the *Chicago Defender*. This newspaper has adhered to all of the democratic ideals of our great country. It has closely followed the regulations set up in the censorship code in order that no information which gives "aid and comfort to the enemy" could be gleaned from its columns. . . . It seems to us that this act contravenes every decent ideal for which America is fighting. It certainly violates the concept of freedom of thought and freedom of speech.[85]

No evidence can be found showing that the army answered Lochard's letter, probably because the order already had been forwarded to camp officers by the time he complained to Stimson and Gibson. But if both the army and the black press assumed that the order would halt suppressions, they were mistaken. In fact, censorship at some camps continued through the summer of 1944. The *Chicago Defender* complained in January about censorship at Vancouver Barracks in Washington and Camp Stewart in Georgia, the *Pittsburgh Courier* and the *Defender* were barred from Fort Benning in Georgia at the end of March, a ban against all black papers at New Orleans's military installations finally was lifted in July after five months, and the *Baltimore Afro-American* reported in August that it had been barred from Fort Huachuca in Arizona.[86] In the *Courier*, Schuyler used the occasion of the Fort Benning censorship to lash out once again at the government on April 8, 1944:

It becomes clearer and clearer that our white folks simply can't take it. . . . When Negro newspapers print the facts and criticise the criminal collusion between officialdom and crackerdom leading to treasonable discrimination against the mistreatment of Negro soldiers and sailors simply because they are colored . . . a cry goes up, not for a change of policy toward the Negroes, but for penalization of suppression of the Negro newspapers.[87]

Such statements by the black press were infrequent by 1944, however. Army suppressions in the camps were all but over, and the army was working more closely with black journalists, feeding them increasing amounts of news about black servicemen. The result was a high percentage of "favorable" news about the army. This was evident in the BPR's weekly "Reports of Trends in the Negro Press" of November 27, 1944. In examining 207 articles from forty-seven black newspapers for the week of November 13–19, the BPR found 127 (63 percent) to be favorable, 39 (18 percent) to be neutral, and only 41 (19 percent) to be unfavorable.[88]

The navy also developed an appreciation for the black press. It had less contact with black journalists during the war than the army, and although its segregationist policies were criticized heavily by the black press, it had not engaged in massive suppressions. Nevertheless, by February 1945, the navy felt compelled to officially point out the dangers of censorship. In its "Guide to the Command of Negro Naval Personnel," the navy said:

> Some concern has been expressed because a good proportion of Negro enlisted men read Negro newspapers which are severely critical of the Navy or because they belong to organizations working for the improvement of racial conditions. It is apparently thought that such contacts may be a source of low morale. This is a doubtful assumption. Commanding officers who have been most successful with colored personnel commonly subscribe to Negro newspapers through the Welfare Fund.
>
> It is true that Negro publications are vigorous and sometimes unfair in their protests against discrimination, but it is also true that they eagerly print all they can get about the successful participation of the Negro in the war. Negroes have to buy them if they want to read Negro news. Censorship and repression of such interests is not in the American tradition. It cannot be made effective, and has the reverse effect of increasing tension, and lowering morale.[89]

Although evidence is lacking, this advice may very well have stemmed from watching the army struggle to find a workable black press policy.

At other government agencies, a noticeable acceptance of the black press also could be seen in the war's final two years. Nowhere was this trend more evident than at the Post Office, where investigations continued until the summer of 1945. Sixty-three issues of seven black publications were inspected between October 1943 and June 1945. They included the *Philadelphia Afro-American* (forty-eight issues); the *New Negro World* (seven issues); *The Black Pilot* of Oregonia, Ohio (four issues); and the *California Eagle* of Los Angeles, the *Afro-American World Almanac* of Chicago, the *Baltimore Afro-American*, and the *Richmond (Va.) Afro-American* (one issue apiece).[90] What was significant about the Post Office's inspections during this period was not the number of publications examined but the reports' overall brevity, which stemmed from the inspectors' belief that it was virtually impossible to take away a black publication's second-class mailing permit. In the first year of the war, a typed inspection report might run five or six pages. By the end of 1943, however, the inspections had declined mostly to one-page statements that represented little more than cursory checks of a publication's contents and an automatic stamp of approval.

Exceptions did occur. One occasion was in October and November of 1943, when the Post Office went to the Justice Department for the final time, seeking advice on the mailability of the *New Negro World*, the *Philadelphia Afro-American*, and the *California Eagle*. In the case of the *California Eagle*, the Post Office examiner wrote a three-page memorandum noting that the issue of October 14, 1943, stressed the imminent possibility of race roits. An example from the front page of the paper's second section said:

Tonight the city is tense. A riot may happen in the next breath. . . .

And somewhere tonight there is a man clearing his throat for the speech he will make after the next riot.

"These niggers have got to be shown their place. Los Angeles is a Southern Town now, and we've gotta let the darkies know it!"

There are presses in our city tonight which will print the stories to start the next riot. . . . "Tonight Mrs. Lula Blotz, attractive housewife, was brutally assaulted by a hulking Negro rapist. . . . "

And somewhere tonight there is the tongue which will send up the first lynch cry . . . "Get That Nigger!"

And the hate is here.

Like devilish electric sparks it bristles out of eyes that remember Mississippi and from the Dixie-accented voice of the street car conductor just in from Oklahoma.

The Post Office's inspector felt that such material would create "fear and hatred of the white race, and racial tension which might easily explode into riots at little or no provocation, resulting in 'murder, arson and assassination.' " Seeking confirmation, he sent the paper to the Justice Department's Clark, who quickly replied on November 15 that it was mailable. As in other Justice Department responses to the Post Office after the summer of 1942, it was a virtual form letter of only four sentences, with no explanation of how the decision had been reached.[91]

As a result, the Post Office inspectors gave up because examinations of black newspapers had become a farce. The public, of course, did not realize what had occurred, and letters continued to arrive from citizens, mostly in the South, who were incensed at the black press. In September 1944, for example, a man in Spartanburg, South Carolina, complained about the black press spreading "hatred and strife between the races." He said that suppressing such publications "would go far toward preventing a farther spread of this dangerous propaganda that is almost like treason in the insidious disservice that it is doing our country."[92] What the Post Office answered, if anything, is unknown.

While the inspectors probably sympathized with such complaints, they were helpless and angry. Whether they verbalized their feelings to superiors at the Post Office is not known, but their irritation definitely crept into numerous reports in 1944 and 1945. In one example, the postmaster in Richmond sent in a July 1944 issue of the *Richmond Afro-American* which carried a front-page article about segregation and mistreatment of blacks in the South. The Post Office's examiner found the article, which was headlined "God-damned Those White Southerners," "inflammatory in character" and agreed that it might incite readers to violate the Espionage Act. However, considering the issue in its entirety, he said that it was impossible to say that the publisher had intended to create the evils proscribed by the Espionage Act or that the paper presented "a clear and present danger" of causing such evils. "In view of this fact," he concluded, "and the liberal policy pursued by the Department in matters affecting freedom of speech and of the press, recommendation for a ruling of nonmailability is not made."[93] The words "liberal policy" appeared again and again. On still another occasion in June 1944, an inspector became bitter in examining the *Philadelphia Afro-American*. "In my opinion the editorial policies of the paper and the reportorial practices definitely tend to increase racial hatreds but the statutes do not cover this type of matter," he concluded.[94]

At the same time that the Post Office examiners were recognizing the futility of attempting to suppress the black press, the Office of Censorship's close inspection of the same publications also was drawing to a close. On February 21, 1944, the agency's district postal censors were told that they no longer needed approval from Washington before black publications could be mailed outside the country.[95] At least two black newspapers, both addressed to Canada, were affected during the order's seven-month existence. The *Chicago Defender* of January 5, 1944, was condemned and not mailed, and the *Pittsburgh Courier's* October 16, 1943, issue was held up until March 3, 1944.[96] In a final move, the Office of Censorship condemned four successive issues of the *Courier* between March 25 and April 15, 1944.[97] The agency's records do not explain why any of these actions were taken. They only show what occurred, without giving any indication of what was considered objectionable in each issue.

Even before the Office of Censorship had made its final condemnation of the *Courier*, several events took place at the White House that signaled a dramatic new acceptance of the black press. Not only did black journalists have their first meeting ever with a president, but a black was allowed to become a White House correspondent. Both were historic occasions.

As historian Graham J. White has noted, the blacks' road to the White House was "protracted, tortuous, and eloquent." They had begun seeking permission to attend Roosevelt's press conferences in 1933, and it was eleven years before they finally succeeded. The stumbling block was the president's Southern secretary, Stephen Early. Time after time, he turned down requests by black journalists because they did not represent daily newspapers. However, as White points out, Early was not consistent in applying this policy. He arranged for Walter Winchell, an outspoken administration supporter, to attend press conferences as often as he wished although he did not fit the formal requirements for admission any more than the black journalists. White claims that Early was able to enforce such racial discrimination only because he had the "tacit approval" of Roosevelt.[98]

But the blacks did not give up. Not only did they keep badgering Early for admission, but they occasionally aired their irritation about Roosevelt refusing to meet with black groups. For example, A. Philip Randolph, one of the country's most prominent blacks, complained in the *Pittsburgh Courier* on April 11, 1942:

> The President does not consider that he has any moral obligation to meet any group of Negroes at any time to consider questions vital to the interest and well-being of Negroes and the government. . . . Practically every other minority group in America have systematic contact with the President. They can call upon the President to meet with their representatives and receive a cordial hearing. The President feels obligated to give consideration to the recommendations of organized labor, the Jews and Catholics and

other minority groups but he has no such attitude toward the Negro.[99]

On May 26 and May 27, 1943, the administration made its first concession to the black press. Reporters from the *Baltimore Afro-American*, the *Chicago Defender*, the *Cleveland Call and Post*, the *Pittsburgh Courier*, and the Associated Negro Press were admitted into the White House and to the House press gallery for twenty-four hours to cover the visit of Liberian President Edwin Barclay.[100] There also was movement behind the scenes. Biddle, an ever-dependable friend of blacks, brought up the subject of having a black journalist at the White House during a luncheon with Roosevelt on July 21, 1943:

> I suggested that the President admit [Ernest E.] Johnson of the Associated Negro Press to the Press conferences. He said I should take it up with Early, but I rejoined that Steve certainly would be against it. He has in mind that this might run into unfavorable congressional opinion as they have excluded Negroes from the Press Gallery. I thought if there was a bonafide daily newspaper he might be represented and the President told me to look into it further.[101]

What information Biddle gathered and whether he reported back to Roosevelt is unknown.

On November 2, 1943, the president received a telegram from John Sengstacke, publisher of the *Chicago Defender*, requesting a presidential conference for the NNPA. The message was referred to Malcolm Ross, chairman of the government's Fair Employment Practice Committee (FEPC), asking for his advice. Ross's choice was interesting because he was a known supporter of blacks. Since the FEPC had been formed on June 25, 1941, it had continually championed the black cause in fighting employment discrimination, a course of which Ross approved. His efforts for racial equality were noted in 1943, when he was named to the Honor Roll of Race Relations, an annual award conferred by the Schomburg Collection of the New York Public

Library on six white groups or individuals who had done the most to improve race relations "in terms of real democracy."[102] At the same time, the *Chicago Defender* named him to its annual honor roll for being one of those who "have contributed most to interracial good feeling by their activities throughout the year."[103] Roosevelt must have known what Ross would say, and yet the president apparently wanted to hear his advice so that he could blame him if even a small move toward equality became a political liability. Ross's reply on November 8 was predictable. He encouraged the president to meet with the NNPA because of "a feeling of disappointment among Negro delegations."[104] The result, less than a week later, was a meeting almost surely ordered by Roosevelt between Early and four NNPA officials—Sengstacke, Howard Murphy of the *Baltimore Afro-American*, C. B. Powell of the *Amsterdam Star–News*, and Carter Wesley of the *Houston Informer*. They began working out the details of accrediting a black White House correspondent, which took almost another three months to arrange, and also presumably discussed an NNPA meeting with the president.[105]

The first result of the negotiations was a meeting of the NNPA with Roosevelt at the White House on February 5, 1944. Thirteen editors and publishers from ten black newspapers met with the president for thirty-five minutes and presented a twenty-one-point statement on blacks' war aims and postwar aspirations.[106] One of those present, P. Bernard Young of the *Norfolk Journal and Guide*, recalled that Roosevelt showed "heightened interest, or even agreement" as the statement was read. "It was obvious that this was no routine audience he was giving the Negro group; he was concentrating his attention on the subject at hand," he wrote. He continued that the conference "hit one tremendous climax after the other." One moment was particularly special because the president demonstrated his trust of the blacks by taking them into his confidence:

The President explained that each year he had the white association of newspaper editors in for a lengthy off-the-record background conference, where all questions could be asked and any question would be answered. He invited us to make our visit an annual one too.

"Come back again about this time next year," he said.

One of the visiting group spoke up: "But, Mr. President, that will be next February or thereabouts."

The President immediately got the point. He laughingly but meaningfully replied:

"Go ahead, make your plans. The invitation still holds."

February, 1945, would be in his fourth term. Thus every member of the NNPA delegation knew almost a year ahead that the President would stand for a fourth term, something then a top-priority topic of discussion.

But it was off the record then.

It is a tribute to the press that none of them ever violated the confidential headline utterance.[107]

Three days later, Harry S. McAlpin attended his first White House press conference as a joint representative of the *Atlanta Daily World*, the only daily black newspaper, and the NNPA.[108] When the conference ended, McAlpin deliberately walked past the president's desk. "As I arrived opposite him," McAlpin recalled, "a genuine smile of friendliness pushed back all the burdensome worries from his face. He extended his hand, which I grasped. The President held on while he said: 'I'm glad to see you, McAlpin, and very happy to have you here.' I managed to say thank you and that I was glad to be there."[109]

The avoidance of massive suppressions was the black press's major milestone in World War II. However, the NNPA's meeting with Roosevelt and McAlpin's presence at the White House also were important moments for the black press, perhaps as significant as the lesser-known meeting between Sengstacke and Biddle in June 1942. Why Roosevelt finally acquiesced to the blacks' demands is unclear. Perhaps Ross and Biddle had persuaded him, or perhaps it was a political gesture aimed at guaranteeing the black vote in the 1944 election.[110] Or maybe, as Sengstacke argues, the president finally realized that Walter White, the executive secretary of the NAACP, was not really the one with whom to meet if he wanted to communicate with the black press. Until that time, said Sengstacke, Roosevelt believed he could tell White something and "Walter would tell everybody else."[111] Whatever the reason, the *Michigan Chronicle* noted the black press's rising prestige on February 19, 1944:

> The minority presses have a tremendous responsibility especially in a time of crisis such as the present. The rising recognition of the Negro Press, we believe, bears witness to the fact that the Negro newspapers have shown themselves worthy of the public trust and have lived up to their responsibilities. The most significant achievement of the Negro Press during this crisis, in our estimation, lies in the fact that the Negro newspapers have brought home to the Negro people of America that this is their war and not merely a "white man's war." . . . We are determined to make this a people's war and we mean all the people, regardless of race, creed or color. It may well be that the tremendous struggle of the Negro Press in this democratic effort is responsible for the recognition which it is receiving today.[112]

Still further milestones came a year later. When Roosevelt died in April 1945, McAlpin was one of thirteen pool reporters who covered the funeral service. Making his selection notable was the fact that only twelve white newsmen and radio announcers originally were scheduled to be present. But Roosevelt's press secretary, Jonathan Daniels, interceded for McAlpin, pointing out that a black representative should be included.[113] A month later, fifteen NNPA publishers, editors, and reporters from twelve newspapers met briefly with Harry S Truman at the White House, urging him basically to support legislation that would benefit blacks. "Knowing that he is from Missouri, I see no reason to expect him to do any unusually generous things for Negroes," wrote the *Houston Informer*'s Carter Wesley, who attended the meeting, "but I doubt that he will do anything vicious where Negroes are concerned, and I suspect that he will follow the Constitution pretty rigidly."[114] That was enough to satisfy the black press for the moment, but they would have to wait another two years before black journalists would be admitted to the congressional press galleries.[115]

Thus, the war ended with the black press enjoying ever-growing prestige and power as well as more access to government officials. The gains were the result of a give-and-take process. After most of the black press toned down considerably, while vocally declaring its patriotism, the government accepted it grudgingly. Blacks could ignore the obvious reluctance because the gains were tangible; not only did the threat of suppression end, but the black journalists also had access to the government, such as at the White House, that they only had dreamed about less than four years before. For the government, these were small concessions, easy to give, but their importance should not be underestimated. Symbolically, they represented equality for the black press, and equality was what the black press was fighting for during World War II.

Just as important was the black press's growing popularity, which reached an unprecedented level at the end of the war. From 1940 to 1945, the combined weekly circulation of black newspapers rose 43 percent, from 1,276,600 to 1,808,060.[116] In a sense, it was the fulfillment of a prediction made by *Pittsburgh Courier* columnist Joseph D. Bibb on October 10, 1942. "When the war ends the colored American will be better off financially, spiritually and economically," he wrote. "War may be hell for some, but it bids fair to open up the portals of heaven for us."[117]

8

"The Ultimate Good Desired Is Better Reached by Free Trade in Ideas"

In April 1955, on the twentieth anniversary of Oliver Wendell Holmes's death, the *New Republic* ran an article by Francis Biddle on the great jurist whom he had served as a secretary from 1911 to 1912. Calling him one of America's "heroes" who "can lift us by the sense of their nobility," he noted that Holmes had valued courage, truth, and tolerance. He particularly praised the latter quality. Holmes was a man of strong beliefs, Biddle pointed out, and yet "he refused to call them [his beliefs] eternal or insist that they must exclude the possibility of other vision." The value of such tolerance, continued Biddle, was stated eloquently in Holmes's 1919 dissent in the *Abrams* case, which involved a poor garment worker who was found guilty of distributing seditious literature. Holmes wrote:

> When men have realized that time has upset many fighting faiths, they have come to believe even more than they believe the very foundations of their own conduct that the ultimate good desired is better reached by free trade in ideas—that the best test of truth is the power of the thought to get itself accepted in the competition of the market, and that truth is the only ground upon which their wishes safely can be carried out. That, at any rate, is the theory of our Constitution. It is an experiment, as all life is an experiment. Every year if not every day we have to wager our salvation upon some prophecy based upon imperfect knowledge. While that experiment is part of our system I think we should be eternally

vigilant against attempts to check the expression of opinions that
we loathe and believe to be fraught with death, unless they so
imminently threaten immediate interference with the lawful and
pressing purposes of the law that an immediate check is required
to save the country.

Equally as important as Holmes's tolerance, Biddle felt, was his
"passion and urgency" for greatness. For example, Holmes
once had admitted to some Harvard undergraduates that he
felt "the secret isolated joy of the thinker, who knows that, a
hundred years after he is dead and forgotten, men who never
heard of him will be moving to the measure of his thought."[1]

Biddle's reverence of Holmes was unmistakable. Throughout
his life, Biddle praised Holmes's legal contributions in speeches,
articles, and books, and he definitely attempted to emulate him.
In September 1941, a *New York Times* reporter interviewed Biddle
and came away convinced that his year with Holmes had been
the "dominant" influence in his life because "it gave point and
direction to all his subsequent mental growth."[2] Another reporter in 1942 noted Holmes's "abiding influence" on Biddle.
"And so it almost seems as if old Justice Holmes, dead these
seven years, is, through his deputy, Biddle, still guarding civil
rights," wrote Beverly Smith in *American Magazine*.[3]

Holmes would have been proud of Biddle. At the Justice
Department he protected civil rights with tenacity. He fought
for aliens, he fought against the internment of the West Coast
Japanese, he fought discrimination directed at blacks. And he
had no reservations about openly defending the rights of these
unpopular causes. Such advocacy of civil rights, which was not
at all common in Washington at that time, was applauded by
the press when Biddle resigned as attorney general in May 1945.
However, as the *Washington Post* noted, "Hearty support of civil
liberties is not the sole measure of an Attorney General's service."[4] Other publications agreed. *Time*, *Newsweek*, *The Nation*,
the *New York Times*, and the *Post* also criticized Biddle, even
labeling him as one of the weakest of the Cabinet members.

Their attacks ranged widely. They complained about his "left-wing righteousness"; his apparent domination at times "by political considerations," particularly in antitrust cases; his willingness to provide "legal justification" for whatever Roosevelt wanted done despite having "very little to go on"; and his lack of "grass-roots" political support, which hurt the administration.[5] Even the black press, which at times he had supported almost alone in high government circles, had little praise for him. In noting that Tom C. Clark would replace Biddle, the *Afro-American* chain of five East Coast newspapers made one of the few editorial comments on the change, and it was complimentary but not effusive. "The U.S. Attorney General's office is trading the North for the South; a liberal for a reactionary; a lawyer for a politician," it said. "The Department of Justice is less likely to prosecute Southern whites for violation of Federal laws."[6]

But what reporters knew little of, and what historians have failed to recognize, was Biddle's wartime contribution to the preservation of freedom of the press. He had the same opportunities to apply the sedition statutes from 1941 to 1945 as did Postmaster General Albert S. Burleson and Attorney General A. Mitchell Palmer from 1917 to 1921. But he chose a different course. This is where Biddle displayed most clearly the inheritance of Holmes and most closely approached the latter's greatness.

Biddle's contribution has gone unrecognized by historians because of the government's limited action against seditionists during World War II. The American Civil Liberties Union, in its annual report in the summer of 1945, noted that only thirty-three persons had convictions sustained during the war for prosecutions involving speech and publications.[7] The Post Office Department, meanwhile, only revoked six second-class mailing permits, and two of those were restored before the war's end. In explaining the general absence of censorship, historians have assumed that it was linked to the relative lack of dissent compared to the earlier war. "With little dissent, there was little suppression by government and private action of the type America had experienced in World War I," wrote Richard S. Kirkendall in 1974.[8] Like many historians, he failed to mention Biddle in any way.

That is an oversight. As this study shows, Biddle played a significant role in the virtual absence of suppressions, and it was his actions, along with the decline in dissent, that determined how the Espionage Act was applied during World War II. Biddle's role was not surprising. He continually stressed the value of freedom of speech and of the press. His view was summed up best when he called "protection of the right to dissent" the "ultimate safeguard" for democracy.[9] Not everyone agreed, as Biddle knew only too well:

> The desire for personal freedom seldom includes an admission that a like freedom be granted to others. It does not seem to us inconsistent to insist on the right to express our own views while we deny the privilege to others. On the contrary, we tend too often to believe, particularly in times of panic, that our freedom to think as we please is endangered by the expression of opposing views, and that to protect the effectiveness of our own point of view, the others must be stifled.[10]

Most historians have failed to recognize the government's strong antilibertarian feeling during World War II. It was not nearly as visible as in the period from 1917 to 1921, but the potential for suppressions was just as great. Roosevelt believed in protecting constitutional rights, including First Amendment freedoms, in peacetime but not necessarily during a war, when victory was a necessity. Nothing must stand in its way. Others agreed. At the Post Office, a number of examiners felt that some black publications, as well as a number of others, should lose their second-class mailing permits because their critical articles were hurting the war effort. And in the Justice Department, Biddle was surrounded by aides who did not share his liberal views on free speech. "We protected the press somewhat—

probably more than we should have," recalled James H. Rowe, Jr., who was an assistant attorney general under Biddle. " . . . If I had had my way, we would have gone after them more than we did."[11] At the FBI, the domineering Hoover, who was a master at compiling damaging information on both individuals and groups, insisted that dissenting journalists and publications were subversive. The Office of Censorship and the army also endorsed censorship.

These were powerful forces, and if unchallenged they might have imposed massive press suppressions, maybe rivaling or even surpassing those of World War I. In their path stood Biddle, a man later described as believing "in the Bill of Rights and in tolerance almost without stint or limit."[12] He stubbornly held his ground, forcing a compromise from Roosevelt. His leadership also frustrated Hoover's attempt to go to court against the black press and ensured that the Post Office would not have Justice Department support if it chose to revoke the second-class permits of black publications. These were important victories for Biddle, who surely derived great satisfaction from them. But with almost the entire drama fought out behind the scenes, few knew of the breadth of his accomplishment. Almost single-handedly, with no apparent regard for the popularity of his actions, he had forced his interpretation of First Amendment press freedom on a reluctant and sometimes angry government.

One of the insiders who knew what had occurred was Grace Tully, Roosevelt's secretary. Four years after the war, she noted that it was "to Biddle's everlasting credit that despite wartime pressures he maintained both the security of the nation and its civil rights."[13] Another person who was aware of Biddle's contribution was Harold L. Ickes, who served as secretary of the Interior under Roosevelt. Looking back in 1952, he noted that although the public was becoming "jittery" about communism when Biddle was named attorney general in 1941, Biddle did not forsake his protection of civil liberties, displaying "a high type of courage." Ickes labeled that "a public service of the highest order" and predicted that Biddle's tenure as attorney general eventually would "stand out in brilliant contrast" with that of Palmer from 1919 to 1921.[14]

This study suggests that Ickes was correct. It is time to reassess Biddle's years at the Justice Department. In the history of the interaction between the federal government and the American press, he was a far more important attorney general than historians have recognized. Antilibertarianism was on the rise, although it was largely hidden from the public, and the press (especially black publications) came extremely close to having massive suppressions imposed on it. Thus, in a basic sense, this study is negative history, an account of something that did not occur. But as Theodore H. White has written, "What does not happen is, sometimes, more significant than what does."[15] In considering World War II and the government's use of the Espionage Act, his point is unquestionably true.

In fighting for civil rights and halting the push for large-scale press suppressions during World War II, Biddle played a role and affirmed values that he had learned from Holmes. Show courage, Holmes had taught him; show tolerance and strive for greatness; leave something that will be remembered. In his 1955 article on Holmes in the *New Republic*, Biddle spoke of what he felt would be Holmes's response if asked to advise a young lawyer. "If you care enough you will achieve something," Biddle wrote, slipping easily into the justice's character that he knew so well. "But you must put everything you have into your work, the whole urge and flight of your soul—and then something more. You must hold only one standard—to live nobly if you are to practice a noble profession."[16] For Biddle, as for Holmes, upholding constitutional rights was the ultimate achievement. It was his noble work, and the black press was one of the principal beneficiaries.

Notes

Chapter 1

1. Memorandum, Herbert Wechsler to Francis Biddle, June 16, 1945, Francis Biddle papers, propaganda-domestic folder, Roosevelt Library, Hyde Park, N.Y.
2. Cabell Phillips, " 'No Witch Hunts,' " *New York Times Magazine*, September 21, 1941, p. 8.
3. Robert A. Bowen to William H. Lamar, September 4, 1919, record group 28, box 68, file 397, National Archives, Washington, D.C.
4. Edwin Mims, *The Advancing South* (New York: Doubleday, 1926), p. 268.
5. George S. Schuyler, "Views and Reviews," *Pittsburgh Courier*, June 27, 1942.
6. Florence Murray, "The Negro and Civil Liberties During World War II," *Social Forces* 24, no. 2 (December 1945): 211.
7. Harry S. McAlpin, "Uncovering Washington," *Atlanta Daily World*, July 11, 1945.
8. Interview, Harry S. McAlpin, March 15, 1983.
9. Walter White, *A Man Called White* (1948; reprint ed., Bloomington: Indiana University Press, 1970), pp. 207–8. Other writers have also occasionally claimed that Roosevelt was pressured to crack down on the black press during World War II. Louie Robinson wrote in *Ebony* in August 1975 that "at least" two unnamed Cabinet members wanted "either severe censorship or outright suppression of the black press" during the war. Since he did not mention the source of his information, he may have been paraphrasing White's book. See Louie Robinson, "The Black Press: Voice of Freedom," *Ebony*, August 1975, pp. 56, 58.

10. George S. Schuyler, *Fifty Years of Progress in Negro Journalism* (1950; reprint ed., Ann Arbor: University Microfilms, 1971), p. 6.

11. Ulysses Lee, *United States Army in World War II: Special Studies: The Employment of Negro Troops*, Vol. 8, no. 8 (Washington, D.C.: Office of the Chief of Military History, U.S. Army, 1966).

12. Lee Finkle, *Forum for Protest* (Cranbury, N.J.: Associated University Presses, 1975).

13. George A. Barnes to Ulric Bell, June 5, 1942, record group 208, 002.11, E-5, box 3, OFF 1941–43, June 1–10 folder, National Archives. According to a Justice Department memorandum in May 1942, "thirty or forty different departments or agencies" were looking at the problem of discrimination against blacks. See Lawrence M. C. Smith, "Memorandum for the Attorney General," May 14, 1942, file 146-28-26, Justice Department, Washington D.C.

14. XXX [pseud.] "Washington Gestapo," *The Nation*, July 24, 1943, pp. 94–95.

15. Beverly Smith, "Everybody's Lawyer," *American Magazine*, April 1942, p. 48.

16. Clinch Calkins, "Wartime Attorney General," *Survey Graphic*, October 1942, p. 421.

17. Edwin Emery and Michael Emery, *The Press and America: An Interpretive History of the Mass Media*, 5th ed. rev. (Englewood Cliffs, N.J.: Prentice-Hall, 1984), pp. 477–80.

Chapter 2

1. Zechariah Chafee, Jr., *Free Speech in the United States* (1941; reprint ed., New York: Atheneum, 1969), pp. 36–38.

2. Woodrow Wilson to Rep. E. Y. Webb, May 22, 1917, as quoted in Donald Johnson, *The Challenge to American Freedoms* (Lexington: University of Kentucky Press, 1963), p. 55.

3. Chafee, *Free Speech*, pp. 38–39.

4. George Juergens, *News from the White House: The Presidential–Press Relationship in the Progressive Era* (Chicago: University of Chicago Press, 1981), pp. 195–96.

5. Chafee, *Free Speech*, pp. 39–41, 100–102.

6. Harry N. Scheiber, *The Wilson Administration and Civil Liberties, 1917–1921* (Ithaca: Cornell University Press, 1960), pp. 61–63.

7. Chafee, *Free Speech*, p. 79.

8. Quoted in Juergens, *News from the White House*, p. 195.

9. Gilbert C. Fite and H. C. Peterson, *Opponents of War, 1917–1918* (Madison: University of Wisconsin Press, 1957), pp. 93–94.

10. Johnson, *The Challenge to American Freedoms*, p. 57.

11. Ibid., p. 60.

12. See Johnson, *The Challenge to American Freedoms*, p. 63; and Juergens, *News from the White House*, pp. 196–99.

13. Quoted in Johnson, *The Challenge to American Freedoms*, p. 63.

14. See Harold L. Nelson and Dwight L. Teeter, *Law of Mass Communications: Freedom and Control of Print and Broadcast Media*, 3rd ed. rev. (Mineola, N.Y.: Foundation Press, 1978), p. 35; and Dorothy Ganfield Fowler, *Unmailable* (Athens: University of Georgia Press, 1977), p. 115.

15. See Lee Finkle, *Forum for Protest* (Cranbury, N.J.: Associated University Presses, 1975), p. 39; and Lawrence D. Hogan, *A Black National News Service: The Associated Negro Press and Claude Barnett, 1919–1945* (Cranbury, N.J.: Associated University Presses, 1984), p. 28.

16. Frederick G. Detweiler, *The Negro Press in the United States* (Chicago: University of Chicago Press, 1922), p. 10.

17. Finkle, *Forum for Protest*, p. 39.

18. Ibid., pp. 44, 47.

19. Emmett J. Scott to George Creel, June 5, 1918, record group 165, MID 10218-154, box 3192, National Archives, Washington, D.C.

20. Having Scott call for the conference ensured that most black editors would attend because of his reputation. After working as a janitor, messenger, and reporter on the white *Houston Post* and then editor of the black *Texas Freeman* (also in Houston), he became Booker T. Washington's private secretary in 1897. He remained with Washington until his death in 1915, during which time he also helped start the National Negro Business League in 1900 and then served as the secretary of the Tuskegee Institute beginning in 1912. He was a special assistant to the secretary of war from 1917 to 1919. For more information on Scott, see John A. Garraty, ed., *Dictionary of American Biography*, Supplement Six, 1956–1960 (New York: Charles Scribner's Sons, 1980), pp. 567–68.

21. "Address to the Committee on Public Information," June 21, 1918, record group 165, MID 10218-154, box 3192, National Archives.

22. Memorandum, J. E. Spingarn to Col. M. Churchill, June 22, 1918, record group 165, MID 10218-154, box 3192, National Archives.

23. Durand Whipple to A. M. Briggs, July 3, 1917, record group 65, entry 12E, box 64A, file O.G. 5911, National Archives.

24. Leo Spitz, "Department Intelligence Office Report," April 25, 1918, record group 165, MID 10218-133, box 3191, National Archives.

25. P. R. Hilliard to Bureau of Investigation, April 17, 1917, record group 65, entry 12E, box 64A, file O.G. 5911, National Archives.

26. Finkle, *Forum for Protest*, p. 46.

27. Military Intelligence documents at the National Archives (record group 165, MID 10218) show that the army investigated forty-seven black publications from 1917 to 1921.

28. Maj. W. H. Loving to Chief, Military Intelligence Branch, May 10, 1918, record group 165, MID 10218-133, box 3191, National Archives.

29. Robert S. Abbott to Maj. W. H. Loving, May 11, 1918, record group 165, MID 10218-133, box 3191, National Archives.

30. Maj. W. H. Loving to Chief, Military Intelligence Branch, May 20, 1918, record group 165, MID 10218-133, box 3191, National Archives.

31. See Finkle, *Forum for Protest*, p. 46; and Roi Ottley, *The Lonely Warrior: The Life and Times of Robert S. Abbott* (Chicago: Henry Regnery, 1955), pp. 155–58.

32. See S. K. Dennis to Attorney General, January 21, 1918, record group 60, file 9-12-725; and J. E. Mitchell to Maj. W. H. Loving, May 25, 1918, record group 165, MID 10218-144, box 3192. Both are in the National Archives. In late 1917, Loving also recommended "a warning talk" with the editors of the black *Boston Guardian* and the *Richmond Planet*, but the records do not indicate if these were ever held. See Maj. W. H. Loving to Chief, Military Intelligence, November 9, 1917, record group 165, MID 10218-47, box 3190, National Archives.

33. S. K. Dennis to Attorney General, January 21, 1918, record group 60, file 9-12-725, National Archives.

34. Elliott M. Rudwick, "W. E. B. DuBois: In the Role of Crisis Editor," *Journal of Negro History* 43, no. 3 (July 1958): 225–26.

35. "Thirteen," *The Crisis*, January 1918, p. 114.

36. Chief, Military Intelligence Branch, to Intelligence Officer, YMCA, New York, May 6, 1918, record group 165, MID 10218-139, box 3191, National Archives.

37. Lt. Col. M. Churchill to Charles H. Studin, June 3, 1918, record group 165, MID 10218-139, box 3191, National Archives.

38. Charles H. Studin to Lt. Col. M. Churchill, June 12, 1918, record group 165, MID 10218-139, box 3191, National Archives.

39. Justice Department to War Department, June 13, 1918, record group 165, MID 10218-139, box 3191, National Archives.

40. Rudwick, "W. E. B. DuBois," p. 226.
41. "Close Ranks," *The Crisis*, July 1918, p. 111.
42. See Finkle, *Forum for Protest*, pp. 48–49; and Rudwick, "W. E. B. DuBois," p. 226.
43. "Our Special Grievances" and "The Reward," *The Crisis*, September 1918, pp. 216–17. In the passage cited, all but the last paragraph comes from "Our Special Grievances," which immediately preceded "The Reward."
44. Fite and Peterson, *Opponents of War, 1917–1918*, pp. 89–90.
45. *Bouldin v. United States*, 261 F. 674 (1919).
46. E. Franklin Frazier, *The Negro in the United States* (New York: Macmillan, 1949), p. 511. Randolph, who came to New York from Jacksonville, Florida, in 1911 at the age of twenty-two, attended the City College of New York for six years and occasionally lectured in economics and the history of blacks at the Rand School of Economics, a New York socialist institution. He went on to become one of the country's most famous blacks as head of the Brotherhood of Sleeping Car Porters and the leader of the March on Washington Movement, which resulted in President Roosevelt's Executive Order 8802 in 1941 establishing the Fair Employment Practice Committee. Owen, who was never as nationally prominent as Randolph, was the better educated of the two, attending Virginia Union before becoming a student of political science and sociology at Columbia University. For more information on them, William H. Harris, *Keeping the Faith* (Urbana: University of Illinois Press, 1977), pp. 27–35; and Theodore Kornweibel, Jr., "The Messenger Magazine: 1917–1928" (Ann Arbor: University Microfilms, 1975), pp. 1–8.
47. Kornweibel, "The Messenger Magazine," pp. 9–10.
48. Ibid., pp. 1–2. Also see Detweiler, *The Negro Press*, p. 171. Harris, in *Keeping the Faith*, p. 29, says Randolph and Owen were released from jail "on the stipulation that they return to their homes, cease their opposition to the government, and register for the draft."
49. "Pro-Germanism Among Negroes," *The Messenger*, July 1918, p. 13.
50. Detweiler, *The Negro Press*, p. 171.
51. See ibid.; and Kornweibel, "The Messenger Magazine," pp. 14–15. The Post Office temporarily had moved against another black publication, the *Richmond Planet*, in 1917 because of an article that criticized the government. "Unless President Wilson speaks out like Col. Roosevelt, unless I am assured that the flag will offer protection to the 12,000,000 colored people in the country, and

unless I am convinced that world democracy includes black men
as well as white men, I shall consider myself a disgrace to my
race and country by freely volunteering to fight for a democracy
across the seas, because I firmly believe and maintain that democracy like charity should begin at home and spread abroad,"
wrote Uzziah Miner. That issue of the *Planet* was held up at the
Richmond Post Office but finally mailed after the paper was warned
that it might lose its second-class mailing permit. See Justine J.
Rector and James S. Tinney, eds., *Issues and Trends in Afro-American Journalism* (Lanham, Md.: University Press of America, 1980),
pp. 40–41.

52. Quoted in Johnson, *The Challenge to American Freedoms*, p. 81.
53. Juergens, *News from the White House*, p. 203.
54. Quoted in Robert K. Murray, *Red Scare: A Study in National Hys-
    teria, 1919–1920* (Minneapolis: University of Minnesota Press, 1955),
    pp. 178–80. Earlier in 1919, the governor of British Honduras
    sought to have *The Negro World* suppressed by the U.S. govern-
    ment because the publication's radicalness was having a bad in-
    fluence on blacks in the colony. The Justice Department replied
    that *The Negro World* contained nothing "upon which this De-
    partment can base any action whatever." See Robert A. Hill,
    " 'The Foremost Radical Among His Race': Marcus Garvey and
    the Black Scare, 1918–1921," *Prologue* 16, no. 4 (Winter 1984):
    219–20.
55. See Parker Hitt to Director, Military Intelligence Division, June
    23, 1921, record group 165, MID 10218-424, box 3197; and "De-
    partment Intelligence Office Report," June 3, 1919, record group
    165, MID 10218-133, box 3191. Both are in the National Archives.
56. See J. W. D. to Bureau of Investigation, September 28, 1921; and
    P-138 to Bureau of Investigation, August 26, 1921. Both are in
    record group 65, entry 12C, box 67, file 202600-2031, National
    Archives.
57. See " 'Crisis' Magazine Held Up in Mails Pending Inquiry," *New
    York Tribune*, May 2, 1919; and John Riley to A. F. Burleson, July
    16, 1919, record group 28, Box 55, file B-240, National Archives.
58. See Maj. Thomas B. Crockett to Director of Military Intelligence,
    June 6, 1919, record group 165, MID 10218-133, box 3191; and
    Agent 800 to Bureau of Investigation, July 16, 1920, record group
    65, entry 12E, box 68B, file O.G. 185161. Both are in the National
    Archives.
59. See "Weekly Radical Report," Bureau of Investigation, October
    17, 1921, record group 65, entry 12C, box 65, file 202600-1768;

and L. Lanier Winslow to Frank Burke, September 25, 1919, record group 65, entry 12E, box 48A, file O.G. 3057. Both are in the National Archives.

60. "Reds Try to Stir Negroes to Revolt," *New York Times*, July 28, 1919.

61. Jay Robert Nash, *Citizen Hoover: A Critical Study of the Life and Times of J. Edgar Hoover and His FBI* (Chicago: Nelson-Hall, 1972), pp. 16–17.

62. Don Whitehead, *The FBI Story: A Report to the People* (New York: Random House, 1956), p. 37.

63. Nash, *Citizen Hoover*, p. 18.

64. See Whitehead, *The FBI Story*, pp. 39–40; Nash, *Citizen Hoover*, pp. 18–19; Fred J. Cook, *The FBI Nobody Knows* (New York: Macmillan, 1964), pp. 87–88; and Hank Messick, *John Edgar Hoover* (New York: David McKay, 1972), p. 13.

65. Cook, *The FBI Nobody Knows*, p. 89.

66. Ibid. Hoover's selection to head the GID was not surprising. Messick, in *John Edgar Hoover*, pp. 11–12, points out that Palmer and Hoover had worked closely together in 1918 in a politically motivated attack on Boies Penrose, a U.S. senator from Pennsylvania. Palmer charged Penrose with receiving political support from brewers, which resulted in a congressional investigation.

67. Stanley Coben, *A. Mitchell Palmer: Politician* (New York: Columbia University Press, 1963), p. 207.

68. Nash, *Citizen Hoover*, p. 23.

69. Whitehead, *The FBI Story*, p. 41.

70. Cook, *The FBI Nobody Knows*, pp. 94–95. It is probable that Hoover built up his file of radicals quickly by beginning with a list compiled by the Bureau of Investigation during World War I of persons suspected of being pro-German. Messick, in *John Edgar Hoover*, p. 12, notes that the list contained such men as William Jennings Bryan and William Randolph Hearst. A link between being pro-German and being a radical was made in 1919 by a Bureau agent, Archibald E. Stevenson, when he told a congressional committee: "German socialism . . . is the father of the Bolsheviki movement in Russia, and consequently the radical movement which we have in this country today has its origin in Germany."

71. Messick, *John Edgar Hoover*, p. 14.

72. Max Lowenthal, *The Federal Bureau of Investigation* (New York: William Sloane Associates, 1950), p. 91.

73. Coben, *A. Mitchell Palmer*, p. 207.

74. Memorandum, J. E. Hoover to Mr. Fisher, September 10, 1919, record group 60, file 9-12-725, National Archives.

75. R. P. Stewart to James F. Byrnes, September 12, 1919, record group 60, file 9-12-725, National Archives. On August 25, 1919, Byrnes had made a speech in the House of Representatives in which he blamed sensational articles in black publications for the country's race problems. He called for the government to prosecute the black press under the Espionage Act. "No greater service can be rendered to the negroes today than to have them know that this Government will not tolerate, on the part of its leaders, action which tends to array them against the Government under which they live, and under which the negro race has made greater progress than it has under any other Government on earth," said Byrnes. See "Blames Race Riots on Negro Leaders," *New York Times*, August 26, 1919.

76. Francis G. Caffey to Attorney General, December 10, 1919, record group 60, file 9-12-725, National Archives.

77. Ibid. Also see Francis G. Caffey to Attorney General, September 17, 1919, and November 3, 1919, both in the same file.

78. Lowenthal, *The Federal Bureau of Investigation*, p. 120.

79. Messick, *John Edgar Hoover*, p. 14. Also see Andrew Buni, *Robert L. Vann of the Pittsburgh Courier* (Pittsburgh: University of Pittsburgh Press, 1974), pp. 106–7.

80. Lowenthal, *The Federal Bureau of Investigation*, p. 121. Detweiler, in *The Negro Press*, p. 171, notes that *The Messenger* ran the statement about being the "most dangerous" in each issue because the editors considered it a compliment.

81. Quoted in Buni, *Robert L. Vann*, p. 108.

82. Murray, *Red Scare*, pp. 178, 230–31. The Lusk Committee hearings of 1919 to 1920 resulted in a multivolume report in April 1920 in which a number of New York based black publications were castigated for appealing to "class consciousness" rather than "seeking to remedy (injustices) . . . in a lawful manner." The committee predicted that the continuation of such "propaganda" would lead to "serious trouble," and it encouraged "loyal and thoughtful" blacks to organize in opposition. See New York Joint Legislative Committee Investigating Seditious Activities, *Revolutionary Radicalism*, Part I, Vol. II (Albany, N.Y.: J. B. Lyon, 1920), pp. 1476, 1520.

83. Murray, *Red Scare*, pp. 230–31.

84. Ibid., pp. 244–46.

85. *Schenck* v. *United States*, 249 U.S. 47 (1919).

86. *United States* ex. rel. *Milwaukee Social Democratic Publishing Co.* v. *Burleson*, 255 U.S. 407 (1921).

87. Messick, *John Edgar Hoover*, p. 34.

88. Quoted in Jerry J. Berman et al., *The Lawless State: The Crimes of the U.S. Intelligence Agencies* (New York: Penguin Books, 1976), p. 95.

89. Ibid.

90. Ibid.

91. Ovid Demaris, *The Director: An Oral Biography of J. Edgar Hoover* (New York: Harper's Magazine Press, 1975), p. 55.

92. Whitehead, *The FBI Story*, pp. 161–62.

93. Ibid., pp. 157–58.

94. Ibid., p. 160.

95. Jack Alexander, "Profiles: The Director—II," *The New Yorker*, October 2, 1937, pp. 22–23.

96. Whitehead, *The FBI Story*, pp. 165–67.

97. Berman et al., *The Lawless State*, p. 96.

98. Ibid., p. 99.

99. Whitehead, *The FBI Story*, pp. 170–71.

100. Ibid., p. 171.

101. Ibid., p. 180. The fate of the GID is unclear. Messick, in *John Edgar Hoover*, pp. 84–85, claims that the GID was dismantled following the public outcry in 1940 because of Hoover's "instinct for self preservation." Messick does not indicate the source of his information, however, and no other historian makes such a claim.

102. "Japanese Propaganda Among the Negro People," *Report on Japanese Propaganda in the United States*, 1939, OF 10B, box 11, Justice Department, FBI Reports, 1939–40 folder, no. 12, Roosevelt Library, Hyde Park, N.Y. The report does not indicate who prepared it, or when the quotes attributed to the two papers appeared.

103. Finkle, *Forum for Protest*, pp. 201–3.

104. Sherman Miles to J. Edgar Hoover, July 11, 1941, record group 165, MID 10110-2452-1174, box 3085, National Archives.

105. Interview, Frank Bolden, January 14, 1983.

106. See J. E. Clegg to Director, Federal Bureau of Investigation, September 30, 1940; Memorandum, John Edgar Hoover to Lawrence M. C. Smith, October 10, 1940; and Memorandum, Hugh A. Fisher to J. Edgar Hoover, November 7, 1940. All are in file 100-122319, Federal Bureau of Investigation, Washington, D.C.

107. Buni, *Robert L. Vann*, pp. 107–8.

108. Ibid., p. 89.

109. Finkle, *Forum for Protest*, p. 131.
110. Ibid., pp. 131–33.
111. Ibid., pp. 143–44.
112. Brig. Gen. W. A. McCain to Quartermaster General, January 30, 1941, record group 165, MID 10110-2663-181, box 3097, National Archives. It was not explained how Military Intelligence convinced the *Courier* that it should run the feature.
113. Maj. G. R. Carpenter to Assistant Chief of Staff, G-2, January 31, 1941, record group 165, MID 10110-2452-993, box 3085, National Archives.
114. Lt. Col. A. R. Bolling, "Report," February 8, 1941, record group 165, MID 10110-2452-974, box 3085, National Archives.
115. See "Memorandum to Officer in Charge," May 16, 1941; Theodore Arter, "Memorandum of Conversation with Mr. Carl Murphy, Publisher of the Afro-American Newspapers," May 20, 1941; and Lt. Col. M. S. Eddy, "Military Intelligence Division Confidential Report," May 22, 1941. All are in record group 165, MID 10218-462, box 3197, National Archives.
116. Finkle, *Forum for Protest*, p. 164.
117. See Seymour Van to Military Intelligence, June 5, 1941, and June 10, 1941. Both are in record group 165, MID 10639-22-13-1, box 3851, National Archives. Prattis was one of the five black journalists who were named in the black special agent's report to Military Intelligence in July 1941. Referring to Prattis's series of articles from army camps, the agent labeled them "sensational" and said they had "caused a great deal of dissatisfaction among the colored soldiers and their families at home." See Sherman Miles to J. Edgar Hoover, July 11, 1941, record group 165, MID 10110-2452-1174, box 3085, National Archives.
118. See Special Agent Report, Federal Bureau of Investigation, October 21, 1941; and John Edgar Hoover to Assistant Chief of Staff, G-2, November 29, 1941. Both are in file 100-31159, Federal Bureau of Investigation. The FBI was slow to respond to the army's June request because the Bureau's special agent in Pittsburgh initially ignored Hoover's July 24 order to investigate the paper. The report was made only after Hoover wrote the agent again on October 4, pointing out that Military Intelligence was "particularly interested in this case." See John Edgar Hoover to Special Agent in Charge, Pittsburgh, Pennsylvania, July 24, and October 4, 1941. Both are in the same file as above.
119. See Lt. Col. S. V. Constant to Assistant Chief of Staff, G-2, July 18, 1941, record group 165, MID 10218-464, box 3197; and Mem-

orandum, Harry L. Twaddle to Assistant Chief of Staff, G-1, September 10, 1941, record group 165, file 15640-114. Both are in the National Archives.

120. Robert P. Patterson to Director of Civilian Defense, September 24, 1941, record group 165, file 15640-115, National Archives.

121. Finkle, *Forum for Protest*, p. 61.

122. Ulysses Lee, *United States Army in World War II: Special Studies: The Employment of Negro Troops*, Vol. 8, no. 8 (Washington, D.C.: Office of the Chief of Military History, U.S. Army, 1966), pp. 65–66.

123. Finkle, *Forum for Protest*, p. 116.

124. Ibid., p. 11.

125. P. L. Prattis, "The Role of the Negro Press in Race Relations," *Phylon* 7, no. 3 (Third Quarter 1946): 274.

126. George S. Schuyler, *Fifty Years of Progress in Negro Journalism* (1950; reprint ed., Ann Arbor: University Microfilms, 1971), p. 6.

127. "The Third Annual Institute of Race Relations—A Summary," *Events and Trends in Race Relations—A Monthly Summary* 4, no. 1 (August 1946): 26. Also see Charles S. Johnson, *Patterns of Negro Segregation* (New York: Harper, 1943), p. 314.

128. See Finkle, *Forum for Protest*, pp. 51–54; Arnold M. Rose, *The Negro's Morale: Group Identification and Protest* (Minneapolis: University of Minnesota Press, 1949), pp. 104–5; and U.S. Department of Commerce, *Negro Newspapers and Periodicals in the United States: 1940*, Negro Statistical Bulletin, no. 1, May 1941, p. 1.

Chapter 3

1. In the first three days of the war, the FBI rounded up 3846 enemy aliens. See Don Whitehead, *The FBI Story: A Report to the People* (New York: Random House, 1956), p. 183.

2. See J. Edgar Hoover, "In Re: Censorship," December 8, 1941; and Memorandum, J. Edgar Hoover to Maj. Gen. Edwin M. Watson, December 9, 1941. Both are in OF 10B, Justice Department, FBI Reports 1941 folder, no. 1039, Roosevelt Library, Hyde Park, N.Y.

3. "Digest of Some of the Leading Cases Involving Matter Held to Be in Violation of the Espionage Act of 1917, and Contra," undated, record group 28, file no. 103777-E, case no. E-347, National Archives, Washington, D.C.

4. Press Release, Office of Censorship, January 14, 1942, record group 28, file no. 103777-E, case no. E-10, National Archives.

5. Stephen T. Early to Kent Cooper, December 21, 1941, Stephen T. Early papers, Byron Price folder, Roosevelt Library.

6. Memorandum, Francis Biddle to Franklin D. Roosevelt, December 9, 1941, Francis Biddle papers, Censorship folder, Roosevelt Library.

7. Private typewritten notes, Francis Biddle, December 19, 1941, Francis Biddle papers, Cabinet Meetings 1941 folder, Roosevelt Library.

8. Graham J. White, *FDR and the Press* (Chicago: University of Chicago Press, 1979), p. 11.

9. For a small sample of what has been written about Roosevelt's fondness for the press and the way he fraternized with journalists, see White, *FDR and the Press*, pp. 5–12; Edwin Emery and Michael Emery, *The Press and America: An Interpretive History of the Mass Media*, 5th ed. rev. (Englewood Cliffs, N.J.: Prentice-Hall, 1984), p. 426; John Tebbel, *The Media in America* (New York: Mentor, 1976), pp. 415–17; and David Halberstam, *The Powers That Be* (New York: Dell, 1980), pp. 20–26.

10. Quoted in White, *FDR and the Press*, p. 50.

11. Ibid., p. 128.

12. Ibid., p. 10.

13. Ibid., pp. 128–30.

14. Francis Biddle, *In Brief Authority* (Garden City, N.Y.: Doubleday, 1962), p. 364.

15. White, *FDR and the Press*, p. 79.

16. See Memorandum, Franklin D. Roosevelt to Homer Cummings, April 18, 1934, 1934 Jan.–Dec., Correspondence of HSC with Franklin D. Roosevelt folder; and John Edgar Hoover, "Memorandum for the Attorney General," May 21, 1938, Attorney General's personal file, 1938–May folder. Both are in the Homer S. Cummings papers (#9973), Manuscripts Department, University of Virginia Library, Charlottesville.

17. See Memorandum, Franklin D. Roosevelt to J. Edgar Hoover, May 20, 1940; and J. Edgar Hoover to Edwin M. Watson, May 22, 1940. Both are in the President's Secretary's file, Justice Dept.–J. Edgar Hoover folder, Roosevelt Library.

18. See J. Edgar Hoover to Stephen T. Early, February 15, 1941; and Memorandum, Stephen T. Early to Franklin D. Roosevelt, February 18, 1941. Both are in OF 4185, Roosevelt Library.

19. Kenneth O'Reilly, "A New Deal for the FBI: The Roosevelt Administration, Control and National Security," *Journal of American History* 69, no. 3 (December 1982): 639, 649–51.

20. Wayne S. Cole, *Roosevelt & the Isolationists, 1932–45* (Lincoln: University of Nebraska Press, 1983), pp. 5–6.
21. Franklin D. Roosevelt to Gen. Edwin Watson, June 12, 1940, OF 10B, Dept. of Justice, FBI 1940 folder, Roosevelt Library.
22. Biddle, *In Brief Authority*, p. 226.
23. Richard W. Steele, "Franklin D. Roosevelt and His Foreign Policy Critics," *Political Science Quarterly* 94, no. 1 (Spring 1979): 25.
24. Arthur Schlesinger, Jr., "Desperate Times," *The New York Review of Books*, November 24, 1983, pp. 37–38. Also see Arthur M. Schlesinger, Jr., "A Comment on 'Roosevelt and His Foreign Policy Critics,' " *Political Science Quarterly* 94, no. 1 (Spring 1979): 33–35.
25. Memorandum, Stephen T. Early to Edwin M. Watson, December 10, 1941, Stephen T. Early papers, Watson, Edwin M.–Memos folder, Roosevelt Library.
26. See White, *FDR and the Press*, p. 55; and Paul F. Healy, *Cissy: The Biography of Eleanor M. "Cissy" Patterson* (Garden City, N.Y.: Doubleday, 1966), pp. 288–89. For information on the December 4 secret war plans article, see Lloyd Wendt, *Chicago Tribune: The Rise of a Great American Newspaper* (Chicago: Rand McNally, 1979), pp. 616–21.
27. See Telegram, Martin Anderson to Stephen T. Early, December 12, 1941; Memorandum, Stephen T. Early to J. Edgar Hoover, December 12, 1941; J. Edgar Hoover to Stephen T. Early, December 12, 1941; and telegrams to Martin Anderson, F. E. Thomason, and W. B. Sorrells, December 12, 1941. All are in the Stephen T. Early papers, FBI folder, Roosevelt Library.
28. White, *FDR and the Press*, p. 53.
29. See Sumner Welles to Franklin D. Roosevelt, January 3, 1942; Memorandum, Stephen T. Early to Franklin D. Roosevelt, January 13, 1942; and Memorandum, Franklin D. Roosevelt to Stephen T. Early, January 17, 1942. All are in the Stephen T. Early papers, President Roosevelt–Memos 1942 folder, Roosevelt Library.
30. Memorandum, Franklin D. Roosevelt to J. Edgar Hoover, January 21, 1942, President's Secretary's file, Justice Dept.–J. Edgar Hoover folder, Roosevelt Library. What apparently bothered Roosevelt in the January issue of *The Galilean* were the statements that the United States deserved the Japanese attack on Pearl Harbor as well as the German and Italian declarations on war. When the Post Office objected to those comments, Pelley agreed to suspend publication. See "Tarnished Silver Shirt," *Newsweek*, April 13, 1942, p. 30.

31. Biddle, *In Brief Authority*, pp, 182–83.
32. Cabell Phillips, " 'No Witch Hunts,' " *New York Times Magazine*, September 21, 1941, p. 8. Also see Francis Biddle, *A Casual Past* (Garden City, N.Y.: Doubleday, 1961), pp. 261–92; and Beverly Smith, "Everybody's Lawyer," *American Magazine*, April 1942, p. 48. Others also noticed Holmes's effect on Biddle. Thomas I. Emerson, who worked for Biddle at the National Labor Relations Board for about a year in the mid-1930s and then was a special assistant to the attorney general in 1940 and 1941, recalled more than forty years later that Holmes had "greatly influenced" Biddle. "He [Biddle] really was committed to the First Amendment position and held it quite deeply," said Emerson. " . . . He felt the press particularly was entitled to state its position. He felt very strongly about that." Interview, Thomas I. Emerson, June 13, 1984.
33. Phillips, " 'No Witch Hunts,' " pp. 8, 28.
34. Biddle, *In Brief Authority*, pp. 164, 258. Roosevelt also told Thomas Corcoran, a close associate, that he thought Biddle might be "too strict at a time like this when . . . we ought to have an attorney general who can close his eyes on occasion." Quoted in Steele, "Franklin D. Roosevelt and His Foreign Policy Critics," p. 22.
35. Ibid., p. 165.
36. Phillips, " 'No Witch Hunts,' " p. 8.
37. Biddle, *In Brief Authority*, p. 169.
38. Francis Biddle, "The Power of Democracy: It Can Meet All Conditions," *Vital Speeches of the Day*, October 15, 1941, p. 9.
39. Phillips, " 'No Witch Hunts,' " p. 8.
40. See Biddle, *In Brief Authority*, pp. 234–35; and "Sedition Cases Dropped," *New York Times*, December 21, 1941.
41. Typescript, "Freedom of Speech in Time of War," address by Wendell Berge over WWDC, Washington, D.C., January 11, 1942, record group 28, file no. 103777-E, case no. E-344, National Archives.
42. "Now Is the Time Not to Be Silent," *The Crisis*, January 1942, p. 7.
43. Ulysses Lee, *United States Army in World War II: Special Studies: The Employment of Negro Troops*, Vol. 8, no. 8 (Washington, D.C.: Office of the Chief of Military History, U.S. Army, 1966), p. 77.
44. "A Hero from the Galley," *Pittsburgh Courier*, January 3, 1942.
45. "Navy Cross for Dorie Miller," *Pittsburgh Courier*, May 16, 1942.
46. George S. Schuyler, "The World Today," *Pittsburgh Courier*, May 23, 1942.

47. "This Is an Example of How the Jim-Crow Policy and the Jim-Crow Attitude Work," *Pittsburgh Courier*, July 25, 1942.
48. "A Hero Returns . . . A Medal He Wears," *Pittsburgh Courier*, December 19, 1942.
49. James G. Thompson, "Should I Sacrifice to Live 'Half American'?" *Pittsburgh Courier*, January 31, 1942.
50. The Double V drawing, which quickly became familiar to blacks throughout the country because of the *Courier's* nationwide circulation, contained the words "Democracy. Double VV victory. At home—abroad." There also were two large Vs with the American symbol—an eagle—between them.
51. "The *Courier's* Double 'V' for a Double Victory Campaign Gets Country-Wide Support," *Pittsburgh Courier*, February 14, 1942. For more information on the *Courier's* Double V campaign, see Pat Washburn, "The *Pittsburgh Courier's* Double V Campaign in 1942," paper delivered at Seventy-fifth Annual Meeting of the Organization of American Historians, Philadelphia, April 1, 1982.
52. Federal Bureau of Investigation, "General Intelligence Survey," February 1942, OF 10B, Justice Dept.–FBI Reports 1942 folder, no. 2076, Roosevelt Library.
53. The possibility that the black press was ignored totally was suggested by Ralph L. Holsinger, an Indiana University journalism professor who read this book while it was being written. He based his conclusion on his personal reminiscences of World War II, when he served in the army and was well aware of black problems in that branch of the service. "For most Americans in 1942," he recalled in 1984, "blacks were like the invisible man on the stair— they simply weren't there. Even in the North, they had their place. Most stayed in that place. As long as they did, they weren't noticed. Blacks were the janitors, the dishwashers, the maids, the sharecroppers. In most places, they were simple not seen as a force."
54. Archivists at the Roosevelt Library confirmed this fact about the president.
55. Lee, *United States Army*, pp. 141–42.
56. Typescript, "Remarks of Colonel E. R. Householder, Officer in Charge of Miscellaneous Division, Adjutant General's Department, War Department, At the Conference of Negro Newspaper Representatives, War Department, Munitions Building, Washington, D.C., December 8, 1941," record group 107, Press Releases folder, National Archives.
57. Ibid.

58. "Newsmen Score War Department Policy," *Chicago Defender*, December 13, 1941.

59. Quoted in Lee, *United States Army*, pp. 142–43.

60. John Morton Blum, *V Was for Victory: Politics and American Culture During World War II* (New York: Harcourt, Brace, Jovanovich, 1976), p. 189.

61. See "Army's Death Penalty Order for Race Mixing Withdrawn," *Pittsburgh Courier*, January 10, 1942; and "Army Limits Number of Colored Nurses," *Pittsburgh Courier*, January 24, 1942.

62. See U.S. Army, "Inflammatory Propaganda," undated, record group 107, file 291.2; Division of Press Intelligence to G-1, December 13, 1941, record group 165, file 15640-129; and Grogan to G-1, February 11, 1942, record group 165, file 15640-136. All are in the National Archives.

63. U.S. Army, "Inflammatory Propaganda."

64. Ibid. The black publications were *Amsterdam News* (New York), *Atlanta World, Baltimore Afro-American, California Eagle* (Los Angeles), *Chicago Defender, Chicago World, Cleveland Call and Post, Houston Informer, Michigan Chronicle* (Detroit), *New York Age, Northwest Enterprise* (Seattle), *Oklahoma City Black Dispatch, Opportunity* (New York), *Pittsburgh Courier, Philadelphia Tribune, San Antonio Register,* and *The Crisis* (New York).

65. Vincent M. Miles, "Seditious and Disloyal Matter Unmailable in Time of War," *The Postal Bulletin*, January 15, 1942, p. 2.

66. The Post Office inspected several hundred publications monthly (an exact figure was not given) between December 7, 1941, and June 30, 1942. Then, in the next three fiscal years respectively, the numbers investigated were 5398, 5537, and 4995. See *Annual Report of the Postmaster General for the Fiscal Year Ended June 30, 1942*, p. 29; *Annual Report of the Postmaster General for the Fiscal Year Ended June 30, 1943*, p. 31; *Annual Report of the Postmaster General for the Fiscal Year Ended June 30, 1944*, p. 49; and *Annual Report of the Postmaster General for the Fiscal Year Ended June 30, 1945*, p. 28. They were published in Washington by the U.S. Government Printing Office in 1942, 1944, 1945, and 1946.

67. See Ernest Malter to Department of Justice, undated (received January 28, 1942); Wendell Berge to Vincent M. Miles, January 28, 1942; and JUH, Memorandum, undated. All are in record group 28, file no. 103777-E, case no. E-13, National Archives. This was not the first government examination of *The Kiplinger Washington Letter*. In 1934, after a complaint from the Democratic National Committee, Attorney General Homer Cummings ordered

an investigation of the publication "to see who is who—and what is behind it all." See William Stanley to Homer Cummings, March 26, 1934; Justice Department, "Re: W. M. Kiplinger," March 28, 1934; and J. Edgar Hoover, "Memorandum for the Assistant to the Attorney General, Mr. William Stanley," April 20, 1934. All are in the Homer S. Cummings papers (#9973), Attorney General's personal file, Memos Re: W. M. Kiplinger and Copies, Kiplinger Washington Agency folder, Manuscript Department, University of Virginia Library.

68. See James S. L. Royle to Ramsey S. Black, February 27, 1942; and Solicitor to Fresno, Calif., postmaster, undated. Both are in record group 28, file no. 103777-E, case no. E-78, National Archives.

69. Richard W. Steele, "Preparing the Public for War: Efforts to Establish a National Propaganda Agency, 1940–41," *American Historical Review* 75, no. 6 (October 1970): 1649.

70. Ibid., p. 1651.

71. Sydney Weinberg, "What to Tell America: The Writers' Quarrel in the Office of War Information," *Journal of American History* 55, no. 1 (June 1968): 75.

72. Steele, "Preparing the Public for War," p. 1652.

73. Ibid.

74. See Office of Facts and Figures, "Reports," undated, record group 44, box 1830, Groups and Organizations–Negroes folder; and documents in record group 44, box 1844, no. 22-28 folder. Both are in the National Archives.

75. J. A. Rogers, "Rogers Says," *Pittsburgh Courier*, February 7, 1942.

76. See Memorandum, John Edgar Hoover to Wendell Berge, January 30, 1942; and Memorandum, Wendell Berge to J. Edgar Hoover, February 5, 1942. Both are in file 100-63963, Federal Bureau of Investigation, Washington, D.C. Also see "The Inquiring Reporter," *Baltimore Afro-American*, December 20, 1941.

77. "Cut the Comedy," *Pittsburgh Courier*, January 17, 1942.

78. A Negro Soldier, "How Would Japs Treat Negroes?" *Pittsburgh Courier*, January 24, 1942.

79. Edgar T. Rouzeau to Franklin D. Roosevelt, February 24, 1942, OF 93, Colored Matters (Negroes), 1942, Jan.–April folder, Roosevelt Library.

80. "Freedom of Negro Press," *Chicago Defender*, December 20, 1941.

81. See [John H. Sengstacke?] to J. Edgar Hoover, December 22, 1941; and J. Edgar Hoover to [John H. Sengstacke?], January 3, 1942. Both are in file 100-122319, Federal Bureau of Investigation. The name of the person corresponding with Hoover has been blacked

out on the documents, but it probably was Sengstacke because he regularly wrote to a number of federal officials during the war.

82. See Moss Hyles Kendrix to Byron Price, undated; JHS to BP, February 23, 1942; and Bryon Price to Moss Hyles Kendrix, February 26, 1942. All are in record group 216, 012-D/8, Negro Press folder, National Archives.

Chapter 4

1. "Attorney General," *Newsweek*, June 8, 1942, p. 32.

2. Clinch Calkins, "Wartime Attorney General," *Survey Graphic*, October 1942, p. 421.

3. Cabell Phillips, " 'No Witch Hunts,' " *New York Times Magazine*, September 21, 1941, p. 8.

4. "Blow to the War Effort," *Time*, June 8, 1942, p. 15.

5. Francis Biddle, *In Brief Authority* (Garden City, N.Y.: Doubleday, 1962), p. 151.

6. Interview, John H. Sengstacke, April 21, 1983.

7. Samuel I. Rosenman, *Working with Roosevelt* (New York: Harper, 1952), p. 321.

8. Biddle, *In Brief Authority*, p. 238.

9. U.S. Congress, *Congressional Record*, 77th Cong., 2d sess., 1942, 88, pt. 2: 2566.

10. Biddle, *In Brief Authority*, p. 238.

11. See Calkins, "Wartime Attorney General," p. 420; and Beverly Smith, "Everybody's Lawyer," *American Magazine*, April 1942, p. 47. Historian Richard W. Steele also has noted that "Biddle served as the administration's conscience, reminding Roosevelt of the purist view of civil liberties." See Richard W. Steele, "Franklin D. Roosevelt and His Foreign Policy Critics," *Political Science Quarterly* 94, no. 1 (Spring 1979): 22.

12. STE, "Memorandum for the President," March 20, 1942, President's Secretary's File, Justice Department folder, Roosevelt Library, Hyde Park, N.Y.

13. Private typewritten notes, Francis Biddle, "March 20, 1942," Francis Biddle papers, Cabinet Meetings, Jan.–June 1942 folder, Roosevelt Library.

14. Francis Biddle, "Taking No Chances," *Collier's*, March 21, 1942, p. 41.

15. *Complete Presidential Press Conferences of Franklin D. Roosevelt*, Vol. 19 (New York: Da Capo Press, 1972), pp. 231–34.

16. See Memorandum, W. B. Woodson to Secretary of the Navy,

March 18, 1942; Memorandum, Frank Knox to President, March 21, 1942; and Memorandum, F. D. R. to Attorney General, March 24, 1942. All are in OF 144, Newspapers 1941–42, Jan.–July folder, Roosevelt Library.

17. Interview, James Henry Rowe, Jr., March 1, 1983.
18. Biddle, *In Brief Authority*, pp. 191, 302.
19. Ibid., p. 108.
20. Ibid., pp. 109–16.
21. Ibid., pp. 213–14.
22. Calkins, "Wartime Attorney General," p. 423.
23. Biddle, *In Brief Authority*, pp. 214–19.
24. James MacGregor Burns, *Roosevelt: The Soldier of Freedom* (New York: Harcourt, Brace, Jovanovich, 1970), p. 215. Historian Geoffrey Perrett has noted that Biddle followed a familiar pattern when pressured on civil liberties issues during the war: "Scapegoats were identified and persecution begun; Biddle would resist official involvement; the pressure on him would increase; he would soon give in." Geoffrey Perrett, *Days of Sadness, Years of Triumph: The American People, 1939–1945* (New York: Coward, McCann & Geoghegan, 1973), p. 358. For an in-depth examination of the Japanese internment and Biddle's role in it, see Peter Irons, *Justice at War* (New York: Oxford University Press, 1983).
25. Biddle, *In Brief Authority*, p. 219.
26. Interview, James Henry Rowe, Jr., March 1, 1983.
27. Calkins, "Wartime Attorney General," p. 423.
28. Interview, James Henry Rowe, Jr., March 1, 1983. For more information on Rowe, see Robert G. Kaiser, "FDR's Era May Have Been Better Than the Founding Fathers'," *Washington Post*, February 27, 1983; and J. Y. Smith, "James H. Rowe, Lawyer, Aide to FDR, Dies at 75," *Washington Post*, June 19, 1984.
29. Interview, James Henry Rowe, Jr., March 1, 1983.
30. Biddle, *In Brief Authority*, pp. 254, 256.
31. Interview, James Henry Rowe, Jr., March 1, 1983. Rowe's anti-press reaction was interesting because of his background. While he was at Harvard, he worked on the *Crimson* during the school year and in the newsroom of his hometown newspaper in Butte during the summer. In his senior year, he had problems deciding whether to become a newspaperman or a lawyer, but he chose the latter when some New York journalists told him what "lousy" jobs they had because of the low pay. Even so, he said in an interview in March 1983 that he remained an admirer of the press until he went to work in the White House. "FDR had no illusions

about the press," Rowe recalled. "I think if he could have been tougher [on it], he would have done it. I agreed with him totally."

32. Memorandum, James Rowe, Jr. to Attorney General, March 23, 1942, Francis Biddle papers, Propaganda–Domestic folder, Roosevelt Library.

33. Ibid.

34. Interview, James Henry Rowe, Jr., March 1, 1983.

35. See "U.S. Cracks Down," *Washington Post*, March 26, 1942; "Naturalized Foes to Lose Citizenship," *New York Times*, March 26, 1942; and "Voices of Defeat," *Life*, April 13, 1942, p. 86.

36. "Nation Starts Cracking Down on the 5th and 6th Columnists," *Newsweek*, April 6, 1942, p. 27.

37. For information about the arrests, indictments, and convictions, see the following in the *New York Times*: "G. W. Christians Accused of Sedition After Writings to Army Camps," March 28, 1942; "Accused of Libel on Gen. M'Arthur," April 1, 1942; "FBI Seizes Pelley on Sedition Charge," April 5, 1942; "Two Accused of Sedition," April 9, 1942; "Indicts 'Crusader' Leader," April 30, 1942; "Head of White Shirts Is Guilty of Sedition," June 5, 1942; "Pelley Is Indicted on Sedition Charge," June 10, 1942; "Convicts Noble, Jones," July 12, 1942; and Leo Egan, "Pelley Convicted on Eleven Counts in Sedition Case," August 6, 1942. Also see "Nation Starts Cracking Down on the 5th and 6th Columnists," *Newsweek*, April 6, 1942, pp. 27–28; "Tarnished Silver Shirt," *Newsweek*, April 13, 1942, pp. 29–30; and "Milquetoast Gets Muscles," *Time*, April 13, 1942, p. 20.

38. "Free Speech in Wartime," *New Republic*, January 4, 1943, p. 5.

39. "Milquetoast Gets Muscles," *Time*, April 13, 1942, p. 20.

40. Michael Williams, "Views & Reviews," *Commonweal*, April 10, 1942, p. 617.

41. William L. Shirer, "The Poison Pen," *Atlantic Monthly*, May 1942, p. 548.

42. Biddle, *In Brief Authority*, p. 238. Biddle's recollection of Roosevelt's persistence at Cabinet meetings was confirmed by Secretary of the Interior Harold L. Ickes, who noted in his diary on April 11, 1942: "One thing the President is interested in . . . is the seditious and subversive newspapers of the country. He presses Biddle on the subject at every Cabinet meeting." Quoted in Richard W. Steele, "American Popular Opinion and the War Against Germany: The Issue of Negotiated Peace, 1942," *Journal of American History* 65, no. 3 (December 1978): 718.

43. See Francis Biddle, "Conference with the President, April 22, 1942," Francis Biddle papers, Franklin D. Roosevelt folder, Roosevelt Library; and "Biddle to Push Sedition Inquiries, Beginning in Chicago, Then Here," *New York Times*, April 23, 1942. Paul F. Healy, in his biography on Patterson, notes that "she was convinced that he [Roosevelt] would have the Justice Department crack down on her or the *Times–Herald* if some wartime justification could be found." The surveillances, of which she apparently was unaware, suggest that she may have been right. See Paul F. Healy, *Cissy: The Biography of Eleanor M. "Cissy" Patterson* (Garden City, N.Y.: Doubleday, 1966), p. 294.

44. Memorandum, FDR to Stephen Early, April 30, 1942, Stephen T. Early papers, President Roosevelt–Memos 1942 folder, Roosevelt Library.

45. See Memorandum, F. D. R. to Attorney General, May 7, 1942, OF 4453, Propaganda folder; Memorandum, Department of Justice, May 19, 1942, Francis Biddle papers, Propaganda–Domestic folder; Francis Biddle to Franklin D. Roosevelt, September 15, 1942, OF 4453, Propaganda folder; and White House report, undated, Francis Biddle papers, Propaganda–Domestic folder. All are in the Roosevelt Library. None of the documents indicates who compiled the clippings Roosevelt sent to Biddle.

46. See Private typewritten notes, Francis Biddle, "May 1, 1942" and "May 7, 1942," Cabinet Meetings, Jan.–June 1942 folder; and Private typewritten notes, Francis Biddle, "May 4, 1942," Franklin D. Roosevelt folder. All are in the Francis Biddle papers at the Roosevelt Library.

47. Typescript, "Roosevelt Fireside Chat," April 28, 1942, President's Personal File 1820, Roosevelt Library.

48. Private typewritten notes, Francis Biddle, "April 24, 1942," Francis Biddle papers, Cabinet Meetings, Jan.–June 1942 folder, Roosevelt Library.

49. Memorandum, James Rowe, Jr., to Francis Biddle, April 29, 1942, Francis Biddle papers, James H. Rowe, Jr., folder, Roosevelt Library.

50. Private typewritten notes, Francis Biddle, "May 1, 1942," Francis Biddle papers, Cabinet Meetings, Jan.–June 1942 folder, Roosevelt Library. This was not the first time Biddle had used clippings to impress the president about the department's activity against seditionists. In an April 22 conference he showed the president a scrapbook "containing the wide publicity on the cases that we

have already instituted." See Francis Biddle, "Conference with the President, April 22, 1942," Francis Biddle papers, Franklin D. Roosevelt folder, Roosevelt Library.

51. Biddle kept Cabinet meeting notes throughout the war, and his notes for the May 22 meeting are the only ones that mention the black press. No other documents can be located that show the black press was discussed at any other wartime Cabinet meeting.

52. Private typewritten notes, Francis Biddle, "May 22, 1942," Francis Biddle papers, Cabinet Meetings, Jan.–June 1942 folder, Roosevelt Library.

53. Nathan Miller, *FDR: An Intimate History* (Garden City, N.Y.: Doubleday, 1983), p. 360.

54. Burns, *Roosevelt: The Soldier of Freedom*, p. 472. Still another historian who has noted Roosevelt's position toward blacks is Neil A. Wynn in *The Afro-American and the Second World War* (London: Paul Elek, 1976), pp. 109–13.

55. Miller, *FDR: An Initmate History*, p. 361.

56. Office of Facts and Figures, "Special Intelligence Report No. 38," May 22, 1942, record group 44, E-171, folder 64, National Archives, Washington, D.C.

57. Robert Durr, *The Negro Press: Its Character, Development and Function* (Jackson: Mississippi Division, Southern Regional Council, 1947), pp. 2–3.

58. F. R. Hammack to Director, Federal Bureau of Investigation, September 4, 1942, file 94–8–1399–7, Federal Bureau of Investigation, Washington, D.C.

59. See Cliff MacKay, "A Note to Mr. Hoover," *Birmingham World*, March 27, 1942. See also John Edgar Hoover to Emory O. Jackson, April 10, 1942; Emory O. Jackson to J. Edgar Hoover, April 20, 1942; Memorandum, L. B. Nichols to Mr. Tolson, April 24, 1942; and J. Edgar Hoover to Emory O. Jackson, April 29, 1942. All are in file 94–8–1399, Federal Bureau of Investigation.

60. Cliff MacKay, "Now Just Who Is Subversive?" *Birmingham World*, July 10, 1942.

61. "Cowing the Negro Press," *Pittsburgh Courier*, March 14, 1942.

62. Interview, Frank Bolden, January 14, 1983. It is impossible to be precise about when the FBI agents visited the *Courier*. Bolden only recalls that it was shortly after the war started, which would put it sometime between December 7, 1941, and June 27, 1942. By the latter date, Bolden was in Arizona as a *Courier* war correspondent, and he was rarely at the paper after that for the

remainder of the war. Therefore, the visit had to have occurred before then.

63. Ibid.
64. See "Publishers to Answer Pegler Challenge," *Chicago Defender*, May 30, 1942; and "Negro Press Will Fight 'Intimidation,' " *California Eagle*, June 4, 1942.
65. Durr, *The Negro Press*, pp. 2–3. Not all of the FBI's subscriptions were made openly, however. In October 1942, the Bureau subscribed to the black *People's Voice* of New York by using a fictitious name. See P. E. Foxworth to Director, Federal Bureau of Investigation, October 21, 1942, file 100–51230–16, Federal Bureau of Investigation.
66. Westbrook Pegler, "Fair Enough," *New York World–Telegram*, April 28, 1942.
67. George S. Schuyler, "The World Today," *Pittsburgh Courier*, May 9, 1942.
68. Marjorie McKenzie, "Pursuit of Democracy," *Pittsburgh Courier*, May 9, 1942.
69. "Is Criticism to Be Suppressed?" *Pittsburgh Courier*, May 16, 1942.
70. "Westbrook Pegler," *Chicago Defender*, May 23, 1942.
71. "Washington to Hush Negro Press," *California Eagle*, May 28, 1942.
72. Moss Hyles Kendrix to Stephen T. Early, March 31, 1942, OF 93, Colored Matters (Negroes) 1942 Jan.–April folder, Roosevelt Library.
73. Luther R. White to Franklin D. Roosevelt, June 1, 1942, OF 93, Colored Matters (Negroes) 1942 May–June folder, Roosevelt Library.
74. "Publishers Pledge Support to President During Crisis," *Pittsburgh Courier*, June 13, 1942.
75. Interview, Billy Rowe, January 3, 1983. James E. Alsbrook, who was a copy reader, feature writer, and proof reader on the *Baltimore Afro-American* from 1941 to 1943, recalled that he heard rumors that "Hoover's boys" were investigating his newspaper because the FBI did not like its tone. However, he never saw any agents visit the paper. Interview, James E. Alsbrook, April 18, 1984.
76. Abstract, Franklin D. Roosevelt to Stephen Early, May 3, 1942, OF 93, Colored Matters X-Refs 1942 folder, Roosevelt Library.
77. Interview, John H. Sengstacke, April 21, 1983. Daisy Bates, who published the *Arkansas State Journal* with her husband, Lucius,

also recalled in a June 9, 1983, interview that the FBI wanted to shut her paper down during World War II. She said the FBI agents made "quite a few visits" to the paper during the war, which did not scare her and had no effect on what the paper wrote, but she cannot remember the specific dates of the visits.

78. Ibid. It is impossible to pinpoint the date of Sengstacke's meeting with Biddle any more precisely than mid-June 1942. Sengstacke does not recall the exact date, and the only document in which the meeting is mentioned is a Post Office memorandum of June 26, 1942, which says the meeting took place "some days ago." See C.W.H., "Memorandum for the Office Files: The Chicago Defender," June 26, 1942, record group 28, file no. 103777–E, case no. E-128, National Archives.

79. See Robert K. Carr, *Federal Protection of Civil Rights: Quest for a Sword* (Ithaca: Cornell University Press, 1947), pp. 24–26; and Biddle, *In Brief Authority*, pp. 154–60.

80. See Biddle, *In Brief Authority*, pp. 152–53; and *Mitchell* v. *United States*, 313 U.S. 80 (1941).

81. Ibid., pp. 166, 169.

82. Calkins, "Wartime Attorney General," p. 423.

83. Interview, John H. Sengstacke, April 21, 1983. The black newspapers used by Biddle in his 1942 meeting with Sengstacke almost certainly were collected by the FBI. On June 2, for example, in what was a routine procedure, Hoover sent Lawrence M. C. Smith, head of the Justice Department's Special War Policies Unit, the *Pittsburgh Courier's* issues of May 16 and May 23 "for your information." This, along with P. B. Young's recollection of the FBI subscribing to numerous black newspapers, suggests that the Bureau had a massive collection of the papers. See J. Edgar Hoover to Lawrence M. C. Smith, June 2, 1942, file 100–31159–9, Federal Bureau of Investigation. For an example of what Biddle apparently had on the table in his meeting with Sengstacke, see the *Pittsburgh Courier's* April 11, 1942, issue, which had a large front-page headline, "Unrest Grows in Army Camps."

84. Smith, "Everybody's Lawyer," p. 52.

85. Interviews, John H. Sengstacke, April 21, 1983, and September 15, 1983.

86. C.W.H., "Memorandum for the Office Files: The Chicago Defender," June 26, 1942, record group 28, file no. 103777–E, case no. E-128, National Archives.

87. Interviews, John H. Sengstacke, April 21, 1983, and September 15, 1983.

88. Under a Freedom of Information Act request, the Justice Department checked its files but was unable to find any "notes, minutes or memoranda" on Sengstacke's June 1942 meeting with Biddle. Miriam M. Nisbet to Pat Washburn, March 23, 1984.

89. See Memorandum, Wendell Berge to Attorney General, March 24, 1942, Jan.–June 1942 folder; Memorandum, Wendell Berge to Attorney General, April 15, 1942, Social Justice folder; Memorandum, Wendell Berge to James Rowe, Jr., April 15, 1942, Social Justice folder; Memorandum, Wendell Berge to Attorney General, April 20, 1942, Social Justice folder; Memorandum, Wendell Berge to Attorney General, April 23, 1942, Jan.–June 1942 folder; Memorandum, Wendell Berge to Attorney General, May 1, 1942, Jan.–June 1942 folder; Memorandum, Wendell Berge to Attorney General, May 20, 1942, Jan.–June 1942 folder; and Memorandum, Wendell Berge to Attorney General, June 25, 1942, Jan.–June 1942 folder. All are in the Wendell Berge papers at the Library of Congress in Washington, D.C. In addition, see a Justice Department report, which was undated but was written in July 1942 (this can be deduced from references in it), on the various sedition investigations. It is in the Francis Biddle papers, Justice Dept. Reports folder, Roosevelt Library.

90. Memorandum, D. E. H. to L. M. C. Smith, May 8, 1942, file 146-28-380, Department of Justice, Washington, D.C.

91. See Lawrence M. C. Smith, "Memorandum for the Attorney General," May 14 and 15, 1942, file 146–28–26, Department of Justice.

92. Lawrence M. C. Smith, "Memorandum for the Attorney General," June 23, 1942, file 146–28–572, Department of Justice.

93. Walter White, *A Man Called White* (1948; reprint ed., Bloomington: Indiana University Press, 1970), pp. 207–8.

94. Lee Finkle, *Forum for Protest* (Cranbury, N.J.: Associated University Presses, 1975), p. 48.

95. Interview, John H. Sengstacke, April 21, 1983.

96. Interview, Frank E. Bolden, January 14, 1983. Bolden specifically recalled when Prattis told him there would be no indictments, because he was back in Pittsburgh for a short rest after covering black troops in Arizona as a war correspondent.

97. Lewis Wood, "28 Are Indicted on Sedition Charge," *New York Times*, July 24, 1942. Other sedition indictments, against essentially the same group, followed in January 1943 and January 1944, as the government tightened up its charges, fearful that the indictments would not be able to withstand a constitutional challenge. The trial, involving twenty-nine extremists, finally began

in April 1944, lasted seven and a half months, and then ended
when the judge died. Eventually, the indictments were dismissed
because of a failure to prosecute. See Cabell Phillips, *The 1940s:
Decade of Triumph and Trouble* (New York: Macmillan, 1975), pp.
114–22; A. A. Hoehling, *Home Front, U.S.A.* (New York: Thomas
Y. Crowell, 1966), pp. 114–15; Burns, *Roosevelt: The Soldier of Freedom*, pp. 453–54; Biddle, *In Brief Authority*, pp. 233–48; and Lawrence Dennis and Maximilian St.-George, *A Trial on Trial: The Great
Sedition Trial of 1944* (National Civil Rights Committee, 1946).

98. Lewis Wood, "28 Are Indicted on Sedition Charge," *New York
Times*, July 24, 1942.

99. "Named in Sedition Indictment," *New York Times*, July 24, 1942.

100. "Indictments And New Spy Hunt Point to Subversion Crack-
down," *Newsweek*, August 3, 1942, p. 26.

101. "Pelley and the Prosecution," *New Republic*, August 17, 1942,
p. 189.

102. See Lloyd Wendt, *Chicago Tribune: The Rise of a Great American
Newspaper* (Chicago: Rand McNally, 1979), pp. 627–36; Biddle, *In
Brief Authority*, pp. 248–51; "Navy Salvo on McCormick," *Newsweek*, August 17, 1942, pp. 64–65; "Navy v. Tribune," *Time*, August 17, 1942, pp. 65–67; "Mystery in Chicago," *Time*, August 31,
1942, pp. 63–64; "Tribune Defeats the Navy," *Newsweek*, August
31, 1942, pp. 65–66; and William D. Mitchell to Francis Biddle,
August 25, 1942, Francis Biddle papers, Propaganda–Domestic
folder, Roosevelt Library.

103. See Memoranda, John Edgar Hoover to Wendell Berge, July 7,
July 10, July 17, and July 18, 1942; and Memorandum, Wendell
Berge to Director, Federal Bureau of Investigation, July 25, 1942.
All are in file 100-20076, Federal Bureau of Investigation.

104. See J. Edgar Hoover to Wendell Berge, May 30, 1942; Memorandum, Wendell Berge to Director, Federal Bureau of Investigation,
June 24, 1942; and John Edgar Hoover to Special Agent in Charge,
Baltimore, July 6, 1942. All are in file 100-63963, Federal Bureau
of Investigation.

105. *Annual Report of the Attorney General of the United States for the Fiscal
Year Ended June 30, 1942* (Atlanta: Federal Prison Industries, 1943),
pp. 6–7.

106. Herbert Wechsler, who was a special assistant to Biddle in 1942,
recalled Roosevelt's pressure on the attorney general to move
against seditionists. He said that it was a "fair assumption" that
Biddle would have lost his job if the Justice Department had not

come up with some indictments. Interview, Herbert Wechsler, March 22, 1985.

Chapter 5

1. Lee Finkle, *Forum for Protest* (Cranbury, N.J.: Associated University Presses, 1975), pp. 105-7.
2. Editorial Cartoon, "Defending America Our Way," *Baltimore Afro-American*, January 31, 1942.
3. Finkle, *Forum for Protest*, p. 107.
4. Emmett J. Scott, "Saboteurs of Morale," *Pittsburgh Courier*, January 24, 1942.
5. "The Courier's Double 'V' for a Double Victory Campaign Gets Country-Wide Support," *Pittsburgh Courier*, February 14, 1942.
6. Pat Washburn, "The *Pittsburgh Courier*'s Double V Campaign in 1942," paper delivered at the Seventy-fifth Annual Meeting of the Organization of American Historians, Philadelphia, April 1, 1982.
7. Richard M. Dalfiume, *Desegregation of the U.S. Armed Forces: Fighting on Two Fronts, 1939-1953* (Columbia: University of Missouri Press, 1969), p. 124.
8. Joseph D. Bibb, "We Remember 1919," *Pittsburgh Courier*, February 7, 1942. In the middle of Bibb's column was the incredible statement, "Now is the time for sedition." Apparently it was a typographical error, but interestingly the paper did not carry a retraction until three weeks later, when Bibb noted that the sentence should have read, "Now is NO time for sedition." There was no explanation of why this was not corrected sooner. See Joseph D. Bibb, "Robeson Is Right," *Pittsburgh Courier*, February 28, 1942.
9. The influential *Chicago Defender* had no one at the OFF meeting because it was not on the original invitation list. Both Chicago Mayor Edward J. Kelly and A. C. MacNeal, the paper's managing editor, contacted OFF Director Archibald MacLeish to find out why the paper was ignored. "Its editorial policies are in complete harmony with the policies of the Washington administration," wrote Kelly. "In fact, this paper has consistently and energetically supported the President. This support, in view of the paper's national circulation, has been most effective. . . . The publishers of the *Defender* are a potent factor in our great system of freedom of the press." MacLeish replied that the paper was excluded

through an "unfortunate oversight" and that it would be included in future meetings. However, no similar meetings were held during the rest of the war. In addition, MacLeish wired MacNeal that the paper could attend the meeting if it wished, but the *Defender* declined the late invitation. See Telegram, A. C. MacNeal to Archibald MacLeish, March 17, 1942; Telegram, Archibald MacLeish to A. C. MacNeal, March 18, 1942; Edward J. Kelly to Archibald MacLeish, March 19, 1942; and Archibald MacLeish to Edward J. Kelly, March 21, 1942. All are in record group 208, 002.11, entry 5, boxes 3 and 4, National Archives, Washington, D.C.

10. "U.S. Asked to Take Firm Stand," *Norfolk Journal and Guide*, March 28, 1942.

11. For articles on the meeting, see Ibid.; William G. Nunn, "Race Leaders Demand Government End Discrimination at OFF Meet," *Pittsburgh Courier*, March 28, 1942; "Leaders Demand That U.S. Clean Own House," *Baltimore Afro-American*, March 28, 1942; Roy Wilkins, "The Watchtower," *Amsterdam Star–News*, March 28, 1942; and "Negro Morale, *The Crisis*, April 1942, p. 111.

12. Archibald MacLeish to Carter W. Wesley, March 24, 1942, record group 208, 002.11, entry 5, box 3, National Archives.

13. Quoted in Dalfiume, *Desegregation of the U.S. Armed Forces*, p. 126.

14. "Negro Morale," *The Crisis*, April 1942, p. 111.

15. George S. Schuyler, "Views and Reviews," *Pittsburgh Courier*, April 11, 1942. In the same issue, also see Schuyler's "The World Today."

16. "Hysteria over Negroes," *Pittsburgh Courier*, May 2, 1942.

17. See Memorandum, Associated Negro Press to Henry A. Wallace, April 16, 1942; Claude A. Barnett to Henry A. Wallace, April 20, 1942; H. A. Wallace to Archibald MacLeish, May 4, 1942; and Archibald MacLeish to Claude A. Barnett, May 18, 1942. All are in record group 208, 002.11, E-5, box 3, Negroes, May 1-30 folder, National Archives.

18. The close monitoring of the black press was part of an overall examination of the U.S. press by OFF and its successor, OWI. OFF began weekly media reports in February 1942 and added monthly reports in March. Both can be found in record group 44, boxes 1720, 1721, and 1844, National Archives. In addition, numerous special reports were compiled. Examples of these include "Radio-Tokyo in the American Press" (February 27, 1942); "Axis News in United States Newspapers" (March 30, 1942); "Foreign-Language Press and the War" (April 7, 1942); "Genesis

of the Anti 40-Hour Week Campaign in Midwestern Newspapers" (April 14, 1942); "Comment on Suppression of Subversive Publications in 32 Metropolitan Papers, April 20–May" (May 21, 1942); "Developing Situation—Government's Informational Policy Antagonizes Public and Press" (November 13, 1942); and "Newspaper Comment on Navy Policies on News and Censorship (October 1–December 15, 1942)" (January 20, 1943). All of these are in record group 44, boxes 1842, 1844, and 1846, National Archives.

19. Bureau of Intelligence, Office of Facts and Figures, "Survey of Intelligence Materials No. 14," March 16, 1942, President's Secretary's File, Office of War Information, Roosevelt Library, Hyde Park, N.Y.

20. Bureau of Intelligence, Office of Facts and Figures, "Special Intelligence Report No. 38," May 22, 1942, record group 44, E-171, box 1844, folder 64, National Archives.

21. Memorandum, Special Services Division to Cornelius Du Bois, June 22, 1942, record group 44, E-171, box 1843, folder 46, National Archives.

22. Memorandum, Special Services Division, Office of War Information, "Recommendations for Survey #30 on the Negro Problem," undated, record group 44, E-171, box 1843, folder 46, National Archives. From the mention of specific events in the memorandum, it is apparent that it was written either July 1 or July 2, 1942.

23. Archibald MacLeish to Francis Biddle, April 27, 1942, record group 208, 002.11, entry 5, box 3, National Archives. Although the document does not have the clippings attached and does not mention from which newspaper they came, a Justice Department memorandum of May 15, 1942, notes that they were from the *Washington Afro-American*. See Lawrence M. C. Smith, "Memorandum for the Attorney General," May 15, 1942, file 146-28-26, Justice Department, Washington, D.C.

24. George A. Barnes to Ulric Bell, May 8, 1942, record group 208, 002.11, E-5, box 3, May 1–30 folder, National Archives.

25. Lawrence M. C. Smith, "Memorandum for the Attorney General," May 15, 1942, File 146-28-26, Justice Department.

26. John H. Sengstacke to Ulric Bell, April 11, 1942, record group 208, 002.11, entry 5, box 3, National Archives.

27. See John H. Sengstacke to Theordore Berry, June 2, 1942, record group 208, 055-S, box 8, National Archives; and Percival Prattis to Pat Prattis, August 1, 1942, Percival Prattis papers, Series B, box 2, People's Committee to Send Dickerson to Congress folder,

Manuscript Division, Moorland–Spingarn Research Center, Howard University, Washington, D.C.

28. See John H. Sengstacke to Byron Price, April 11, 1942; John H. Sengstacke to Eleanor Roosevelt, April 14, 1942; and John H. Sengstacke to Byron Price, June 3, 1942. All are in record group 216, 012-D/8, Negro Press folder, National Archives.

29. For information on the Office of Censorship's voluntary code of wartime practices, see the news release announcing it on January 14, 1942. This can be found in record group 28, file no. 103777-E, case no. E-10, National Archives.

30. Memorandum, Bill Steven to Byron Price, March 11, 1942, record group 216, file 012, Propaganda folder, National Archives.

31. J.H.S, to Byron Price, April 17, 1942, record group 216, 012-D/8, Negro Press folder, National Archives. Which *Pittsburgh Courier* article Sorrells was referring to is unknown.

32. See Archibald MacLeish to Byron Price, March 12, 1942; and Byron Price to Archibald MacLeish, March 14, 1942. Both are in record group 216, 012-D/8, Negro Press folder, National Archives. The Censorship Policy Board was established by Roosevelt when he created the Office of Censorship on December 19, 1941. Its purpose was to "advise the Director of Censorship with respect to policy and the coordination and integration of the censorship" ordered by the president. Serving originally with Walker on the eight-person board were the vice-president, the secretary of the Treasury, the secretary of War, the secretary of the Navy, the attorney general, the director of the Office of Facts and Figures, and the director of the Office of Government Reports. In June 1942, the latter two members were replaced by the director of the Office of War Information. See White House, "Executive Order: Establishing the Office of Censorship and Prescribing Its Functions and Duties," December 19, 1941, Frank C. Walker papers, box 49, Censorship Board folder, University of Notre Dame Archives, Notre Dame, Ind.; and *Federal Records of World War II, Civilian Agencies*, Vol. 1 (Washington, D.C.: U.S. Government Printing Office, 1950), p. 321.

33. William O. Walker to Byron Price, undated; and Byron Price to William O. Walker, May 18, 1942. Both are in record group 216, 012-D/8, Negro Press folder, National Archives.

34. An example of action taken by the Office of Censorship occurred in late May and early June of 1942 with the *Washington Times–Herald*. When the paper ran an article about 2100 officers going to London to set up a branch of the War Department, Price angrily

wrote publisher Eleanor Patterson, complaining that the story violated the censorship guidelines and wanting to know why it was published. He also threatened to publicly castigate the paper, but did not do so when Patterson apologized for the oversight and promised that there would be "no recurrence of this mistake." See Memorandum, Stephen Early to Byron Price, May 29, 1942; Byron Price to Eleanor Patterson, May 29, 1942; Byron Price to Stephen Early, May 30, 1942; Telegram, Eleanor Patterson to Byron Price, June 1, 1942; and Byron Price to Eleanor Patterson, June 2, 1942. All are in the Stephen T. Early papers, box 14, Byron Price folder, Roosevelt Library.

35. The army began planning for the wartime censorship of mail moving in and out of the country in September 1939, and it immediately put the plans into effect when Pearl Harbor was bombed on December 7, 1941. Roosevelt then delegated mail censorship to the Office of Censorship when the agency was established on December 19, but the army's censorship personnel were not transferred there formally until March 15, 1942. See Office of Censorship, "General Outline of Testimony to Be Given Before the Senate Judiciary Committee with Respect to H.R. 7151," undated; and Byron Price to Sam Rayburn, January 21, 1943. Both are in the Frank C. Walker papers, box 49, Censorship Board folder, University of Notre Dame Archives. Also see *Federal Records of World War II*, pp. 318–19.

36. See Col. George C. Van Dusen to Lt. Col. W. Preston Corderman, March 9, 1942; and Maj. Chet W. Wadsworth to District Postal Censor, Miami, March 14, 1942. Both are in record group 216, file 007-B/2, National Archives. Also see Jas. R. Stewart, "Let's Face the Truth," *New Negro World*, February 1942, pp. 1–2.

37. Office of Censorship, "National Censorship Form," March 28, 1942, record group 216, 012-D/8, Negro Press folder, National Archives.

38. See Telegrams, Van Dusen to CCC, August 4, August 7, and August 23, 1942. All are in record group 216, file 007-B/2, National Archives. Both the August 7 telegram (about the *New Negro World*) and the August 23 telegram (about the *Pittsburgh Courier*) have the word "condemn" written on them. However, it is unclear whether either was condemned because no documents can be located to show that such an order was given to the district postal examiner.

39. See I. Kingsley Hope to the *Chicago Defender*, April 20, 1942; John H. Sengstacke to Byron Price, June 3, 1942; and Byron Price to

John H. Sengstacke, June 12, 1942. All are in record group 216, 012-D/8, Negro Press folder, National Archives.

40. Francis Biddle, *In Brief Authority* (Garden City, N.Y.: Doubleday, 1962), p. 186.

41. "War Department Denies Ban on Newspapers and Magazines," *Pittsburgh Courier*, March 8, 1941.

42. Adjutant General's Office, War Department, "Donations of Reading Material to Service Club Libraries," June 24, 1941, record group 407, AG 461, National Archives. Also see 1st Lt. Elias C. Townsend to Assistant Chief of Staff, G-2, Atlanta, July 1, 1941, record group 165, MID 10110-2452-1160, box 3085, National Archives.

43. War Department, "Special Service Officer," May 12, 1942, record group 407, file 062.11, TM 21-205, National Archives.

44. Adjutant General's Office, War Department, "Undesirable Literature in Camps," June 18, 1942, record group 407, AG 461, National Archives.

45. See Ibid.; Adjutant General's Office, War Department, "Undesirable Literature in Camps," June 28, 1942; and A. Hoeppel to Adjutant General, July 7, 1942. All are in record group 407, AG 461, National Archives.

46. See " 'No Clamp for Press'—Stimson," *Pittsburgh Courier*, May 30, 1942; and "For Alien-Tongue Press," *New York Times*, May 22, 1942.

47. McGeorge Bundy and Henry L. Stimson, *On Active Service in Peace and War* (New York: Harper, 1947), pp. 461–64.

48. John J. McCloy to Francis Biddle, March 24, 1942, record group 107, ASW 291.2 (Negro Troops 1942), box 35, National Archives.

49. U.S. Army, "Inflammatory Propaganda," undated, record group 107, file 291.2, National Archives.

50. G-2, "Japanese Racial Agitation among American Negroes," April 15, 1942, record group 107, file 291.2, National Archives. The army's wartime investigation of the black press was not limited solely to reports from camp officers and examinations of black publications. Military Intelligence also placed an undercover agent on the *Michigan Chronicle* in Detroit, and he worked there undetected throughout the war, claims Sengstacke. No other such incidents are known. Interview, John H. Sengstacke, April 21, 1983.

51. Eugene Katz to William Bryant, May 15, 1942, record group 44, entry 170, box 1830, Groups and Organizations–Negroes folder, National Archives.

52. Memorandum, Maj. Gen. George V. Strong to Assistant Chief of Staff, G-3, May 29, 1942, record group 165, 291.21, box 43, Volume 1 Thru August 1943 folder, National Archives.

53. Memorandum, Maj. Gen. George V. Strong to Assistant Chief of Staff, G-3, June 17, 1942, record group 165, 291.21, box 43, Volume 1 Thru August 1943 folder, National Archives. The black press discovered the statistical survey in mid-May, when an enlisted man at Fort Eustis in Virginia gave one of the questionnaires to a reporter from the *Norfolk Journal and Guide*. Out of thirty wide-ranging questions, ten dealt with black newspapers. The questions included, "Do you think that the Negro newspapers are serving the best interests of the Negro?" "Do [you] think the attacks against the army, navy and government by Negro newspapers are helping to improve the situation?" "Do you think that Negro newspapers have much influence over colored soldiers?" and "Do you think that Negro newspapers tend to make the Negro dissatisified?" P. B. Young, president of the *Journal and Guide*, thought the questionnaire came from the Office of Facts and Figures and wrote MacLeish on May 21 to ask for the "motive" behind it. Assistant OFF Director Ulric Bell told Young that an investigation would be made to determine its origin and purpose, but no documents show that Young ever received any information. A comparison of the questionnaire sent in by Young with statistics cited by the army in its June 17 report leaves little doubt that the questionnaire was the one used by the army in its survey. See P. B. Young to Archibald MacLeish, May 21, 1942; and Ulric Bell to P. B. Young, Sr., May 26, 1942. Both are in record group 208, E-5, box 6, folder 033, Jan.–May 30, National Archives.

54. Truman K. Gibson, Jr., to Roy Wilkins, April 10, 1942, record group 107, Hastie Files, Press folder, National Archives.

55. Roy Wilkins to Truman K. Gibson, Jr., May 7, 1942, record group 107, Hastie Files, Press folder, National Archives.

56. William H. Hastie to Roy Wilkins, May 11, 1942, record group 107, Hastie Files, Press folder, National Archives.

57. Truman K. Gibson, Jr., to Roy Wilkins, May 22, 1942, record group 107, Hastie Files, Press folder, National Archives.

58. See Memorandum, William H. Hastie to John J. McCloy, June 30, 1942; and Memorandum, John J. McCloy to Judge Hastie, July 2, 1942. Both are in record group 107, ASW 291.2 (Negro Troops 1942), box 35, National Archives.

59. John H. Sengstacke to John J. McCloy, July 11, 1942, record group

107, ASW 291.2 (Negro Troops 1942), box 35, National Archives.

60. Ulysses Lee, *United States Army in World War II: Special Studies: The Employment of Negro Troops*, Vol. 8, no. 8 (Washington, D.C.: Office of the Chief of Military History, U.S. Army, 1966), p. 383.

61. Memorandum, Maj. Gen. A. D. Surles to Assistant Chief of Staff, G-3, August 31, 1942, record group 165, 291.21, box 43, Volume 1 Thru August 1943 folder, National Archives.

62. Maxine Block, ed., *Current Biography: Who's Who and Why, 1940* (New York: H. H. Wilson, 1940), pp. 833–35.

63. Beverly Smith, "Everybody's Lawyer," *American Magazine*, April 1942, p. 52.

64. Post Office Department, Press Release, September 21, 1941, Frank C. Walker papers, box 101, 9/20/41 French Lick Springs, Ind., Democratic Editorial Assn. of Indiana folder, University of Notre Dame Archives.

65. "Address of Hon. Frank C. Walker, Postmaster General of the United States, delivered from the steps of the Sub-Treasury Building, New York, N.Y., at the Celebration of the 150th Anniversary of the Bill of Rights, September 25, 1941," Frank C. Walker papers, box 101, 9/25/41 150th Anniversary Bill of Rights Sub. Treasury Bldg. New York City folder, University of Notre Dame Archives.

66. "Tarnished Silver Shirt," *Newsweek*, April 13, 1942, p. 30. Herbert Wechsler, who worked in the Justice Department from 1940 to 1946 and knew Walker, recalled that the postmaster general was always seeking favorable publicity. "He was a politician," said Wechsler. "He would just do what people liked, what would look good." Interview, Herbert Wechsler, March 22, 1985.

67. See "Voices of Defeat," *Life*, April 13, 1942, p. 86; and Walter K. Belknap to Calvin W. Hassell, April 14, 1942, record group 28, file no. 103777-E, case no. E-47, National Archives.

68. Private typewritten notes, Francis Biddle, "March 20, 1942," Francis Biddle papers, Cabinet Meetings, Jan.–June 1942 folder, Roosevelt Library.

69. Memorandum, James Rowe, Jr., to Francis Biddle, April 29, 1942, Francis Biddle papers, James H. Rowe, Jr., folder, Roosevelt Library. According to Rowe, Walker took a "beating" from Roosevelt.

70. See Memoranda, Wendell Berge to the Attorney General, May 1 and May 20, 1942, Wendell Berge papers, box 24, Jan.–June 1942 folder, Library of Congress, Washington, D.C. Also see the following *New York Times* articles: "Philadelphia Paper Barred from Mail," May 1, 1942; "Mails Shut to X-Ray as Seditious Weekly,"

May 2, 1942; "Publicity, A Weekly, Barred from Mails," May 9, 1942; "Herold Loses Mail Right," May 15, 1942; and "Mails Closed to X-Ray," June 9, 1942. Also see Post Office Department, "Second Class Cases," March 4, 1944; and Post Office press releases of April 26, May 5, May 9, and June 8, 1942. All are in the Frank C. Walker papers, box 46, Committee on Freedom of the Press (Lasswell) folder, University of Notre Dame Archives.

71. Post Office Department, Press Release, June 8, 1942, Frank C. Walker papers, box 46, Committee on Freedom of the Press (Lasswell) folder, University of Notre Dame Archives.

72. "Coughlin Weekly Ends Publication," *New York Times*, May 5, 1942.

73. William L. Shirer, "The Poison Pen," *Atlantic Monthly*, May 1942, pp. 548, 550.

74. *Annual Report of the Postmaster General for the Fiscal Year Ended June 30, 1942* (Washington, D.C.: U.S. Government Printing Office, 1942), p. 29. Included among the publications examined during the war's first seven months were some of the country's largest white newspapers: the *Chicago Daily News*, the *Chicago Herald–American* and *PM*. By the time the war ended, the Post Office also had examined issues of *The New Republic*, the *Hartford Courant*, the *Detroit Free Press*, the *New York Daily News*, the *Chicago Tribune*, the *Minneapolis Tribune*, and the *New York World–Telegram*. Some of the examinations were extensive. Both the *Chicago Tribune* and the *New York Daily News* were studied for thirty months, the *Minneapolis Tribune* was examined for sixteen months, and the *Detroit Free Press* was checked for fifteen months. For information on the examinations, see record group 28, file no. 103777-E, case nos. E-3-A, E-109, E-111, E-111-A, E-111-C, E-129, E-135, E-185-A, E-185-B, E-187, E-220, E-263, E263-A, E-263-B, E-263-C, E-444, and E-444-A, National Archives.

75. Private typewritten notes, Francis Biddle, "May 22, 1942," Francis Biddle papers, Cabinet Meetings, Jan.–June 1942 folder, Roosevelt Library.

76. Solicitor to Third Assistant in Division of Classification, May 7, 1942, record group 28, file no. 103777-E, case no. E-56, National Archives.

77. Manherz to O'Brien, May 15, 1942, record group 28, file no. 103777-E, case no. E-56, National Archives.

78. See Memoranda, Manherz to O'Brien, May 25, May 26, May 28, May 29, and June 26, 1942. All are in record group 28, file no. 103777-E, case no. E-56, National Archives.

79. Information on the examinations can be found in record group
    28, file no. 103777-E, case nos. E-122, E-128, E-134, and E-208,
    National Archives. In addition to the examination of individual
    issues, the Post Office solicitor compiled a list of about 600 pos-
    sibly seditious items in the *Chicago Defender, Pittsburgh Courier,*
    and *People's Voice* in late May 1942 and sent it to the Justice
    Department. The latter was unimpressed. An in-house memo-
    randum concluded that "in no manner do the findings give a
    rounded description of the contents of the Negro press" because
    only "undesirable" items were included in the Post Office's list
    of articles. See Memorandum, "Re: The Negro Press," June 2,
    1942, file 146-28-380, Justice Dept.
80. See Lawrence M. C. Smith to Calvin W. Hassell, July 22,
    1942; Vincent Miles to Cleveland Postmaster, July 24, 1942;
    M. F. O'Donnell to Solicitor, August 4, 1942; Memorandum,
    O'Brien to Breen, August 7, 1942; Calvin W. Hassell to L. M. C.
    Smith, August 6, 1942; Chester T. Lane to Calvin Hassell, August
    19, 1942; and Vincent M. Miles to Cleveland Postmaster, August
    20, 1942. All are in record group 28, file no. 103777-E, case no.
    E-208, National Archives.
81. J. Percy H. Johnson, ed., *N. W. Ayer & Son's Directory of Newspapers
    and Periodicals, 1942* (Philadelphia: N. W. Ayer & Son, 1942), pp.
    231, 1252–53.
82. See Memoranda, Breen to O'Brien, June 8 and June 10, 1942. Both
    are in record group 28, file no. 103777-E, case no. E-134, National
    Archives.
83. Calvin W. Hassell to L. M. C. Smith, June 10, 1942, record group
    28, file no. 103777-E, case no. E-134, National Archives.
84. See Memorandum, Ralph S. Boyd to Lawrence M. C. Smith, June
    30, 1942; and L. M. C. Smith to Calvin Hassell, June 30, 1942.
    Both are in record group 28, file no. 103777-E, case no. E-134,
    National Archives.
85. Memorandum, G. Breen to O'Brien, July 7, 1942, record group
    28, file no. 103777-E, case no. E-134, National Archives. This was
    not the first time during this period that the Justice Department
    had angered the Post Office over seditious publications. Several
    months before, Biddle and Assistant Attorney General Rowe had
    met with Walker on the controversial *Social Justice* case. Walker
    stressed that he wanted the Justice Department's backing if he
    attempted to take away the publication's second-class mailing
    permit, and Biddle promised to support him. However, Biddle
    became busy with other wartime matters and did not provide all

of the public support he had promised, giving the misleading impression that the Post Office was moving against the publication primarily by itself. As it turned out, Coughlin ceased publication before a hearing on his second-class mailing permit. However, Walker was so angry at Biddle for not keeping his word on a matter that could have caused the Post Office great embarrassment that, as Rowe recalled, Walker refused to speak to Biddle for the remainder of the war, although they saw each other constantly at Cabinet meetings. Interview, James Henry Rowe, Jr., March 1, 1983.

86. Calvin W. Hassell to L. M. C. Smith, November 24, 1942, record group 28, file no. 103777-E, case no. E-304, National Archives.

87. Memorandum, O'Brien to Haynes, November 23, 1942, record group 28, file no. 103777-E, case no. E-292, National Archives.

88. Lucius C. Harper, "Dustin' Off the News," *Chicago Defender*, May 30, 1942.

89. C.W.H., "Memorandum for the Office Files: The Chicago Defender," June 26, 1942, record group 28, file no. 103777-E, case no. E-128, National Archives. Whether Walker or the journalists requested the meeting is unknown.

90. John H. Sengstacke to Frank C. Walker, July 11, 1942, record group 28, file no. 103777-E, case no. 128, National Archives.

91. See Washburn, "The *Pittsburgh Courier*'s Double V Campaign in 1942"; and Pat Washburn, "The *Pittsburgh Courier* and Black Workers in 1942," paper delivered at the Sixty-sixth Annual Meeting of the Association for Education in Journalism and Mass Communication, Corvallis, Ore., August 8, 1983.

92. Photograph, *Pittsburgh Courier*, May 23, 1942.

93. A number of researchers have noted this conservatism and the effect it had on the black press. For example, see Lunabelle Wedlock, *The Reaction of Negro Publications and Organizations to German Anti-Semitism* (Washington, D.C.: Howard University Studies in the Social Sciences, III, no. 2, 1942), pp. 116–17.

94. There was no question that the excess profits tax resulted in more advertising. A black publishers' magazine noted in February 1944 that the tax had brought about a "mild advertising boom" in black publications since the U.S. entered the war. See "A Memo to Negro Advertising Men," *PEP: Negro Publisher, Editor and Printer*, February 1944, p. 21.

95. The first large white corporation to advertise in the *Pittsburgh Courier* during World War II was Philip Morris, which bought a quarter-page ad on April 11, 1942. The ad was not a total surprise.

In the summer of 1941, Philip Morris placed experimental ads in three large black newspapers to see what effect they would have. See Vera Chandler Foster and Jessie P. Guzman, "The Negro Press," in *Negro Year Book, 1941–46*, ed. Jessie Parkhurst Guzman (Tuskegee, Ala.: Tuskegee Institute, 1947), p. 390.

96. Thomas Sancton, "The Negro Press," *New Republic*, April 26, 1943, p. 560.
97. Vishnu V. Oak, *The Negro Newspaper* (Yellow Springs, Ohio: Antioch Press, 1948), pp. 47–48.
98. Interview, John H. Sengstacke, April 21, 1983.
99. See John H. Sengstacke to Franklin D. Roosevelt, July 29, 1942; Stephen Early to John H. Sengstacke, August 4, 1942; Elmer Davis to Stephen Early, September 5, 1942; and Franklin D. Roosevelt to John Sengstacke, September 9, 1942. All are in the President's Personal File 6943, Roosevelt Library.
100. John H. Sengstacke to Truman K. Gibson, August 31, 1942, record group 107, Hastie Files, Press folder, National Archives.

Chapter 6

1. For more information on the examinations, see record group 28, file no. 103777-E, case nos. E-56, E-208, E-280, and E-292, National Archives, Washington, D.C.
2. Memorandum, O'Brien to Manherz, November 7, 1942, record group 28, file no. 103777-E, case no. E-280, National Archives.
3. Memorandum, O'Brien to Haynes, November 23, 1942, record group 28, file no. 103777-E, case no. E-292, National Archives.
4. See Memoranda, O'Brien to Haynes, December 2, 1942, record group 28, file no. 103777-E, case no. E-292, National Archives; and Lawrence M. C. Smith to Calvin W. Hassell, January 22 and 29, 1943, file 146-28-380, Justice Dept., Washington, D.C.
5. See Calvin W. Hassell to L. M. C. Smith, October 21, October 28, November 7, November 16, November 27, and December 29, 1942. All are in record group 28, file no. 103777-E, case no. E-56, National Archives.
6. See Memorandum, Breen to O'Brien, October 14, 1942, file 146-7-64-354; and Lawrence M. C. Smith to Calvin W. Hassell, December 8, 1942, and January 29, 1943, file 146-28-380, Justice Dept.
7. See Memoranda, Manherz to O'Brien, November 6 and December 31, 1942, and February 4, 1943. All are in record group 28, file no. 103777-E, case no. E-56, National Archives.
8. Memorandum, Manherz to O'Brien, November 13, 1942, record

group 28, file no. 103777-E, case no. E-56, National Archives.
9. Memorandum, Coral Sadler to D. W. Barco, October 29, 1942, file 146-7-64-354, Justice Dept. For an example of how such reasoning was followed in future Justice Department decisions involving the black press, see Memorandum, Barrington Moore, Jr., to Eugene F. Roth, December 24, 1942, in the same file.
10. Memorandum, D. Newcomb Barco, Jr., to Lawrence M. C. Smith, October 29, 1942, file 146-7-64-354, Justice Dept.
11. Examples of typical Justice Department replies to the Post Office can be found in record group 28, file no. 103777-E, case no E-56, National Archives.
12. Interview, Herbert Wechsler, March 22, 1985.
13. Memorandum, Breen to O'Brien, October 3, 1942, record group 28, file no. 103777-E, case no. E-208, National Archives.
14. See Calvin W. Hassell to L. M. C. Smith, October 6, 1942; and Lawrence M. C. Smith to Calvin W. Hassell, October 16, 1942. Both are in record group 28, file no. 103777-E, case no. E-208, National Archives.
15. Calvin W. Hassell to L. M. C. Smith, November 24, 1942, record group 28, file no. 103777-E, case no. E-304, National Archives.
16. WCO'B, "Memorandum," December 1, 1942, record group 28, file no. 103777-E, case no. E-326, National Archives.
17. See Ibid.; and C.W.H., "Memorandum," December 2, 1942. Both are in record group 28, file no. 103777-E, case no. E-326, National Archives. These are the only known accounts of the conference. Under a Freedom of Information Act request, the Justice Department checked its files but was unable to find any "notes, minutes or memoranda" on the December 1, 1942, meeting. Miriam M. Nisbet to Pat Washburn, March 23, 1984.
18. Memorandum, Breen to O'Brien, January 12, 1943, record group 28, file no. 103777-E, case no. E-208, National Archives.
19. See U.S. Congress, *Congressional Record*, 78th Cong., 1st sess., 1943, 89, pt. 2: 1819–21; and Dorothy Ganfield Fowler, *Unmailable* (Athens: University of Georgia Press, 1977), pp. 146–47. In addition to congressional pressure for more suppressions, Post Office files show that the department received numerous letters from citizens demanding an end to seditious publications. For example, a New York attorney complained to the Post Office on June 28, 1943, about material mailed by "subversive elements." "Such lawless use of the mails cannot be defended under the constitutional guarantees of free speech," wrote Jerome F. Cohen. "The Constitution was intended to promote 'a more perfect Union'

of our people, and was never intended to constitute a license to incite one group against another by the spread of poisonous propoganda [sic]." Jerome F. Cohen to Frank C. Walker, June 28, 1943, record group 28, file no. 103777-E, case no. E-12, National Archives. Also see case nos. E-3-A and E-16 in the same file.

20. *Annual Report of the Postmaster General for the Fiscal Year Ended June 30, 1943* (Washington, D.C.: U.S. Government Printing Office, 1944), p. 31.

21. Post Office Department, "Second Class Cases," March 4, 1944, Frank C. Walker papers, box 46, Committee on Freedom of the Press (Lasswell) folder, University of Notre Dame Archives, Notre Dame, Ind. The *Boise Valley Herald* had its permit revoked on October 8, 1942, after the Post Office concluded that it was attempting "to embarrass and defeat the Government in its effort to prosecute the war to a successful termination." *The Militant* lost its permit on March 3, 1943. According to a letter from Attorney General Biddle, which was read at the revocation hearing, "Since December 7, 1941, this publication has openly discouraged participation in the war by the masses of the people. It is permeated with the thesis that the war is being fought solely for the benefit of the ruling groups and will serve merely to continue the enslavement of the working classes." Biddle added that the publication derided democracy and the "four freedoms," attacked Britain, charged that the United States was a "Fascist" collaborator, and incited race problems. Biddle's letter was particularly interesting because it showed a willingness to continue helping the Post Office with sedition cases on a limited basis, even after the December 1942 impasse. See Post Office press releases of October 9, 1942, and March 8, 1943. Both can be found in the Frank C. Walker papers, box 46, Committee on Freedom of the Press (Lasswell) folder, University of Notre Dame Archives.

22. *Freedom in Wartime* (New York: American Civil Liberties Union, 1943), p. 55.

23. See *Annual Report of the Postmaster General for the Fiscal Year Ended June 30, 1944* (Washington, D.C.: U.S. Government Printing Office, 1945), p. 49; *Annual Report of the Postmaster General for the Fiscal Year Ended June 30, 1945* (Washington, D.C.: U.S. Government Printing Office, 1946), p. 28; *In Defense of Our Liberties* (New York: American Civil Liberties Union, 1944), p. 43; and *Liberty on the Home Front* (New York: American Civil Liberties Union, 1945), p. 48.

24. "Conference Held Between Mr. O'Brien And Attorneys of the

Espionage Section," July 16, 1943, record group 28, file no. 103777-E, case no. E-326, National Archives.

25. It is impossible to determine the exact date of the meeting. Walter White, in *A Man Called White*, mentions only that it was in December 1942. White's diary for that month has a notation for December 1, "3 Prs. R. at White House," but the subject of their meeting is not listed. This is the only meeting with the president listed that month in the diary. However, neither Roosevelt's appointment calendar nor the White House "Usher's Diary" shows that the president met with White on December 1, 1942, or any other day that month. Donald B. Schewe, former assistant director of the Roosevelt Library in Hyde Park, N.Y., has suggested that the two may have met "informally, at some other place other than the White House." He also noted that White's conversation may have taken place when White was at the White House to see someone else, in which case neither the appointment calendar nor the "Usher's Diary" would have shown him meeting with Roosevelt. See Walter White, *A Man Called White* (1948; reprint ed., Bloomington: Indiana University Press, 1970), pp. 207–8; Walter White, "1942 Diary," James Weldon Johnson Memorial Collection, Manuscripts, Walter F. White, Miscellaneous 58, Collection of American Literature, The Beinecke Rare Book and Manuscript Library, Yale University, New Haven, Conn.; and Donald B. Schewe to Pat Washburn, October 10, 1980.

26. Walter White to Carter Wesley, January 16, 1943, Arthur Barnett Spingarn papers, box 10, Jan. 1–Feb. 11, 1943, folder, Library of Congress, Washington, D.C.

27. Walter White, *A Man Called White*, early manuscript version, typescript, episode 17, pp, 7–8, James Weldon Johnson Memorial Collection, Manuscripts, Walter F. White, 14, Collection of American Literature, The Beinecke Rare Book and Manuscript Library, Yale University. In the final version of his book, White (p. 208) mentioned that editors of the twenty-four largest black newspapers were invited to the conference, but he did not say who or how many came.

28. "Washington to Hush Negro Press," *California Eagle*, May 28, 1942.

29. Interview, John H. Sengstacke, April 21, 1983. Sengstacke's account of the conference is the only other one besides White's in *A Man Called White* (p. 208).

30. White, *A Man Called White*, p. 208.

31. Wallace Lee, "Negro Digest Poll," *Negro Digest*, February 1943, p. 54. The black press knew, however, that it could not afford to

tone down completely. On the same day that White was meeting with the editors in New York, the *Pittsburgh Courier* reported a poll that showed 91.2 percent of the respondents approving of the black press's campaign "for the full integration of the race into the life of America." While such a result was gratifying to black publishers, it also was a warning from readers that circulation, which was the lifeblood of the black press, might decline if the newspapers toned down. See "Citizens Endorse Crusade of the Negro Press," *Pittsburgh Courier*, January 23, 1943.

32. White, *A Man Called White*, p. 208. Even if the story of the WPB's cutback is true, it still is unclear wheri it began. White's book suggests that it started after his talk with Roosevelt. However, in an early draft of the book, he wrote that before his meeting with the president he had learned that "a quiet movement was under way to eliminate or greatly weaken Negro newspapers by denying them newsprint." Why he changed his story between the early draft of the book and the final draft is unknown. See White, *A Man Called White*, early manuscript version, p. 5.

33. Interview, John H. Sengstacke, April 21, 1983.

34. John T. McCutcheon, Jr., to Pat Washburn, June 23, 1983.

35. Peter B. B. Andrews, "History of the Printing and Publishing Division (During World War II—1941–45)," October 31, 1945, p. 115, record group 179, WPB 052.2408 R, National Archives. For other denials that the WPB discriminated illegally against any publications, see Donald J. Sterling to Donald M. Nelson, April 27, 1943, record group 179, file 052.2402, WPB–Personnel folder; and Memorandum, Bertrand Fox to J. A. Krug, January 2, 1945, record group 179, WPB 552.51, Newsprint-Supply folder. Both are in the National Archives.

36. "Statement to the Truman Committee by Carroll Hanson, Chief of the Newspaper Section, Printing and Publishing Division, War Production Board," undated, record group 179, WPB 052.2404, WPB–Administration folder, National Archives. Although this document is undated, material in it indicates that it was written in the first five months of 1944.

37. In 1960, George Schuyler, the *Pittsburgh Courier*'s outspoken and widely read World War II columnist, told an interviewer that the government "felt that it couldn't be in the position [during the war] of being accused of having curtailed the Negro press, by cutting its quota of newsprint." However, this cannot be taken as evidence that no illegal cutback ever occurred, because Schuyler had nothing to do with the business end of the newspaper.

It could have occurred without him knowing about it. Interview, George S. Schuyler to William Ingersoll, November 7, 1960, p. 584, "The Reminiscenses of George S. Schuyler," copywritten by the Trustees of Columbia University in the City of New York, 1975, and used by their permission.

38. G-2, "The Negro Problem and Its Factors," November 9, 1942, record group 165, MID 291.2, G-2 Regional Files, 1933–44, box 3020, National Archives.

39. See Mrs. Dwight T. Reed, "Mother of Demoted Camp Lee Soldier Writes AFRO," *Baltimore Afro-American*, January 2, 1943; and "St. Paul Civic Groups Ask Investigation of Camp Lee," *Norfolk Journal and Guide*, January 2, 1943.

40. See Maj. Gen. James E. Edmonds to Adjutant General, December 31, 1942; and Memorandum, Col. J. S. Leonard to Chief of Staff, March 16, 1943. Both are in ASW 291.2, box 35, Negro Troops–Committee folder, National Archives.

41. See Ulysses Lee, *United States Army in World War II: Special Studies: The Employment of Negro Troops*, Vol. 8, no. 8 (Washington, D.C.: Office of the Chief of Military History, U.S. Army, 1966), p. 158; and Memorandum, Adjutant General's Office to John J. McCloy, August 27, 1942, record group 107, ASW 291.2, box 35, Negro Troops–Committee folder, National Archives.

42. See Memorandum, Col. J. S. Leonard to Chief of Staff, March 16, 1943; and Col. J. S. Leonard, "Minutes of Meeting of Advisory Committee on Negro Troop Policies," March 22, 1943. Both are in record group 107, ASW 291.2, box 35, Negro Troops–Committee folder, National Archives.

43. See Col. F. S. Doll to Assistant Chief of Staff, G-2, February 20, 1943, file 100-63963-28, Federal Bureau of Investigation, Washington, D.C.: and Ira F. Lewis to Maj. Gen. A. D. Surles, April 9, 1943, record group 107, Special Assistant to the Secretary of War (Hastie files), Press folder, National Archives. It is unclear whether the editors from the *Courier* and the *Afro-American* told the other black newspapers about Prattis's talk with Surles. On April 19, in a "confidential" message to subscribing editors, the Associated Negro Press noted rumors that editors from the two largest black papers had been called to Washington to discuss what the soldier had said in his trial testimony. Whether the ANP ever discovered, however, that the story represented more than a rumor is unknown. Evidence also is lacking to show that anyone from the *Afro-American* talked to army officials about the soldier's testimony. In the same letter to editors, the ANP said it was

rumored in Chicago that the Post Office was "holding, opening, examining and copying" mail to the news service and then sending it to the FBI. The ANP admitted that it had been unable to determine if this was true, but it advised editors to check their mail. "These are war times," it said, "and while these rumors may be unfounded we think we should share them with you for the protection of the craft." A copy of the ANP note was obtained by the Justice Department, which supports the rumor of mail being opened, and sent to the Post Office in early May. Lawrence M. C. Smith to Calvin Hassell, May 5, 1943, record group 28, file no. 103777-E, case no. E-446, National Archives.

44. Typescript, "Remarks of Colonel E. R. Householder, Officer in Charge of Miscellaneous Division, Adjutant General's Department, War Department, At the Conference of Negro Newspaper Representatives, War Department, Munitions Building, Washington, D.C., December 8, 1941," record group 107, Press Releases folder, National Archives.

45. D. P. Ludwig, "Special Comment of the Agent on the 'Pittsburgh Courier' Case," May 15, 1943, file 100-31159-148, Federal Bureau of Investigation.

46. See Memorandum, Col. Lathe B. Row to Inspector General, July 16, 1943; and Memorandum, Brig. Gen. Philip E. Brown to John J. McCloy, July 24, 1943. Both are in record group 107, 291.2, Negro Troops folder, National Archives.

47. See "Confiscate Defender in Dixie Camp," *Chicago Defender*, July 24, 1943; and "Church Council Raps Dixie Attempts to Halt Sale of Negro Newspapers," *Chicago Defender*, July 31, 1943. It was not surprising that only Northern black newspapers apparently had problems in the South. Historian Lee Finkle has noted that by the summer of 1942, many Southern black papers had toned down and become cautious after attacks on the black press by three nationally known journalists: Virginius Dabney, editor of the *Richmond Times-Dispatch*; Westbrook Pegler, a nationally syndicated columnist; and Mark Ethridge, publisher of the *Louisville Courier–Journal* and *Times*. The papers backed off because they did not want to jeopardize a friendly relationship with Southern white liberals. An Office of Facts and Figures report of June 1942 substantiated the fact that Southern black newspapers could not be as bold as their Northern counterparts. "Negro newspapers in the South must, if they wish to exist, be more careful than newspapers in the North," it said. See Lee Finkle, *Forum for Protest* (Cranbury, N.J.: Associated University Presses, 1975), pp. 63–65;

and Bureau of Intelligence, Office of Facts and Figures, "Special Intelligence Report No. 48," June 25, 1942, record group 44, E-171, box 1845, National Archives.

48. Interview, Frank Bolden, January 14, 1983. Also see file 146-7-64-354, Justice Dept.; and files 44-682 and 100-31159, Federal Bureau of Investigation.

49. S. I. Hayakawa, "Second Thoughts," *Chicago Defender*, August 7, 1943. The black press was not without its white defenders, although none of them had the stature of Howard, Hearst, or McCormick. As historian Lee Finkle his noted in *Forum for Protest* (pp. 77–78), the "liberal white press began to defend the black press" in late 1942 and early 1943, when it "became aware of the paradox of a democratic America continuing its racial proscriptions while fighting Hitler." Among the publications supporting the black press were the *New Republic*, *The Nation*, and the *Harvard Guardian*. For a discussion of the white press's criticism and support of the black press during World War II, see Finkle, *Forum for Protest*, pp. 62–87.

50. Lee, *United States Army*, p. 384.

51. Ibid., pp. 380–81. Also see John J. McCloy to Herbert B. Elliston, August 5, 1943, record group 107, ASW 291.2 (Negro Troops), National Archives.

52. See Truman K. Gibson, Jr., to Carter Wesley, July 15, 1943; and Carter Wesley to Truman K. Gibson, Jr., August 3, 1943. Both are in record group 107, Special Assistant to the Secretary of War (Hastie files), Press folder, National Archives.

53. See Moss Hyles Kendrix to Byron Price, February 10, 1943; N. R. Howard to Byron Price, February 15, 1943; and Byron Price to Moss Hyles Kendrix, February 16, 1943. All are in record group 216, 012-D/8, Negro Press folder, National Archives.

54. The secrecy maintained by the censors was impressive considering the scope of their operations. In January 1943, for example, more than 1 million pieces of mail and about 70,000 cables, all moving in and out of the United States, passed daily through twenty postal stations and seventeen cable stations run by censors throughout the country. To ensure the secrecy of the mail and cables being examined, according to Price, the censors signed secrecy pledges and worked in guarded rooms, and any information taken from the mail or cables was delivered by a locked pouch only to government officials who promised that "the material will be used only for war purposes," according to Price. See *Federal Records of World War II, Civilian Agencies*, Vol. 1 (Wash-

ington, D.C.: U.S. Government Printing Office, 1950), p. 319; and Byron Price to Sam Rayburn, January 21, 1943, Frank C. Walker papers, box 49, Censorship Board folder, University of Notre Dame Archives.

55. It is surprising that the Office of Censorship did not also suppress *The Crisis* at this time. On January 9, 1943, Military Intelligence wrote to the chief postal censor to remind him that several issues of the magazine had been placed on the "not approved for export" list during the previous year. (This does not appear in the Office of Censorship records.) Even so, copies of *The Crisis* had shown up in Puerto Rico, and G-2 feared that the magazine's "highly inflammatory" articles would create problems between Americans and blacks in Latin America. It asked the censor to examine each issue of *The Crisis* closely, because Military Intelligence felt that the magazine's editorial policy was "inimical to the best interests of the United States in the Latin-American Theater." There is no evidence, however, that *The Crisis* was held up by censors at this time. Col. C. Knudsen to Chief Postal Censor, January 9, 1943, record group 216, file 007-B/2, National Archives.

56. See L. M. Quinn to District Postal Censor, March 11 and March 12, 1943; Charles W. Sherrill to Chief Postal Censor, March 13, 1943; M. A. J. Healy to District Postal Censor, March 16, 1943; Col. George C. Van Dusen to Chief Postal Censor, March 19, 1943; and Lt. Col. N. V. Carlson to L. M. Quinn, March 25, 1943. All are in record group 216, file 007-B/1, Condemned for Export folder, National Archives. The *Chicago Defender* was not the only publication that mistakenly had a "condemned" issue returned at this time. The same thing happened to the *Daily Worker*, a communist paper in New York. Col. George C. Van Dusen to Chief Postal Censor, March 21, 1943, record group 216, file 007-B/2, National Archives.

57. Office of Censorship, *"Political: Charges of Discrimination Toward Negroes,"* October 7, 1942, file 62-62736-2-8977, Federal Bureau of Investigation.

58. See Byron H. Spinney to Chief Postal Censor, May 14, 1943, record group 216, file 007-B/2, National Archives. It is unclear what is meant by the statement that "inflammatory racial material [in the *Racial Digest*] has frequently been condemned by this Station." No documents can be located showing that the Office of Censorship previously "condemned" an issue of the *Racial Digest* from export. It is possible that the district postal censor had

considered previous issues to be unmailable, only to be overruled by the chief postal censor.

59. See Eliot Janeway, "Fighting a White Man's War," p. 1, and "Are Negroes Citizens?" p. 13. Both are in *Racial Digest*, April 1943.

60. Rhoza A. Walker, "The Fifth Freedom," *Racial Digest*, April 1943, pp. 20–21.

61. M. A. J. Healy to District Postal Censor, May 19, 1943, record group 216, file 007-B/2, National Archives.

62. E. L. Harvey to Otten, May 24, 1944, record group 216, file 007, Complaints and Inquires P–Q folder, National Archives. The Office of Censorship order of July 27, 1943, cannot be located, and Harvey's letter to Otten is the only document that mentions it.

63. Black journalists continued to write to Roosevelt throughout this period of the war to assure him of the black press's loyalty. For example, the New Orleans Press Club wrote such a letter in October 1942, and the managing editor of the *Negro Digest* sent the president a similar message a month later. See Leon Lewis to Franklin D. Roosevelt, October 2, 1942; and John H. Johnson to Franklin D. Roosevelt, November 19, 1942. Both are in OF 93, box 5, Colored Matters (Negroes), 1942, July–Oct. folder, Roosevelt Library.

64. "Sengstacke, N.N.P.A. President," *PEP: Negro Publisher, Editor and Printer*, July 1943, p. 4.

65. "Colored Newspaper Publishers Confer with War Management," *Norfolk Journal and Guide*, July 24, 1943.

66. Carter Wesley, "Ram's Horn," *Houston Informer*, July 24, 1943.

67. War Production Board, Newspaper Industry Advisory Committee, "Summary of Meeting," October 19–20, 1943, record group 179, file 651.305 M, Newspapers–Industry Advisory Committee Meetings 1942–43 folder, National Archives. One of the black newspapers apparently caught in the newsprint crunch was the *Pittsburgh Courier*, whose circulation almost doubled during World War II. Ordinarily a twenty-four-page paper, it cut back to twenty pages on September 18, 1943, and remained between sixteen and twenty pages for the rest of the war. Readers were never given an explanation for the cutback.

68. "Minority Problems Laid Before Vice President, Other Officials," *Atlanta Daily World*, July 20, 1943.

69. The best account of the Searles affair appears in an Associated Negro Press article ("Probe to Be Made of Editor Suddenly Inducted Following Lynching Exposed by Paper") from an uniden-

tified paper in the Vertical Files, Newspapers III, at the Schomburg Center for Research in Black Culture in New York. The ANP story ran August 7, 1943, in the *Chicago Defender* ("Hit Revenge Draft of Ga. Race Editor"), but the *Defender* only used slightly more than half of the ANP article, and therefore its account was not nearly as detailed.

70. Finkle, *Forum for Protest*, pp. 83–84.
71. Memoradum, John J. McCloy to General Marshall, July 21, 1943, record group 107, ASW 291.2, Negro Troops box, Race–Alphabetical folder, National Archives.
72. John J. McCloy to John H. Sengstacke, August 5, 1943, record group 107, ASW 291.2 (Negro Troops), Civilian Aide files, National Archives.
73. John H. Sengstacke to John J. McCloy, August 26, 1943, record group 107, ASW 291.2 (Negro Troops), Civilian Aide files, National Archives.
74. See Office of War Information, Bureau of Intelligence, "Negroes in a Democarcy at War," September 4, 1942, record group 44, E-170, box 1830, Groups and Organizations II folder; Memorandum, Special Services Division to R. Keith Kane, November 2, 1942, record group 44, E-171, box 1843, folder 14; and Office of War Information, Bureau of Intelligence, "Project Outline," January 12, 1943, record group 44, E-170, box 1828. All are in the National Archives.
75. See Lawrence M. C. Smith to Milton Starr, January 29 and March 4, 1943, file 146-7-64-354, Justice Dept.
76. " 'OWI Feeds Negro Press with Paternalistic Pap'—Barnett," *Pittsburgh Courier*, November 28, 1942.
77. "Sengstacke, N.N.P.A. President," p. 4.
78. Finkle, *Forum for Protest*, p. 84.
79. "Negro Publishers to Advise OWI," *Amsterdam Star–News*, September 4, 1943.

Chapter 7

1. Robert Durr, *The Negro Press: Its Character, Development and Function* (Jackson: Mississippi Division, Southern Regional Council, 1947), pp. 2–3.
2. U.S. Congress, Senate Select Committee to Study Governmental Operations with Respect to Intelligence Activities, *Supplementary Detailed Staff Reports on Intelligence Activities and the Rights of Amer-*

icans, Vol. III, 94th Congress, 2d sess., 1976, S. Rept. 94-755, p. 403.

3. Ibid., pp. 404–5.
4. Ibid., p. 406.
5. Ibid., p. 405.
6. Ibid., pp. 410–11.
7. Ibid., pp. 412–17. Also see Jerry J. Berman et al., *The Lawless State: The Crimes of the U.S. Intelligence Agencies* (New York: Penguin, 1976), pp. 98–101.
8. Kenneth O'Reilly, "A New Deal for the FBI: The Roosevelt Administration, Control and National Security," *Journal of American History* 69, no. 3 (December 1982): 639. William W. Turner, who became an FBI agent in 1951, recalled finding the same political biases referred to by O'Reilly. "Very many agents in the FBI, I learned, were hostile not only to avowed Communists but to the entire left-of-center spectrum," he wrote. ". . . Once inside the Bureau subculture, the agent was indoctrinated in the belief that only J. Edgar Hoover's early recognition and exposure of the Communist menace had preserved the American way of life. The enemy was not only Communists and socialists, but 'those liberals' and 'dangerous-thinking one worlders.' . . . Agents who carried these demon beliefs into the field were plainly predisposed to slant reports, subconsciously if not deliberately." See William W. Turner, *Hoover's FBI: The Men and the Myth* (Los Angeles: Sherbourne Press, 1970), pp. 197–98.
9. W. G. Banister to Director, Federal Bureau of Investigation, November 23, 1942, file 100-20076, Federal Bureau of Investigation, Washington, D.C.
10. Francis Biddle, *In Brief Authority* (Garden City, N.Y.: Doubleday, 1962), p. 261.
11. Stephen Gillers and Pat Watters, eds., *Investigating the FBI* (Garden City, N.Y.: Doubleday, 1973), pp. 338–39.
12. Ibid.
13. Ovid Demaris, *The Director: An Oral Biography of J. Edgar Hoover* (New York: Harper's Magazine Press, 1975), p. 167.
14. Ibid., p. 168.
15. A sample of the FBI's World War II investigative reports on blacks and communism can be found in the agency's monthly "General Intelligence Survey in the United States." These are in OF 10B, FBI Reports 1942–45 folders, Roosevelt Library, Hyde Park, N.Y.
16. Demaris, *The Director*, p. 158. For a brief discussion of Communist attempts to recruit blacks in the 1920s and 1930s and why they

failed, see Benjamin Quarles, *The Negro in the Making of America*, rev. ed. (New York: Macmillan, Collier, 1969), pp. 204–7.

17. XXX [pseud.], "Washington Gestapo," *The Nation*, July 24, 1943, pp. 94–95.

18. David Wise, *The American Police State: The Government Against the People* (New York: Random House, 1976), p. 298. Also see Bill Brown and William C. Sullivan, *The Bureau: My Thirty Years in Hoover's FBI* (New York: W. W. Norton, 1979), pp. 268–69.

19. Sanford J. Ungar, *FBI* (Boston: Little, Brown, 1975), pp. 255–56, 328.

20. David J. Garrow, *The FBI and Martin Luther King, Jr.: From "Solo" to Memphis* (New York: W. W. Norton, 1981), p. 153.

21. Neil A. Wynn, "Black Attitudes Toward Participation in the American War Effort, 1941–45," *Afro-American Studies* 3, no. 1 (June 1972): 17–18.

22. Ibid., p. 18.

23. "Cut the Comedy," *Pittsburgh Courier*, January 17, 1942.

24. Joseph D. Bibb, "What Is He Thinking?" *Pittsburgh Courier*, May 16, 1942.

25. See Joseph D. Bibb, "Fools and Fanatics," *Pittsburgh Courier*, October 3, 1942; and "Black Hitler Gone," *Pittsburgh Courier*, January 9, 1943.

26. "The Pacific Movement," *Pittsburgh Courier*, August 8, 1942.

27. A. Philip Randolph, "Pro-Japanese Activities Among Negroes," *The Black Worker*, September 1942, p. 4.

28. Louis Martin, "Fifth Column Among Negroes," *Opportunity*, December 1942, pp. 358–59.

29. Interview, Frank Bolden, January 14, 1983.

30. George S. Schuyler, "Views and Reviews," *Pittsburgh Courier*, October 3, 1942.

31. "The Negro Press," *PEP: Negro Publisher, Editor and Printer*, September 1943, p. 19.

32. Martin, "Fifth Column Among Negroes," p. 359.

33. Ralph Matthews, "The Big Parade," *Baltimore Afro-American*, October 11, 1941.

34. See Lee Finkle, *Forum for Protest* (Cranbury, N.J.: Associated University Presses, 1975), pp. 200–201; Horace Cayton, "Our Confusion," *Pittsburgh Courier*, November 6, 1943; and "No Prejudice in Red Army," *Chicago Defender*, March 18, 1944.

35. Interview, Billy Rowe, January 3, 1983.

36. Interview, Frank Bolden, January 14, 1983.

37. Federal Bureau of Investigation, "Survey of Racial Conditions in

the United States," undated, pp. 359, 370, OF 10B, #2420, Justice
Dept., FBI, Reports folder, Roosevelt Library. A letter which was
sent with the report to the White House indicates that it was
completed in September 1943.

38. Interviews, Billy Rowe, January 3, 1983; Frank Bolden, January
14, 1983; and John H. Sengstacke, April 21, 1983.
39. Interview, Frank Bolden, January 14, 1983.
40. "PEP Salutes . . . Carl Murphy," *PEP: Negro Publisher, Editor and
Printer*, November 1943, p. 10. In another example of black ad-
miration for communism, the *Cleveland Call and Post* endorsed
Arnold S. Johnson, Ohio's communist leader, for a seat on Cleveland's Board of Education in October 1943. The paper said it
supported him because he recognized "the value of our schools
as agencies for making democracy live and work." The Communist Party's *Daily Worker* was ecstatic in announcing the endorsement. See "Ohio Negro Paper Backs Communist," *Daily
Worker*, October 22, 1943.
41. Interview, Billy Rowe, January 3, 1983.
42. Interview, John H. Sengstacke, April 21, 1983.
43. Interview, Frank Bolden, January 14, 1983. Examples of Hoover's
ongoing investigation of the connection between Communists
and blacks, with occasional references to the black press, can be
found in OF 4245G at the Roosevelt Library.
44. See E. E. Conroy to Director, FBI, March 18, 1943; Memorandum,
John Edgar Hoover to Wendell Berge, April 12, 1943; Memorandum, Wendell Berge to Director, Federal Bureau of Investigation,
April 30, 1943; Memorandum, John Edgar Hoover to Wendell
Berge, July 1, 1943; and Memorandum, Wendell Berge to Director,
Federal Bureau of Investigation, July 12, 1943. All are in file 100-
51230, Federal Bureau of Investigation.
45. See Memoranda, John Edgar Hoover to Wendell Berge, November
24, 1942; Wendell Berge to Director, Federal Bureau of Investigation, December 7, 1942; John Edgar Hoover to Wendell Berge,
March 26, 1943; John Edgar Hoover to Wendell Berge, May 3,
1943; John Edgar Hoover to Wendell Berge, May 29, 1943; John
Edgar Hoover to Wendell Berge, June 8, 1943; Wendell Berge to
Director, Federal Bureau of Investigation, June 12, 1943; and Wendell Berge to Director, Federal Bureau of Investigation, August
23, 1943. All are in file 100-63963, Federal Bureau of Investigation.
46. Federal Bureau of Investigation, "Survey of Racial Conditions in
the United States," p. 1. This was not the only report by the FBI
in 1943. The subjects of others included Venezuela (March), Chile

(March), El Salvador (April), Austrian group activities in the United States (May), Argentina (June), strategic facilities in Latin America (June), Unión Nacional Sinarquista (July), Cuba (August), Costa Rica (September), enemy sabotage equipment (November), Nationalist Party of Puerto Rico (November), and the Spanish Falange in the Western Hemisphere (December).

47. Walter Yust, ed., *1944 Britannica Book of the Year* (Chicago: Encyclopaedia Britannica, 1944), pp. 580–81.
48. J. Edgar Hoover to Maj. Gen. Edwin M. Watson, September 24, 1943, OF 10B, #2420, Justice Dept., FBI, Reports folder, Roosevelt Library. Roosevelt probably had more than a passing interest in Hoover's report. During the previous December and January, the president had directed Attorney General Biddle to confer with a number of blacks and whites about the country's black situation. Biddle's conclusion on January 29 was sobering. "There is widespread discontent among Negroes," he wrote Roosevelt. " . . . Politically I think the administration is losing the support of the Negro population." See Private typewritten notes, Francis Biddle, "December 11, 1942," Cabinet Meetings, July–Dec. 1942 folder; and Memorandum, Francis Biddle to Franklin D. Roosevelt, January 29, 1943, Civil Rights/Fair Employment folder. Both are in the Francis Biddle papers, Roosevelt Library.
49. Federal Bureau of Investigation, "Survey of Racial Conditions in the United States," pp. 1–2.
50. The report did not explain why it mentioned less than half of the country's black publications. If only those had been listed that were considered inflammatory, the reason for those selected would be clear, but in fact fifty-seven publications were mentioned but not criticized. They may have been included to give the survey "balance." The strangest absence in the report was the *Chicago World*. Not only was it among the country's ten largest black publications, with a circulation of almost 30,000, but it had also been at the heart of the dispute in late 1942 between the Justice Department and the Post Office.
51. Federal Bureau of Investigation, "Survey of Racial Conditions in the United States," pp. 406–7.
52. Ibid., pp. 34, 342, 360.
53. Ibid., p. 430.
54. *Editor & Publisher, The Fourth Estate: 1944 International Year Book Number* (New York: Editor & Publisher, 1944), p. 182.
55. Federal Bureau of Investigation, "Survey of Racial Conditions in the United States," p. 445.

56. Historian Eric Foner warned researchers in February 1984 about the dangers of blindly using FBI documents. "Reports of intelligence agents and paid informers cannot be taken at face value," he wrote. "More often than not, investigating agents revealed their own prejudices and preconceptions more accurately than . . . reality." See Eric Foner, "Roots of Black Power," *New York Times Book Review*, February 5, 1984, p. 25.

57. Federal Bureau of Investigation, "Survey of Racial Conditions in the United States," pp. 433–42.

58. Ibid., p. 443.

59. Ibid., pp. 443–44.

60. Ibid., pp. 445–47.

61. Ibid., pp. 448–51.

62. Ibid., pp. 451–53.

63. Ibid., pp. 454–59. In connection with the *Pittsburgh Courier*'s pro-Japanese activities, the FBI reported that Schuyler apparently had been invited to visit Japan in 1938 or 1939 and had written several pro-Japanese articles upon his return. At the same time, it said Rogers had been entertained by Japanese officers in Ethiopia and allegedly had promised "favorable publicity" for Japan when he returned to the United States.

64. Interview, Herbert Wechsler, March 22, 1985.

65. Francis Biddle, "Taking No Chances," *Collier's*, March 21, 1942, p. 40.

66. Biddle, *In Brief Authority*, p. 255. Before the new cafeteria was built, Biddle was criticized in August 1942 by New Orleans's black *Louisiana Weekly* for the segregated eating facilities at the Justice Department. See "What Is Biddle's Game—Or Does He Give a Damn About Democracy for the Negro?" *Louisiana Weekly*, August 8, 1942.

67. Jonathan Daniels, *White House Witness, 1942–1945* (Garden City, N.Y.: Doubleday, 1975), p. 27. In a number of places in his book, Daniels noted the discrimination that blacks dealt with in Washington during the war.

68. Malcolm Ross, *All Manner of Men* (New York: Reynal & Hitchcock, 1948), p. 22.

69. Biddle, "Taking No Chances," p. 41. Wechsler, who was a special assistant to the attorney general from 1940 to 1944 and an assistant attorney general for the next two years, recalled that Biddle was "very hostile" to any prosecutions of publications during the war. Interview, Herbert Wechsler, March 22, 1985.

70. *Annual Report of the Attorney General of the United States for the Fiscal*

Year Ended June 30, 1943 (Atlanta: Federal Prison Industries, 1944), p. 6.

71. "Biddle Lauds Race Press As Loyal to U.S.," *Amsterdam Star–News*, February 20, 1943.

72. Biddle, *In Brief Authority*, pp. 151–52.

73. See Memorandum, John Edgar Hoover to Tom C. Clark, October 11, 1943; Tom C. Clark to Director, Federal Bureau of Investigation, November 9, 1943; J. Edgar Hoover to Tom C. Clark, December 16, 1943; and Tom C. Clark to Director, Federal Bureau of Investigation, January 1, 1944. All are in file 100-122319, Federal Bureau of Investigation.

74. See Federal Bureau of Investigation Report, December 31, 1943; J. Edgar Hoover to Tom C. Clark, February 2, 1944; and Memorandum, Tom C. Clark to Director, Federal Bureau of Investigation, February 23, 1944. All are in file 100-63963, Federal Bureau of Investigation. Also see Tom C. Clark to Director, Federal Bureau of Investigation, May 24, 1944, file 100-31159, Federal Bureau of Investigation.

75. See Federal Bureau of Investigation Report, November 10, 1944; John Edgar Hoover to Tom C. Clark, November 29, 1944; and Tom C. Clark to Director, Federal Bureau of Investigation, December 9, 1944. All are in file 100-63963, Federal Bureau of Investigation. Also see *Hartzel* v. *United States*, 322 U.S. 680 (1944). It is unknown why Clark took six months to conclude that the *Hartzel* decision made further investigations of the *Afro-American* chain unnecessary.

76. See John Edgar Hoover to Tom C. Clark, February 22, 1945, file 100-31159-204; and Tom C. Clark to Director, Federal Bureau of Investigation, March 1, 1945, file 146-7-64-354. Both are at the Justice Dept., Washington, D.C.

77. Truman K. Gibson, Jr., to Assistant Secretary of War, October 23, 1943, record group 107, ASW 291.2 (Negro Troops), Civilian Aide files, National Archives, Washington, D.C.

78. Truman K. Gibson, Jr., to Assistant Secretary of War, December 20, 1943, record group 107, ASW 291.2 (Negro Troops), Race–Alphabetical folder, National Archives.

79. Harry S. McAlpin, "Un-Covering Washington," *Atlanta Daily World*, July 11, 1945.

80. Ulysses Lee, *United States Army in World War II: Special Studies: The Employment of Negro Troops*, Vol. 8, no. 8 (Washington, D.C.: Office of the Chief of Military History, U.S. Army, 1966), pp. 384–85.

81. Truman K. Gibson, Jr., to Adjutant General, October 29, 1943,

record group 107, Special Assistant to the Secretary of War (Hastie files), Press folder, National Archives. On at least three occasions, black press complaints about bans were unjustified. In July 1943, the *People's Voice* said that black soldiers at Camp Shelby in Mississippi had been told they could not read black papers "published north of Mississippi." An army investigation in August showed that this was untrue. A month later, the *Baltimore Afro-American* claimed it had been barred from Camp Sutton in North Carolina, but Gibson pointed out that it was not sold in the post exchange because no one had asked for it. Then, the *Houston Informer* said in December 1943 that black papers had been prevented from reaching black soldiers on maneuvers in the desert. Gibson replied this was untrue and pointed out that the *Pittsburgh Courier* had a reporter with the troops. See War Department, M.I.D., "People's Voice," August 30, 1943, file 100-51230-68, Federal Bureau of Investigation. Also see Truman K. Gibson, Jr., to Carl Murphy, September 23, 1943; Carter Wesley to Truman K. Gibson, Jr., December 7, 1943; and Truman K. Gibson, Jr., to Carter Wesley, December 22, 1943. All are in record group 107, Special Assistant to the Secretary of War (Hastie files), Press folder, National Archives.

82. See Lee, *United States Army*, p. 385; and Truman K. Gibson, Jr., to Col. Stanley J. Grogan, November 22, 1943, record group 107, Special Assistant to the Secretary of War (Hastie files), Press folder, National Archives.

83. "No Ban on Race Papers in Camps; Army Rules," *Pittsburgh Courier*, November 13, 1943.

84. See Truman K. Gibson, Jr., to Col. Stanley J. Grogan, November 22, 1943, record group 107, Special Assistant to the Secretary of War (Hastie files), Press folder, National Archives; and Lee, *United States Army*, p. 385.

85. Metz T. P. Lochard to Henry L. Stimson, December 1, 1943, record group 107, Special Assistant to the Secretary of War (Hastie files), Press folder, National Archives. In the same folder, see John A. Rector to *Chicago Defender*, November 13, 1943; and Metz T. P. Lochard to Truman K. Gibson, Jr., December 2, 1943.

86. See Charles P. Browning to Truman K. Gibson, Jr., January 8 and 24, 1944, record group 107, Special Assistant to the Secretary of War (Hastie files), Press folder, National Archives; George S. Schuyler, "The World Today," *Pittsburgh Courier*, April 8, 1944; "Army Lifts Ban on Papers," *PEP: Negro Publisher, Editor and Printer*, July 1944, p. 16; and Ida M. Smith to Maj. Gen. A. D. Surles,

August 24, 1944, record group 107, Special Assistant to the Secretary of War (Hastie files), Press AFRO folder, National Archives.

87. Schuyler, "The World Today."

88. Bureau of Public Relations, "Report of Trends in the Negro Press," November 27, 1944, record group 107, box 223, entry 91, Assistant Secretary of War, Civilian Aide to the Secretary Subject file, 1940–47, Negro Press Analysis, National Archives.

89. Morris J. MacGregor and Bernard C. Nalty, eds., *Blacks in the United States Armed Forces: Basic Documents*, Vol. VI (Wilmington: Scholary Resources, 1977), p. 12.

90. For information on the Post Office's investigations, see record group 28, file no. 103777-E, case nos. E-3-C, E-208-A, E-419, E-440, and E-464, National Archives; and file 146-28-1227, Justice Dept.

91. See Kieferle to O'Brien, November 5, 1943; Calvin W. Hassell to Tom C. Clark, November 8, 1943; and Tom C. Clark to Calvin W. Hassell, November 15, 1943. All can be found in file 146-28-1227, Justice Dept.

92. Archibald Rutledge to Postmaster General, September 9, 1944, record group 28, file no. 103777-E, case no. E-3-A, National Archives. Other letters can be found in case nos. E-12 and E-16.

93. See Fergus McRee to Solicitor, July 29, 1944; and Memorandum, Breen to O'Brien, August 1, 1944. Both are in record group 28, file no. 103777-E, case no. E-419, National Archives.

94. Memorandum, Manherz to Breen, June 17, 1944, record group 28, file no. 103777-E, case no. E-419, National Archives.

95. E. L. Harvey to Otten, May 24, 1944, record group 216, file 007, Complaints and Inquires P–Q folder, National Archives. No information can be located showing why the order was rescinded.

96. See Ibid.; and William H. Walsh to District Postal Censor, January 7, 1944, record group 216, file 007-B/2, National Archives.

97. E. L. Harvey to Otten, May 24, 1944, record group 216, file 007, Complaints and Inquires P–Q folder, National Archives.

98. Graham J. White, *FDR and the Press* (Chicago: University of Chicago Press, 1979), pp. 18–19.

99. " 'Need Frank Talk with President'—Randolph," *Pittsburgh Courier*, April 11, 1942. Another such example was "Conferences with President Sought," *Pittsburgh Courier*, September 12, 1942.

100. "Negro Reporters at White House," *PM*, May 27, 1943.

101. Private typewritten notes, Francis Biddle, "July 21, 1943," Francis Biddle papers, Franklin D. Roosevelt folder, Roosevelt Library.

102. Anna Rothe, ed., *Current Biography: Who's News and Why, 1944* (New York: H. W. Wilson, 1945), pp. 565–66.
103. "Outstanding Leaders of the Year," *Chicago Defender*, January 1, 1944.
104. "SENGSTACKE, John H.—Pres., Negro Newspaper Publishers Association, Chicago, Ill., The Chicago Defender," November 2, 1943, OF 10, Justice Dept., Abstracts 1943 folder, Roosevelt Library.
105. Memorandum, MB to Ruth Jane, November 12, 1943, OF 36, Press (Newspapers), Colored Repre. folder, Roosevelt Library. "MB" probably was Mary McLeod Bethune, who was Roosevelt's special adviser on minority affairs and director of the Division of Negro Affairs for the National Youth Administration. She apparently was partly responsible for getting a black White House correspondent and arranging a meeting of the NNPA with Roosevelt. Interviews, Harry S. McAlpin, March 15, 1983; and John H. Sengstacke, April 21, 1983.
106. "Negro's War Aims Told to President," *Pittsburgh Courier*, February 12, 1944. The papers represented included the *Amsterdam Star–News* (New York), the *Atlanta Daily World*, the *Baltimore Afro-American*, the *Chicago Defender*, the *Cleveland Call and Post*, the *Houston Informer*, the *Michigan Chronicle* (Detroit), the *Norfolk Journal and Guide*, the *Pittsburgh Courier*, and the *Washington Tribune*. The statement was drawn up by an NNPA committee chaired by Percival Prattis of the *Pittsburgh Courier*. See Percival Prattis to Pat Prattis, February 5, 1944, Percival Prattis papers, series B, box 4, Letters to Pat folder, Manuscript Division, Moorland–Spingarn Research Center, Howard University, Washington, D.C.
107. "Off the Record," *PEP: Negro Publisher, Editor and Printer*, May 1945, pp. 10–11.
108. McAlpin, one of about twenty black Washington correspondents, covered the capital for the *Chicago Defender* before joining the White House press corps. At that point he switched to the *Daily World* because it was the only daily black paper. The more prosperous *Defender*, however, secretly continued to pay his salary. Interviews, Harry S. McAlpin, March 15, 1983; and John H. Sengstacke, April 21, 1983.
109. Harry S. McAlpin, typewritten autobiographical manuscript, used with the author's permission. Early usually introduced new reporters to Roosevelt, but why he did not do so with McAlpin is unknown.

110. Roosevelt unquestionably recognized the importance of the black vote. "In the presidential election of 1936 Roosevelt received from 70 to 80 per cent of ballots cast by Negroes, and in the campaign of 1940 he did almost as well," noted historian Benjamin Quarles. "The winning of the colored vote was important, since the Negro by 1940 had come to hold the balance of power in some ten states outside the South." See Quarles, *The Negro in the Making of America*, p. 213.

111. Interview, John H. Sengstacke, April 21, 1983.

112. "Publishers at the White House," *Michigan Chronicle*, February 19, 1944.

113. "At FDR Rites," *PEP: Negro Publisher, Editor and Printer*, May 1945, p. 11; and Interview, Harry S. McAlpin, March 17, 1983. Although Daniels was from North Carolina, his intercession in McAlpin's behalf was not surprising. As historian Frank Freidel has noted, Daniels was "in the forefront of a generation of young Southerners" during the 1930s, 1940s, and 1950s who attempted to hasten an end to discrimination against blacks in the South. "There was never a time when Daniels was not firm in his opposition to prejudice whether because of race or religion," Freidel continued. However, that did not mean he fully supported the black press's wartime campaign to end discrimination and injustices. "Some Negro leaders irritate me to anger, when in the 'Double V' language of two victories or none, they discuss conditions precedent upon which full Negro participation for America in this war depends," Daniels wrote in November 1942. "I know they are not in fact talking for the rank and file of their people who share with all southerners the sort of headlong loyalty upon which a fighting America can always depend." See Jonathan Daniels, "New Patterns for Old," *Survey Graphic*, November 1942, p. 487; and Jonathan Daniels, *White House Witness, 1942–1945*, pp. xi–xii.

114. See "NNPA Committee to DC," *PEP: Negro Publisher, Editor and Printer*, July 1945, p. 11; Carter Wesley, "Ram's Horn," *Houston Informer*, June 9, 1945; and Harry McAlpin, "Publishers, Walter White See President Truman," *Chicago Defender*, June 2, 1945. Those papers represented at the meeting with Truman included the *Baltimore Afro-American*, the *Chicago Defender*, the *Cleveland Call and Post*, the *Houston Informer*, the *Kansas City Call*, the *Louisville Defender*, the *Michigan Chronicle*, the *Minneapolis Spokesman*, the *Norfolk Journal and Guide*, the *Pittsburgh Courier*, the *St. Louis Argus*, and the *Washington Tribune*.

115. Finkle, *Forum for Protest*, p. 85.

116. See Ibid., p. 53; and U.S. Department of Commerce, *Negro Newspapers and Periodicals in the United States: 1940*, Negro Statistical Bulletin no. 1, May 1941, p. 1.
117. Joseph D. Bibb, "We Gain by War," *Pittsburgh Courier*, October 10, 1942.

Chapter 8

1. Francis Biddle, "The Humanism of Mr. Justice Holmes," *New Republic*, April 11, 1955, pp. 10–13.
2. Cabell Phillips, " 'No Witch Hunts,' " *New York Times Magazine*, September 21, 1941, p. 8. A reporter for *Survey Graphic* also noted that Holmes had provided "direction" to Biddle's legal career. See Clinch Calkins, "Wartime Attorney General," *Survey Graphic*, October 1942, p. 422.
3. Beverly Smith, "Everybody's Lawyer," *American Magazine*, April 1942, p. 48.
4. "New Blood in Cabinet," *Washington Post*, May 24, 1945.
5. See Ibid.; "Cabinet Changes," *New York Times*, May 24, 1945; "The Cabinet Changes," *The Nation*, June 2, 1945, p. 616; "The Cabinet: Shake-Up!" *Time*, June 4, 1945, pp. 22–23; and " 'Three to Make Ready,' " *Newsweek*, June 4, 1945, pp. 36–37.
6. "Biddle Out, ? In," *Washington Afro-American*, June 2, 1945. It is possible that the black press's reaction to Clark and its reluctance to praise Biddle were mainly because of an incident in 1944. According to a *PM* article on October 8, both Clark and Victor Rotnem, head of the Justice Department's Civil Liberties Unit, used the word "nigger" during an interview with a reporter. The *Afro-American* chain, in a front-page editorial, promptly called Clark and Rotnem a "distinct liability" to the administration and asked for an immediate investigation. "Colored people do not want four years more of a Department of Justice which has prosecutors like these two," it said. A week later, the chain noted that a Justice Department public relations official said both men denied using the offensive word, and he called the *PM* article "stupidly incorrect." *PM's* managing editor, however, stood behind the accuracy of the story and called for the ouster of Clark and Rotnem. Finally, on October 28, in the third straight front-page story in the *Afro-American* chain, a letter appeared from Biddle in which he claimed that the language attributed to them was "grossly inaccurate." He continued by reviewing some of the Justice Department's investigations into discrimination and

crimes against blacks. "I know of no other administration where the rights of colored people have been so aggressively defended and prosecutions so vigorously brought," wrote Biddle. "As long as I am attorney general, I shall see to it that the rights of colored people—in fact the rights of all minority groups—are protected so far as they can be protected under the Federal laws." Editor Carl Murphy applauded Biddle's "assurance" that blacks' rights would be safeguarded by the Justice Department, but he called for a further investigation to determine "the truth of the alleged charges." Whether that was done is unknown. See the following articles in the *Baltimore Afro-American*: "The Department of Injustice," October 14, 1944; "*PM* Puts Finger on Justice Dept.," October 21, 1944; and "Attorney General's Letter to *Afro* Editor," October 28, 1944.

7. *Liberty on the Home Front* (New York: American Civil Liberties Union, 1945), pp. 33–34. According to the ACLU, twenty-five of the individuals belonged to obscure black religious sects, six were native Americans, one was a German alien, and one was a naturalized German.

8. Richard S. Kirkendall, *The United States, 1929–1945: Years of Crisis and Change* (New York: McGraw-Hill, 1974), p. 221.

9. Francis Biddle, "Security and Liberty," *New Republic*, August 14, 1950, p. 11.

10. Francis Biddle, *The Fear of Freedom* (Garden City, N.Y.: Doubleday, 1952), pp. 1–2.

11. Interview, James H. Rowe, Jr., March 1, 1983.

12. Thomas H. Eliot, "Gentleman, Scholar and New Dealer," *New York Times Book Review*, November 11, 1962, p. 1.

13. Grace Tully, *F.D.R., My Boss* (New York: Charles Scribner's Sons, 1949), p. 180.

14. Biddle, *The Fear of Freedom*, p. xvii. Herbert Wechsler, who was a special assistant to the attorney general from 1940 to 1944 and an assistant attorney general the next two years, agrees with Ickes that Biddle was a "great" attorney general. "He was a superb lawyer, a splendid statesman, an extremely strong and courageous man," said Wechsler. "He was not a politician in the ordinary sense of the word." Interview, Herbert Wechsler, March 22, 1985.

15. Theodore H. White, *In Search of History: A Personal Adventure* (1978; reprint ed., New York: Warner Books, 1981), p. 628.

16. Biddle, "The Humanism of Mr. Justice Holmes," p. 13.

Fishel, Leslie H., Jr., and Benjamin Quarles. *The Black American: A Documentary History*. New York: William Morrow, 1970.

Fite, Gilbert C., and H. C. Peterson. *Opponents of War, 1917–1918*. Madison: University of Wisconsin Press, 1957.

Fowler, Dorothy Ganfield. *Unmailable*. Athens: University of Georgia Press, 1977.

Franklin, John Hope. *From Slavery to Freedom*. New York: Alfred A. Knopf, 1956.

Frazier, E. Franklin. *The Negro in the United States*. New York: Macmillan, 1949.

Freedom in Wartime. New York: American Civil Liberties Union, 1943.

Garraty, John A., ed. *Dictionary of American Biography*, Supplement Six, 1956–1960. New York: Charles Scribner's Sons, 1980.

Garrow, David J. *The FBI and Martin Luther King, Jr.: From "Solo" to Memphis*. New York: W. W. Norton, 1981.

Gillers, Stephen, and Pat Watters, eds. *Investigating the FBI*. Garden City, N.Y.: Doubleday, 1973.

Guzman, Jessie Parkhurst, ed. *Negro Year Book, 1941–46*. Tuskegee, Ala.: Tuskegee Institute, 1947.

Halberstam, David. *The Powers That Be*. New York: Alfred A. Knopf, 1979.

Harris, William H. *Keeping the Faith*. Urbana: University of Illinois Press, 1977.

Healy, Paul F. *Cissy: The Biography of Eleanor M. "Cissy" Patterson*. Garden City, N.Y.: Doubleday 1966.

Hill, Roy L. *Who's Who in the American Negro Press*. Dallas: Royal, 1960.

Hoehling, A. A. *Home Front, U.S.A.* New York: Thomas Y. Crowell, 1966.

Hogan, Lawrence D. *A Black National News Service: The Associated Negro Press and Claude Barnett, 1919–1945*. Cranbury, N.J.: Associated University Presses, 1984.

Hoke, Henry. *It's a Secret*. New York: Reynal & Hitchcock, 1946.

Ickes, Harold L. *The Secret Diary of Harold L. Ickes*, Vol. III. New York: Simon and Schuster, 1954.

In Defense of Our Liberties. New York: American Civil Liberties Union, 1944.

Irons, Peter. *Justice at War*. New York: Oxford University Press, 1983.

Johnson, Charles S. *Patterns of Negro Segregation*. New York: Harper, 1943.

Johnson, Donald. *The Challenge to American Freedoms*. Lexington: University of Kentucky Press, 1963.

Johnson, J. Percy H., ed. *N. W. Ayer & Son's Directory of Newspapers and Periodicals, 1942*. Philadelphia: N. W. Ayer & Son, 1942.

Juergens, George. *News from the White House: The Presidential-Press Relationship in the Progressive Era*. Chicago: University of Chicago Press, 1981.

Kirkendall, Richard S. *The United States, 1929–1945: Years of Crisis and Change*. New York: McGraw-Hill, 1974.

La Brie, Henry G., III, ed. *Perspectives of the Black Press: 1974*. Kennebunkport, Maine: Mercer House, 1974.

Lee, Ulysses. *United States Army in World War II: Special Studies: The Employment of Negro Troops*, Vol. 8, no. 8. Washington, D.C.: Office of the Chief of Military History, U.S. Army, 1966.

Liberty on the Home Front. New York: American Civil Liberties Union, 1945.

Lofton, John. *The Press As Guardian of the First Amendment*. Columbia: University of South Carolina Press, 1980.

Lowenthal, Max. *The Federal Bureau of Investigation*. New York: William Sloane Associates, 1950.

MacGregor, Morris J., and Bernard C. Nalty, eds. *Blacks in the United States Armed Forces: Basic Documents*, Vol. VI. Wilmington: Scholarly Resources, 1977.

Messick, Hank. *John Edgar Hoover*. New York: David McKay, 1972.

Miller, Nathan. *FDR: An Intimate History*. Garden City, N.Y.: Doubleday, 1983.

Mims, Edwin. *The Advancing South*. New York: Doubleday, 1926.

Morris, Harry W., and Charles W. Simmons, eds. *Afro-American History*. Columbus, Ohio: Charles E. Merrill, 1972.

Murray, Robert K. *Red Scare: A Study in National Hysteria, 1919–1920*. Minneapolis: University of Minnesota Press, 1955.

Myrdal, Gunnar. *An American Dilemma*. New York: Harper, 1944.

Nash, Jay Robert. *Citizen Hoover: A Critical Study of the Life and Times of J. Edgar Hoover and His FBI*. Chicago: Nelson-Hall, 1972.

Nelson, Harold L., and Dwight L. Teeter. *Law of Mass Communications: Freedom and Control of Print and Broadcast Media*. 3rd ed. rev. Mineola, N.Y.: Foundation Press, 1978.

Oak, Vishnu V. *The Negro Newspaper*. Yellow Springs, Ohio: Antioch Press, 1948.

Ottley, Roi. *'New World A-Coming': Inside Black America*. Boston: Houghton Mifflin, 1943.

Ottley, Roi. *The Lonely Warrior: The Life and Times of Robert S. Abbott*. Chicago: Henry Regnery, 1955.

Overstreet, Bonaro, and Harry Overstreet. *What We Must Know About Communism.* New York: W. W. Norton, 1958.

Perrett, Geoffrey. *Days of Sadness, Years of Triumph: The American People, 1939–1945.* New York: Coward, McCann & Geoghegan, 1973.

Phillips, Cabell. *The 1940s: Decade of Triumph and Trouble.* New York: Macmillan, 1975.

Quarles, Benjamin. *The Negro in the Making of America.* Rev. ed. New York: Macmillan, Collier, 1969.

Rauch, Basil, ed. *The Roosevelt Reader.* New York: Holt, Rinehart and Winston, 1960.

Rector, Justine J., and James S. Tinney, eds. *Issues and Trends in Afro-American Journalism.* Lanham, Md.: University Press of America, 1980.

Rose, Arnold M. *The Negro's Morale: Group Identification and Protest.* Minneapolis: University of Minnesota Press, 1949.

Rosenman, Samuel I. *Working with Roosevelt.* New York: Harper, 1952.

Ross, Malcolm. *All Manner of Men.* New York: Reynal & Hitchcock, 1948.

Rothe, Anna, ed. *Current Biography: Who's News and Why, 1944.* New York: H. W. Wilson, 1945.

Scheiber, Harry N. *The Wilson Administration and Civil Liberties, 1917–1921.* Ithaca: Cornell University Press, 1960.

Schuyler, George S. *Fifty Years of Progress in Negro Journalism.* Reprint of 1950 ed. Ann Arbor, Mich.: University Microfilms, 1971.

Scott, Emmett J. *Scott's Official History of the American Negro in the World War.* Chicago: Homewood Press, 1919.

Tebbel, John. *The Media in America.* New York: Thomas Y. Crowell, 1974.

Tully, Grace, *F.D.R., My Boss.* New York: Charles Scribner's Sons, 1949.

Turner, William W. *Hoover's FBI: The Men and the Myth.* Los Angeles: Sherbourne Press, 1970.

Ungar, Sanford J. *FBI.* Boston: Little, Brown, 1975.

Wedlock, Lunabelle. *The Reaction of Negro Publications and Organizations to German Anti-Semitism.* Washington, D.C.: Howard University Studies in the Social Sciences, III, no. 2, 1942.

Wendt, Lloyd. *Chicago Tribune: The Rise of a Great American Newspaper.* Chicago: Rand McNally, 1979.

White, Graham J. *FDR and the Press.* Chicago: University of Chicago Press, 1979.

White, Theodore H. *In Search of History: A Personal Adventure.* Reprint of 1978 ed. New York: Warner Books, 1981.

White, Walter. *A Man Called White.* Reprint of 1948 ed. Bloomington: Indiana University Press, 1970.

Whitehead, Don. *The FBI Story: A Report to the People.* New York: Random House, 1956.

Wise, David. *The Politics of Lying: Government Deception, Secrecy, and Power.* New York: Random House, 1973.

Wise, David. *The American Police State: The Government Against the People.* New York: Random House, 1976.

Wolseley, Roland E. *The Black Press, U.S.A.* Ames: Iowa State University Press, 1971.

Wynn, Neil A. *The Afro-American and the Second World War.* London: Paul Elek, 1976.

Yust, Walter, ed. *1944 Britannica Book of the Year.* Chicago: Encyclopaedia Britannica, 1944.

Monographs

Bishop, Robert L., and LaMar S. Mackay. "Mysterious Silence, Lyrical Scream: Government Information in World War II." *Journalism Monographs* 19 (1971).

Pember, Don R. "The Smith Act As a Restraint on the Press." *Journalism Monographs* 10 (1969).

Journals and Periodicals

Alexander, Jack. "Profiles: The Director—II." *The New Yorker,* October 2, 1937, pp. 21–26.

"Along the Personal Front." *PEP: Negro Publisher, Editor and Printer,* July 1943, p. 15.

"Are Negroes Citizens?" *Racial Digest,* April 1943, pp. 13–14.

"Army Lifts Ban on Papers." *PEP: Negro Publisher, Editor and Printer,* July 1944, p. 16.

"At FDR Rites." *PEP: Negro Publisher, Editor and Printer,* May 1945, p. 11.

"Attorney General." *Newsweek,* June 8, 1942, p. 32.

Biddle, Francis. "The Power of Democracy: It Can Meet All Conditions." *Vital Speeches of the Day,* October 15, 1941, pp. 5–9.

Biddle, Francis. "Taking No Chances." *Collier's,* March 21, 1942, p. 21.

Biddle, Francis. "Security and Liberty." *New Republic,* August 14, 1950, pp. 11–14.

Biddle, Francis. "The Humanism of Mr. Justice Holmes." *New Republic,* April 11, 1955, pp. 10–13.

Black Gregory D., and Clayton R. Koppes. "What to Show the World: The Office of War Information and Hollywood, 1942–1945." *Journal of American History* 64 (1977): 87–105.

"Blow to the War Effort." *Time*, June 8, 1942, p. 15.

Bond, Horace Mann. "Should the Negro Care Who Wins the War?" *Annals of the American Academy of Political and Social Science* 223 (1942): 81–84.

Boudin, Louis B. " 'Seditious Doctrines' and 'Clear and Present Danger' Rule, Part I." *Virginia Law Review* 38 (1952): 143–86.

Brown, Warren H. "A Negro Looks at the Negro Press." *Saturday Review of Literature*, December 19, 1942, pp. 5–6.

Burma, John H. "An Analysis of the Present Negro Press." *Social Forces* 26 (1947): 172–80.

"The Cabinet Changes." *The Nation*, June 2, 1945, pp. 616–17.

"The Cabinet: Shake-Up!" *Time*, June 4, 1945, pp. 22–23.

Calkins, Clinch. "Wartime Attorney General." *Survey Graphic*, October 1942, pp. 420–24.

"Close Ranks." *The Crisis*, July 1918, p. 111.

"Cover." *PEP: Negro Publisher, Editor and Printer*, April 1945, p. 2.

Dabney, Virginius. "Press and Morale." *Saturday Review of Literature*, July 4, 1942, pp. 5–6.

"Damper on Press Move." *PEP: Negro Publisher, Editor and Printer*, November 1945, pp. 15–16.

Daniels, Jonathan. "New Patterns for Old." *Survey Graphic*, November 1942, pp. 485–87.

Davis, Ralph N. "Negro Newspapers and the War." *Sociology and Social Research* 27 (1943): 373–80.

DeVoto, Bernard. "Sedition's General Staff." *Harper's Magazine*, June 1942, pp. 109–12.

Durr, Clifford J. "Report on Certain Alleged Practices of the FBI." *Lawyers Guild Review* 10 (1950): 185–201.

Eliot, Thomas H. "Gentleman, Scholar and New Dealer." *New York Times Book Review*, November 11, 1962, p. 1.

Foner, Eric. "Roots of Black Power." *New York Times Book Review*, February 5, 1984, p. 1.

"Free Speech in Wartime." *New Republic*, January 4, 1943, pp. 547–48.

"The Front Page of the Negro Press." *Events and Trends in Race Relations—A Monthly Summary* 4 (1947): 377.

"Further Cuts in Newsprint in '44 Forecast by Nelson." *PEP: Negro Publisher, Editor and Printer*, October 1943, p. 11.

Hancock, Gordon B. "The Negro Press—Its Duty Today." *PEP: Negro Publisher, Editor and Printer*, February 1944, p. 4.

"Harry S. McAlpin." *PEP: Negro Publisher, Editor and Printer*, March 1944, p. 6.

High, Stanley. "How the Negro Fights for Freedom." *Reader's Digest*, July 1942, pp. 113–18.

Hill, Robert A., " 'The Foremost Radical Among His Race': Marcus Garvey and the Black Scare, 1918–1921." *Prologue* 16, no. 4 (Winter 1984): 214–31.

"Indictments and New Spy Hunt Point to Subversion Crackdown." *Newsweek*, August 3, 1942, pp. 26–27.

"Iron Cross." *Newsweek*, December 28, 1942, pp. 30–31.

Janeway, Eliot. "Fighting a White Man's War." *Racial Digest*, April 1943, pp. 1–3.

Johnson, Ernest E. "The Negro Press Reacts to the War." *Interracial Review*, March 1942, pp. 39–41.

Johnson, Ernest E. "Ted Poston Leaves OWI." *PEP: Negro Publisher, Editor and Printer*, August–October 1945, pp. 27–28.

Johnson, Ernest E. "The Washington News Beat." *Phylon* 7 (1946): 126–31.

Jones, Lester M. "The Editorial Policy of Negro Newspapers of 1917–18 As Compared with That of 1941–42." *Journal of Negro History* 29 (1944): 24–31.

"Jos. Bibb Deserves Monument." *Negro Printer and Publisher*, August 1941, pp. 1–3.

Lee, Wallace. "Negro Digest Poll." *Negro Digest*, February 1943, p. 54.

"Major Accomplishments: Negro Newspaper Publishers Association." *PEP: Negro Publisher, Editor and Printer*, February 1944, p. 32.

Martin, Louis. "Fifth Column Among Negroes." *Opportunity*, December 1942, pp. 358–60.

"A Memo to Negro Advertising Men." *PEP: Negro Publisher, Editor and Printer*, February 1944, p. 21.

"Milquetoast Gets Muscles." *Time*, April 13, 1942, p. 20.

Murray, Florence. "The Negro and Civil Liberties During World War II." *Social Forces* 24 (1945): 211–16.

"Mystery in Chicago." *Time*, August 31, 1942, pp. 63–64.

"Nation Starts Cracking Down on the 5th and 6th Columnists." *Newsweek*, April 6, 1942, pp. 27–28.

"Navy Salvo on McCormick." *Newsweek*, August 17, 1942, pp. 64–65.

"Navy v. Tribune." *Time*, August 17, 1942, pp. 65–67.

"The Negro Market: An Appraisal." *Tide*, March 7, 1947, pp. 15–18.

"Negro Morale." *The Crisis*, April 1942, p. 111.

"The Negro Press." *PEP: Negro Publisher, Editor and Printer*, September 1943, p. 19.

"Negro Press." *Tide*, September 1, 1944, pp. 84–86.

"The New Cabinet Posts." *Commonweal*, June 8, 1945, p. 180.

"Newsprint Cut Again." *PEP: Negro Publisher, Editor and Printer*, October 1943, p. 7.

"NNPA Committee to DC." *PEP: Negro Publisher, Editor and Printer*, July 1945, pp. 11–12.

"No Censorship Here." *PEP: Negro Publisher, Editor and Printer*, September 1943, p. 24.

"Now Is the Time Not to Be Silent." *The Crisis*, January 1942, p. 7.

Oak, V. V. "What About the Negro Press?" *Saturday Review of Literature*, March 6, 1943, pp. 4–5.

"O'Donnell's $50,000." *Time*, February 8, 1943, pp. 62–63.

"O'Donnell's Victory." *Newsweek*, February 8, 1943, pp. 74–76.

"Off the Record." *PEP: Negro Publisher, Editor and Printer*, May 1945, pp. 9-11.

"One Point of View—The Fascist Viewpoint." *PEP: Negro Publisher, Editor and Printer*, December 1943, p. 21.

O'Reilly, Kenneth. "A New Deal for the FBI: The Roosevelt Administration, Control and National Security." *Journal of American History* 69 (1982): 638–58.

Ottley, Roi. "The Negro Press Today." *Common Ground*, Spring 1943, pp. 11–18.

"Our President." *The Crisis*, March 1918, p. 216.

"Our Special Grievances." *The Crisis*, September 1918, pp. 216–17.

Paul, Angus. "A Pioneering Black Scientist; Roosevelt and Black Voters." *Chronicle of Higher Education*, October 26, 1983, p. 12.

"Pelley and the Prosecution." *New Republic*, August 17, 1942, p. 189.

"PEP Enters the Scene." *PEP: Negro Publisher, Editor and Printer*, July 1943, p. 3.

"PEP Salutes . . . Carl Murphy." *PEP: Negro Publisher, Editor and Printer*, November 1943, p. 10.

Phillips, Cabell. " 'No Witch Hunts.' " *New York Times Magazine*, September 21, 1941, p. 8.

Poston, Ted. "The Negro Press." *The Reporter*, December 6, 1949, pp. 14–16.

Prattis, P. L. "The Role of the Negro Press in Race Relations." *Phylon* 7 (1946): 273–83.

Prattis, P. L. "Racial Segregation and Negro Journalism." *Phylon* 8 (1947): 305–14.

"Press Prexy Lauds Negro Papers in Lincoln U. Talk." *PEP: Negro Publisher, Editor and Printer*, January 1944, p. 8.

"Pro-Germanism Among Negroes." *The Messenger*, July 1918, p. 13.

Ragan, Fred D. "Justice Oliver Wendell Holmes, Jr., Zechariah Chafee, Jr., and the Clear and Present Danger Test for Free Speech: The First Year, 1919." *Journal of American History* 58 (1971): 24–45.

Randolph, A. Philip. "Pro-Japanese Activities Among Negroes." *The Black Worker*, September 1942, p. 4.

"The Reward." *The Crisis*, September 1918, p. 217.

Robinson, Louie. "The Black Press: Voice of Freedom." *Ebony*, August 1975, pp. 52–58.

Rudwick, Elliott M. "W. E. B. DuBois: In the Role of Crisis Editor." *Journal of Negro History* 43 (1958): 214–40.

Sancton, Thomas. "The Negro Press." *New Republic*, April 26, 1943, pp. 557–60.

Schell, Orville. "Rounding Up Americans." *New York Times Book Review*, January 1, 1984, p. 22.

Schlesinger, Arthur M., Jr. "A Comment on 'Roosevelt and His Foreign Policy Critics.' " *Political Science Quarterly* 94 (1979): 33–35.

Schlesinger, Arthur, Jr. "Desperate Times." *The New York Review of Books*, November 24, 1983, pp. 36–38.

"Selective Service." *PEP: Negro Publisher, Editor and Printer*, July 1943, p. 2.

"Sengstacke, N.N.P.A. President." *PEP: Negro Publisher, Editor and Printer*, July 1943, p. 4.

Shirer, William L. "The Poison Pen." *Atlantic Monthly*, May 1942, pp. 548–52.

Sitkoff, Harvard. "Racial Militancy and Interracial Violence in the Second World War." *Journal of American History* 58 (1971): 661–81.

Smith, Beverly. "Everybody's Lawyer." *American Magazine*, April 1942, pp. 47–52.

"Statement of Negro War Aims." *PEP: Negro Publisher, Editor and Printer*, June 1944, p. 39.

Steele, Richard W. "Preparing the Public for War: Efforts to Establish a National Propaganda Agency, 1940–41." *American Historical Review* 75 (1970): 1640–53.

Steele, Richard W. "American Popular Opinion and the War Against Germany: The Issue of Negotiated Peace, 1942." *Journal of American History* 65 (1978): 704–23.

Steele, Richard W. "Franklin D. Roosevelt and His Foreign Policy Critics." *Political Science Quarterly* 94 (1979): 15–32.

Stewart, Jas. R. "Let's Face the Truth." *New Negro World*, February 1942, pp. 1–2.

"Tarnished Silver Shirt." *Newsweek*, April 13, 1942, pp. 29–30.

"The Third Annual Institute of Race Relations—A Summary." *Events* and Trends in Race Relations—A Monthly Summary* 4 (1946): 21–28.

"Thirteen." *The Crisis*, January 1918, p. 114.

" 'Three to Make Ready.' " *Newsweek*, June 4, 1945, pp. 36–38.

"Tribune Defeats the Navy." *Newsweek*, August 31, 1942, pp. 65–66.

"U.S. Sends Fascist Noble to Prison for Five Years." *Life*, August 3, 1942, p. 32.

"Voices of Defeat." *Life*, April 13, 1942, pp. 86–100.

"Walker in Cabinet." *Newsweek*, September 9, 1940, p. 19.

Walker, Rhoza A. "The Fifth Freedom." *Racial Digest*, April 1943, pp. 18–22.

Weinberg, Sydney. "What to Tell America: The Writers' Quarrel in the Office of War Information." *Journal of American History* 55 (1968): 73–89.

Wilkerson, Doxey A. "The Negro Press." *Journal of Negro Education* 26 (1947): 511–21.

Williams, Michael. "Views & Reviews." *Commonweal*, March 27, 1942, p. 561.

Williams, Michael. "Views & Reviews." *Commonweal*, April 10, 1942, pp. 617–18.

Wynn, Neil A. "Black Attitudes Toward Participation in the American War Effort, 1941–45." *Afro-American Studies* 3 (1972): 13–19.

XXX [pseud.]. "Washington Gestapo." *The Nation*, July 24, 1943, pp. 92–95.

Published Government Documents

Annual Report of the Attorney General of the United States for the Year 1918. Washington, D.C.: Government Printing Office, 1918.

Annual Report of the Attorney General of the United States for the Year 1919. Washington, D.C.: Government Printing Office, 1919.

Annual Report of the Attorney General of the United States for the Year 1920. Washington, D.C.: Government Printing Office, 1920.

Annual Report of the Attorney General of the United States for the Year 1921. Washington, D.C.: Government Printing Office, 1921.

Annual Report of the Attorney General of the United States for the Fiscal Year Ended June 30, 1942. Atlanta: Federal Prison Industries, 1943.

Annual Report of the Attorney General of the United States for the Fiscal Year Ended June 30, 1943. Atlanta: Federal Prison Industries, 1944.

Annual Report of the Attorney General of the United States for the Fiscal Year Ended June 30, 1944. Atlanta: Federal Prison Industries, 1945.

Annual Report of the Attorney General of the United States for the Fiscal Year Ended June 30, 1946. Atlanta: Federal Prison Industries, 1947.

Annual Report of the Postmaster General for the Fiscal Year Ended June 30, 1942. Washington, D.C.: Government Printing Office, 1942.

Annual Report of the Postmaster General for the Fiscal Year Ended June 30, 1943. Washington, D.C.: Government Printing Office, 1944.

Annual Report of the Postmaster General for the Fiscal Year Ended June 30, 1944. Washington, D.C.: Government Printing Office, 1945.

Annual Report of the Postmaster General for the Fiscal Year Ended June 30, 1945. Washington D.C.: Government Printing Office, 1946.

Federal Records of World War II, Civilian Agencies, Vol. 1. Washington, D.C.: U.S. Government Printing Office, 1950.

Miles, Vincent M. "Seditious and Disloyal Matter Unmailable in Time of War." *The Postal Bulletin,* January 15, 1942, p. 2.

New York Joint Legislative Committee Investigating Seditious Activities. *Revolutionary Radicalism,* Part I, Vol. II. Albany: J. B. Lyon, 1920.

U.S. Congress, House. *Congressional Record.* 77th Cong., 2d sess., 1942, 88, pt. 2: 2566.

U.S. Congress, House. *Congressional Record.* 78th Cong., 1st sess., 1943, 89, pt. 2: 1819–21.

U.S. Congress, Senate. Select Committee to Study Governmental Operations with Respect to Intelligence Activities. *Federal Bureau of Investigation,* Vol. 6. 94th Cong., 1st sess., 1976, S. Res. 21.

U.S. Congress, Senate. Select Committee to Study Governmental Operations with Respect to Intelligence Activities. *Intelligence Activities and the Rights of Americans,* Vol. II. 94th Cong., 2d sess., 1976, S. Rept. 94–755.

U.S. Congress, Senate. Select Committee to Study Governmental Operations with Respect to Intelligence Activities. *Supplementary Detailed Staff Reports on Intelligence Activities and the Rights of Americans,* Vol. III. 94th Cong., 2d sess., 1976, S. Rept. 94–755.

U.S. Congress, Senate. Select Committee to Study Governmental Operations with Respect to Intelligence Activities. *Supplementary Reports on Intelligence Activities,* Vol. VI. 94th Cong., 2d sess., 1976, S. Rept. 94–755.

U.S. Department of Commerce. *Negro Newspapers and Periodicals in the United States: 1940.* Negro Statistical Bulletin no. 1, May 1941.

U.S. Department of Commerce. *Negro Newspapers and Periodicals in the United States: 1943.* Negro Statistical Bulletin no. 1, August 1944.

U.S. Department of Justice. *Investigation Activities of the Department of Justice.* Washington, D.C.: U.S. Government Printing Office, 1919.

Unpublished Dissertations and Papers

Kornweibel, Theodore Jr. "The Messenger Magazine: 1917–1928." Ph.D. dissertation, Yale University, 1971. Ann Arbor: University Microfilms, 1975.

Washburn, Pat. "The Pittsburgh Courier's Double V Campaign in 1942." Paper given at Seventy-fifth Annual Meeting of the Organization of American Historians, April 1, 1982, at Philadelphia.

Washburn, Pat. "The Pittsburgh Courier and Black Workers in 1942." Paper given at Sixty-sixth Annual Meeting of the Association for Education in Journalism and Mass Communication, August 8, 1983, at Corvallis, Ore.

Law Cases

Bouldin v. *United States*, 261 F. 674 (1919).

Dunne v. *United States*, 138 F.2d 137 (1943).

Hartzel v. *United States*, 322 U.S. 680 (1944).

Mitchell v. *United States*, 313 U.S. 80 (1941).

Schenck v. *United States*, 249 U.S. 47 (1919).

United States ex. rel. *Milwaukee Social Democratic Publishing Co.* v. *Burleson*, 255 U.S. 407 (1921).

Interviews

Alsbrook, James E. April 18, 1984, in Athens, Ohio.

Bates, Daisy. June 9, 1983, telephone conversation.

Bolden, Frank. October 31, 1980, telephone conversation; November 21, 1980, telephone conversation; January 14, 1983, in Pittsburgh; and January 19, 1983, telephone conversation.

Emerson, Thomas I. June 13, 1984, telephone conversation.

McAlpin, Harry. March 15, 1983, telephone conversation; and March 17, 1983, in Fairfax, Va.

Rowe, Billy. January 3, 1983, in New Rochelle, N.Y.

Rowe, James Henry Rowe, Jr. March 1, 1983, in Washington, D.C.

Sengstacke, John H. April 21, 1983, in Chicago; and September 15, 1983, telephone conversation.

Wechsler, Herbert. March 22, 1985, telephone conversation.

Correspondence

McCutcheon, John T., Jr. June 23, 1983.
Nisbet, Miriam M. March 23, 1984.
Schewe, Donald B. October 10, 1980.

Index